TALKING WITH YOUR CHILD ABOUT A TROUBLED WORLD

Also by Lynne S. Dumas
(with Emily Koltnow)

CONGRATULATIONS! YOU'VE BEEN FIRED

TALKING WITH YOUR CHILD ABOUT A TROUBLED WORLD

LYNNE S. DUMAS

FAWCETT COLUMBINE

NEW YORK

A Fawcett Columbine Book
Published by Ballantine Books

Copyright © 1992 by Lynne S. Dumas

All rights reserved under International and Pan-American Copyright Conventions. Published in the United States by Ballantine Books, a division of Random House, Inc., New York, and simultaneously in Canada by Random House of Canada Limited, Toronto.

Library of Congress Catalog Card Number: 91-72952

ISBN: 0-449-90797-X

Design by Holly Johnson
Cover design by Kristine V. Mills

Manufactured in the United States of America

First Ballantine Books Trade Edition: May 1992
10 9 8 7 6 5 4 3 2 1

To Stephen and David,
who deserve to grow up in the best of all worlds,
but who will do just fine in this one.

And to my husband, Dominick Scotto,
with more love than I can write.

Contents

Acknowledgments

Writing this book without the help of some very special people would not have been possible. So let me thank them now: my perceptive and thoughtful editor, Joëlle Delbourgo; my agent and publishing ally, Lynn Seligman; Andrea Linne, who I know shares my delight in seeing this project come to fruition; my loving family; and all my smart and supportive pals, especially Priscilla Orr, Betsy Mangan, Elise Marton, and Susan Franz.

Special thanks to my wise and encouraging panel of reviewers: David Fassler, who gave of himself above and beyond anything I could have hoped for and who has become a valued friend; Ellen Bassuk, whose honesty, frankness, and grasp of the issues pushed me to do more and to do it better than I thought I could; Myron Belfer, whose sharp eye and good sense saved me from more than a few blunders; Elizabeth Weller, who always managed to find time for me despite her daunting work schedule; and Fred Kaeser, whose keen insights and sunny manner never failed to brighten my thoughts.

Finally, I'd like to express my appreciation to all the experts who gave of their time and talent so generously. I've named each of you at the end of the appropriate chapter, but up front, let me say a collective and sincere "thanks" for all your help.

TALKING WITH YOUR CHILD ABOUT A TROUBLED WORLD

INTRODUCTION

When I was a teacher, I used to worry about my students a good deal. And not just about whether they were grasping the classroom lessons of the day, but about how what I said and how I said it would color their perceptions and affect their view of life as they hurtled toward adulthood.

Today, though I've traded in my chalk for a word processor and my young students for a broader audience of readers, I'm still concerned. I see a society that has grown increasingly complex, confronting parents with a wide array of complicated issues that are difficult to understand and even harder to explain.

And that's why I wrote this book. To offer parents and

3

caretakers guidance in talking with young children ages four to eleven about the most sensitive and powerful issues of our troubled world—issues like AIDS, homelessness, racial prejudice, war, and the environment. In addition to these rather global concerns, I also address some more personal but nonetheless disquieting topics affecting today's families, such as divorce, dealing with the elderly, sexual abuse, drugs and alcohol, job loss, and coping with a loved one's cancer.

But there's another reason why I wrote this book and, more important, why I believe you will benefit from reading it: We love our kids. And not just our own children—the ones we gave birth to and are trying hard to raise—but all kids today who are faced with one tough task: growing up happy in a troubled and troubling world. As my good friend Carley, who, like me, never had children of her own, once remarked, "The way I see it, children are a collective responsibility. They are an essential part of our present and all of our future. So it's up to each and every one of us to do whatever we can to make their lives as rich and satisfying as possible." I couldn't agree more.

Now, I know some parents may balk at the appropriateness of discussing some of these delicate subjects with young children. But remember, your kids are already hearing about these subjects from TV, movies, magazines, and schoolyard friends. If *you* don't talk to them—and answer their questions—they'll get their "facts" from someone else. Then you'll be denied an invaluable opportunity to offer your children accurate information in a context that's comfortable for you.

Also, as the more than 120 child psychiatrists, psychologists, sociologists, scientists, doctors, and educators whose ideas and opinions I've collected and synthesized in this book confirm, talking with your children about these issues won't hurt them—but making these issues taboo will. Instead, opening up clear lines of communication with your kids will help them to become not only happy children but confident teenagers and, finally, healthy, well-adjusted adults.

How to Use This Book

If I've done my job well, *Talking with Your Child About a Troubled World* will serve as a resource for every parent, a starting-off point to get you thinking about these subjects and discussing them effectively with your child. To begin, read through chapter 1; it offers the essential rules of thumb you need to know in talking with your child about anything. Then peruse the other chapter titles and pick and choose according to your—and your child's—needs. If, for instance, you're struggling with a divorce, or about to head into one, go straight to the chapter on divorce and read it through. Or if your kids become frightened by the homeless man they see lying on the street, flip directly to that chapter instead. Each issue has its own chapter that includes a quick course in the subject at hand, concrete tips (geared to different age levels) for talking with your child about the particular issue, questions that children typically ask (and sample answers to guide you in your responses), and a resource guide for further information.

One final point to keep in mind as you read this book: Trust yourself. Every child is different. But if you rely on your parental instincts to apply the information and advice offered here and adapt them to the abilities and interest levels of your own unique youngsters, you will find yourself becoming more confident and successful in guiding your children through our troubled world.

Chapter One

FIRST THINGS

FIRST

What You Need to Know Before

Talking with Your Child

About Anything

Four-year-old Brian climbed up on his mother's lap, peered into her face, and asked, "Mommy, where did I come from?" A bit cowed by the suddenness and import of his question, but wanting to offer her impressionable youngster all the information he might need, his mother launched into a detailed account of sexual intercourse, explaining every action involved and ending with the message that sex should never be undertaken without the mutual under-standing and respect of a loving partner.

"Oh," said little Brian, scrambling off his mother's lap. "My friend Tommy came from Florida."

I know . . . it's an old joke. But it's a favorite of mine

not only because it always makes me laugh, but because it so vividly illustrates what we need to remember when talking with young kids. That is, it reminds us to listen to our children's questions and to hear what they are really asking. Even more important, it tells us that children will understand what they are able to understand when they are ready to understand it. And not one moment before.

Kids grow and learn according to their own timetable. At each age, particularly in the early years, they reach new and exciting developmental levels, not only in their expanding ability to achieve physical mastery over themselves and their environment—to creep, crawl, walk, and run—but in their ability to think and react as well. Trying to introduce a concept that is beyond the reach of a young child's emotional and cognitive levels will be a futile exercise not only for you as a parent and caregiver, but for your child as well. At best, he won't understand what you're talking about and will dismiss the subject altogether. At worst, he'll pick up only disjointed bits of information and arrange them in such a way as to confuse or even frighten him.

Explaining to a four-year-old that her pet dog had to be "put to sleep" may make her afraid to fall asleep at bedtime. Telling a five-year-old that AIDS is caused by a "bug" may make him fearful of all insects. Clearly, then, you need first to understand what your child is able to comprehend both psychologically and cognitively at each individual stage of development before you attempt to discuss any complex issues (and particularly the ones in this book) with him. Here follows a brief overview of these general developmental stages. (For more detailed information on children's growth and development, check the Readings for Parents section at the end of this chapter.)

The Key Developmental Stages

INFANCY

During the first year of life, babies learn about their immediate world—their own bodies and the environment that they can touch, see, hear, smell, and feel. They are completely egocentric, primarily concerned with the world as it relates to their physical comfort. Infants begin to bond at birth, particularly with parents and siblings. Healthy babies raised in a caring, safe, and stable environment start learning to trust. When Mommy smiles at them, they respond, smiling and cooing in delight. At this stage, parents are beginning to lay the foundation for their baby's successful transition into toddlerhood.

TODDLERHOOD

One- and two-year-olds are still egocentric, but they show an increased interest in their surroundings. Curiosity leads them to explore anything within reach, but their short attention spans make them easily distracted.

Toddlers are developing an awareness of their separateness; that is, they are discovering that they are distinct from Mom or Dad. That growing sense of self hits hard during "the terrible twos" when, as every parent knows, "no" becomes the favorite word in most toddlers' embryonic vocabulary.

As toddlers grow more certain of their physical abilities, they begin to test their world's boundaries. Parents often find themselves trailing behind an energetically mobile two-year-old as he explores every nook and cranny of his expanding environment.

During toddlerhood, kids rarely ask their parents many difficult questions, at least not ones about the complex issues covered in this book. That's because toddlers do not as yet have the vocabulary to frame adequate questions and because their cognitive development—their ability to think logically and abstractly—is still at its most formative stage.

THE PRESCHOOL YEARS

Although three- and four-year-olds intensify their interaction with their environment, they still see themselves as the center of the universe. Since they view the world *solely* from their own perspective, they cannot distinguish between their own point of view and anyone else's. If Daddy divorces Mommy and leaves home, the four-year-old is likely to blame himself for his father's disappearance. "Daddy left home because I was bad" is not an unlikely rationale in the mind of a preschooler.

Preschoolers also think in concrete terms. They focus on external, observable events rather than unseen ones, understanding the world primarily through what they see, touch, smell, taste, and hear. Abstract thoughts are still beyond most preschoolers. If, for instance, a four-year-old learns that Grandma has died, his first question might be "Well, where did she go?" If you explain that Grandma's soul has gone to heaven, he might ask, "When will she come back?" Sophisticated concepts like the finality of death are not within the cognitive grasp of the typical preschooler.

At this stage, kids also engage in magical thinking. For example, they believe that events which occur contiguously have a cause-and-effect relationship, so that a four-year-old may announce, "I know why Uncle Bobby got AIDS

. . . because he visited us for Thanksgiving." Magical thinking also allows kids to believe that their thoughts, wishes, or feelings can cause events to occur. If a young child wishes her alcoholic father would go away and never come back—and then he is killed in an auto accident—the child may well believe that her wish caused the tragedy.

Preschoolers have language and are beginning to engage in "symbolic play." A three-year-old may imitate a train whistle while pushing a block of wood along the floor in a pretend game of railroad engineer. Child-care specialists often capitalize on preschoolers' ability to enjoy symbolic play by using toys to prepare them for traumatic events. Pediatricians often use a doll to represent the "patient" in order to explain to the child who needs surgery what an IV or operating room is.

Because preschoolers are beginning to think symbolically, they are at a wonderful age to try "bibliotherapy," the current term for using books to teach children about all aspects of life. *Losing Uncle Tim,* for instance, helps very young children understand how losing a loved one to AIDS might feel.

What's more, just as books provide an excellent teaching tool for children, paying close attention to children's "symbolic" drawings and fantasy play, particularly puppet and doll play, can give parents great insight into their children's concerns. For example, one five-year-old who never voiced any anxiety about his parents' divorce suddenly began drawing vivid pictures of a sad little boy standing all alone in a very big house. When his mother asked her son to explain what the picture was about, he said that the "divorced boy" in the drawing was sad because "he got left all alone with no one to take care of him." His response, then, gave his mom the perfect opportunity to draw her youngster out about his fears and to reassure him that he would never be abandoned. (FYI: older children may also reveal their concerns symbolically through art and play; thus, parents should tune into such nonverbal expressions for important clues as to what's on their kids' minds.)

Another aspect of this developmental stage is the child's ability to attend to only one aspect of reality at a time. As Piaget explained in his renowned work on children's intellectual development, a young child who sees the same amount of water being poured into a tall thin beaker as into a short, fat one will still believe that the tall, thin beaker has more water in it simply because, once the water is poured, that beaker *looks* fuller. In more personal terms, the preschooler, who can attend to only one concrete fact at a time, may have difficulty understanding how, after a divorce, Daddy can still be his father, but not Mommy's husband.

It's also difficult for a preschooler to comprehend that he can experience more than one feeling at a time. Emotionally, his world is either black or white, with few, if any, shades of gray. If Mommy denies him something he wants, he may feel "all mad" at Mommy. He has difficulty understanding that he can be mad at Mommy and love her, too, or just as important, that Mommy can be mad at him and love him at the same time.

EARLY SCHOOL AGE

Children ages five through seven are still relatively egocentric, although they are beginning to be able to see things from another person's point of view. They can be quite sympathetic and empathetic, particularly toward other children who may be crying or having a difficult time.

These youngsters also can think about two concepts simultaneously. They are able to realize, for example, that four jellybeans grouped closely together equal the same number of jellybeans as four spaced far apart. Emotionally, they are beginning to understand that Mom always loves them, even when she punishes them for being naughty.

Early-school-age youngsters are concerned with their bodies' integrity; they're able to understand that their body is important and that it is *theirs*. A statement like "We need to eat good foods because it will keep our bodies strong and healthy" makes perfect sense to a five-, six- or seven-year-old.

Children at this stage of life view the world with great interest. They are highly observant and curious, and ask innumerable questions in an ongoing effort to make rational sense of the world around them. Their ability to remember facts and ideas is developing, though at this stage, short-term memory is much stronger than its long-term counter-part.

By the time youngsters reach the age of eight or so, they are capable of understanding fairly abstract concepts. Whereas a five-year-old may have difficulty grasping the finality of death, the ten-year-old understands that when someone dies, he will never return. Consequently, children at this stage may think, and sometimes worry, about the future. They become more introspective; some may start writing journals or keeping diaries. Youngsters at this stage enjoy interactive play that allows them to demonstrate mastery over their burgeoning physical and intellectual skills. They are resourceful problem-solvers and may work hard at discovering successful solutions.

At this age, children move away from magical "there's a monster under the bed" fears and into more reality-based anxieties. Youngsters may worry about passing a spelling test, being accepted by their peers, or having their house blown away by an impending tornado.

PRE-ADOLESCENCE

Children ages eleven to twelve demonstrate a strong capacity to differentiate between themselves and others. They are able to feel deep sympathy for and empathy toward others less fortunate than themselves.

Cognitively, they are quite capable of thinking in hypothetical terms; they understand that if X were to happen, then Y would result. Children of this age also have strong short- and long-term memory skills.

Pre-adolescents also are developing a stronger sense of self. Correspondingly, they are often highly introspective and concerned with their competence. Also, they are much more social; peer pressure begins to mount in the pre-adolescent stage.

Pre-adolescents also evince great interest in what is happening to their bodies. They are intensely interested in and curious about breast changes, the growth of pubic hair, and the early onset of menstruation.

While these developmental stages provide useful insights into how children grow, they are by no means carved in stone. Each child develops at her own individual pace, and variations on these themes are commonplace. It is not unusual for very young children to ask some precocious questions, like "Mommy, I saw two men hug each other. Are they gay?" which popped out of a five-year-old, or "If

I don't wash my hands before dinner will I get AIDS?" which came from a four-year-old child.

Nonetheless, understanding these basic developmental stages enables us to communicate effectively with our children, neither overwhelming them with too much information nor underestimating their abilities to comprehend. When seasoned with a large dose of sensitivity to your own child's abilities within each developmental level, such understanding helps us explain the complexities of our world to youngsters as simply and clearly as possible.

Sixteen Essential Rules of Thumb for Talking with Your Child About Anything

As you will see in the upcoming chapters, the words you use and the messages you convey when talking with your child vary from issue to issue. But the following guidelines hold true no matter what the topic of discussion.

1. Create an Open Environment.

Children are curious. They have questions about anything and everything. Yet when it comes to such sensitive issues as AIDS, homelessness, racism, or divorce, they will raise their questions only if they feel you will be receptive. It's up to you, then, as parents, to create the kind of open environment where any query—on any issue—can be asked freely and without fear of consequence.

How do you foster such an atmosphere? By being encouraging, supportive, and positively reinforcing. Giving a child a quick, curt answer, or worse, a reprimand, whenever she asks a sensitive or tricky question will put an immediate end to discussion. What you need to do instead is to respond in a way that tells your child her questions are always welcome.

Here's what I mean. If your child asks, "How many people are homeless?" try not to answer with "How do I know! Just eat your lunch," no matter how busy or upset you are at the time. Instead, try something like "That's an interesting question, but you know, I'm not sure. Let's look it up after you eat your lunch." That way, you not only validate their curiosity but also leave open the door for plenty of important discussion.

2. Consider Your Child's Temperament.

Whether your child is easygoing or fussy, outgoing or shy, demonstrative or reserved will affect the way you respond to his questions. As Harvard developmental psychologist Dr. Nancy Cotton explains, "Suppose you are planning a picnic, and your child, who tends to be a worrier, asks, 'But what if it rains?' Responding with 'Oh, don't worry about that' will only make him more anxious because you are not taking his concerns seriously."

Now I realize that intuitively, you'll want to offset his negativism by cheering your child up. But, says Cotton, that approach will have the opposite effect. You have a better chance of calming his fears and opening up communication if you say, "Well, I don't think it's going to rain, but if it does, we'll spread a blanket over the living room rug and hold the picnic inside."

On the other hand, suppose your child is extremely

cheerful, and always sees the bright side of every situation. Her knee-jerk optimism could sometimes make it difficult for her to confront negative feelings, like the sadness or anger she may feel when her grandmother dies. In that case, you may need to help her out by saying, "It's okay to feel sad about Grandma, and maybe even a little angry because she's left us. But we know she didn't want to leave us and that she loved us very much. Grandma will always be in our hearts because we love her, too."

3. Respect Your Child's Feelings.

Allowing children to express their feelings openly— even when they spring from what you feel is a silly event— will help insure that they'll always come to you when they have a serious problem. The child who screams out in dismay because his big sister tossed his teddy bear out of his favorite TV-watching seat can be better handled by a brief word of comfort—"Teddy's okay. He just got bounced a bit, but he's fine now"—than by an angry "Don't be such a baby. Nobody hurt *you*!"

Here's the point: Rather than trying to argue your child out of her feelings, legitimize them instead. That way, you let her know that she's an important individual whose feelings always count.

Respecting your child's feelings will also help you tune into his cues as to when he's had enough. Suppose, for instance, you're answering your nine-year-old's questions about AIDS. Feel free to give the child as much information as he wants, but if he says, "I want to go out and play now," or "I don't want to talk about this," don't force the issue. "Back up—but don't back off," as child and adolescent psychiatrist Dr. Alan Cohen, medical director of Laurel Oaks Hospital, likes to put it. Just try to introduce the subject at another time.

4. Know Your Child's Cognitive Limits.

As we've already discussed, there are limits to what children can understand at different developmental stages. Providing a detailed explanation of the sociological determinants of homelessness is well beyond the cognitive reach of the six-year-old who wants to know why the man is sleeping on the street. To avoid talking over the head of your youngster, first clarify exactly what he is asking and what he already knows. If, for instance, your child asks you what war is, ask him what *he thinks* war is. If he says "I think it's like when Ninja Turtles fight the bad guys," then you have a sense of the level of information he's seeking and you can tailor your explanations to fit his age and developmental level.

5. Always Be Honest.

Recently, I spoke with a mother who, rather than explain to her four- and six-year-old sons that the family dog had died, told them that their pet was very sick and had to go live at the vet's from now on. Not surprisingly, the kids became extremely upset and confused, especially when, during a trip to the vet with their cat the following week, the dog was nowhere in sight.

I wondered, on hearing this story, how trusting of others these children would grow up to be. For, as child psychiatrist David Fassler has said to me, "Once you've lied to a kid, no matter what your intentions, you usually don't get a second chance to set the record straight. You've damaged the relationship of trust." Whatever your child's age, he deserves honest answers and explanations. It's honesty that strengthens your child's ability to trust. Also, when you don't provide a straightforward answer, kids may make up their own, and their fantasy explanation is often more frightening than any real and honest response you could have offered.

6. If You Don't Know Something, Admit It.

I'm always amazed by how many parents I meet who incorrectly believe that if their children learn that Mom and Dad don't know *everything,* they won't look up to them. It's simply not true. Kids accept "I don't know" and "Let's find out." And it's much better for them to hear than false information supplied by an insecure parent.

Also remember that as a parent, you don't need to answer more questions than you're ready to answer. It's perfectly acceptable to say, "I'm not sure about that. I need to think it over a bit, but we'll talk about it another time"— as long as you *do* talk about it again. Following up lets your child know that his concerns are important to you—and that goes a long way toward building your youngster's self-esteem.

In that same vein, it's also okay to postpone a discussion for a more appropriate time. For instance, a woman I know was negotiating a tricky turn in fierce rush-hour traffic when her nine-year-old son suddenly asked, "Mom, what's a condom?" "I didn't know what to do," she told me. "I was so taken aback that I made a sharp left without signaling and almost smashed into a truck. But what the heck do you say?"

Actually, an appropriate response isn't all that complicated. It's perfectly okay to say something like "Boy, that's an important question, but with all this traffic, I can't talk to you about it now. Let's talk about it later, after dinner." And then make sure you do.

7. Don't Leave Big Gaps.

While you may not want or need to share all the details of a particular situation or issue with your child, try not to leave big gaps, either. Young children will fill in those holes themselves and, in the process, generate a good deal of confusion and concern.

A case in point: In a misguided attempt to shield their daughter from her mother's upcoming surgery, the parents of four-year-old Elizabeth told her that "Mommy is going away for a while" instead of explaining that she had to go to the hospital for an operation. After her mother left, the youngster became extremely and uncharacteristically agitated. When the baby-sitter asked her what was wrong, she answered, "I made Mommy leave. I didn't eat all my carrots"—a perfect example of the preschooler's egocentric thinking. To avoid such misunderstandings, be sure to fill in as many details as your child can understand.

8. Be Careful What You Promise.

Never promise a child something over which you have no control. Suppose Grandma becomes very ill and has to go to the hospital, and your ten-year-old comes to you and says, "I'm worried that Grandma will die." Try not to falsely reassure the youngster by promising that "Grandma will be just fine" if you're not sure that she will. Instead, say something like "Well, I'm a little worried, too, because Grandma is very sick. And sometimes when people get very, very sick and are as old as Grandma is, they do die. But the doctors will take extra good care of her and there's a good chance she'll get well again." This simple, honest, and direct approach really will serve your child better.

9. Use Age-appropriate Language.

Always speak to your child in language she can understand. For instance, when David Fassler and his colleagues were researching the current AIDS literature before writing a children's book on the subject, they found that often publications written for young children used words like "transmission" and "transfusion" that few kids understand. So Fassler and his colleagues took great pains to use simple, basic words that even very young children could comprehend.

There's no particular rule that dictates which language is appropriate for which age; much depends on the verbal abilities of the individual. The best advice is to use simple, short words and straightforward explanations, and to trust your parental instincts as to the language your child can understand.

10. Get Feedback.

One of the best ways to figure out if your child has understood a certain subject is to ask him. Let a little time pass after an important discussion, then ask him to tell you what he remembers about the conversation and what he understands. For example, a commercial on recycling may lead you and your seven-year-old into a conversation about the environment. But a week later, when you ask your son "Do you remember what I told you about recycling?" you find he's gotten some of the information a little backward.

Now that you're aware of it, though, you have the opportunity to correct any misconceptions and fill in any gaps.

11. Listen Patiently.

As any parent or caretaker of a young child knows, it can feel like forever before your youngster gets his story out. Sometimes he'll begin with "Mom, know what?" and then launch into a ten-minute-long series of unrelated statements before finally telling you "what."

As adults, we feel tempted to finish the child's sentences for him, filling in words and phrases in an effort to hear the point some time within this century. Well, here's some advice: resist the impulse. He'll recount his tale in his own time and when he's ready. By listening patiently, you'll allow him to work at his own pace and convey to him the message that he's worthy of your time.

Patience also comes in handy when answering your child's questions. Since most young children can only process small pieces of information at any one time, they probably won't learn all they need to know about a particular topic in a single discussion. Therefore, they'll ask the same questions again and again over time. Such repetition is normal, so be prepared and tolerant.

12. Give Yourself Some Time Out.

Once an issue has fired a child's imagination, he can be unrelenting in wanting to question you about it. While you don't want to dampen his enthusiasm, you may also reach a saturation point. Whether you're home all day and bombarded with questions or are hit with a barrage of queries the moment you walk in the door after a grueling workday, as a parent you're sometimes too drained to cope.

When that happens, call time-out and put further discussion off for a while. Just say, "Daddy's too tired right now. Let's talk about that after dinner, when I've had a chance to rest." Then make sure you follow up at that time.

13. Establish Eye Contact.

Think about it. How many times do you answer your child's questions while folding clothes, preparing for your next day's meeting, or pushing a shopping cart through the supermarket? For most parents caught up in the hectic routines of contemporary life, actually making eye contact while they're talking to their children becomes an all too rare event.

Still, it's important to find times to talk to your youngster when you can look her in the eye. Direct eye contact adds more conviction to your message: after all, which would you pay more attention to, a comment your boss made as she was running out the door, or the one she made when she looked you right in the eye? Second, facing your child when you speak with her helps build self-esteem by letting her know she's worthy of your undivided attention.

14. Speak Separately to Kids of Different Ages.

If your children are widely spaced in age, it's best to talk with them separately, even if you want to discuss the same general subject. The reason is that children at such varied developmental levels need different information, have different sensitivities, and require different vocabularies. Also, older children often will dominate the discussion, and may well inhibit the younger ones from speaking.

15. Examine Your Own Motives.

If you feel compelled to discuss a subject in which your child has shown no interest—even though whenever you bring it up he immediately tunes out—you may want to examine why you're so committed to this issue. Perhaps, as Cohen suggests, it's because you may be "extremely concerned about a particular topic, like sex or war or adoption, and want to take the pressure off yourself by speaking in great detail to your kids." Be sure, then, to take your own psychological pulse to see why it is you feel pressured to talk about the subject so fully. If it has more to do with making *you* feel better than with helping your children, you may want to think twice before bringing the issue up again.

16. Know When Your Child Needs Professional Help.

Whenever anything upsetting happens in a child's life—a new baby arrives, the family relocates, your child changes schools—a certain degree of "symptomatology" may emerge. That is, your child may become clingy, have trouble sleeping, lose his appetite, show such regressive behavior as bed-wetting, thumb sucking, or playing with long-outgrown baby toys. He may suddenly become more aggressive and pick fights with the other kids, or experience a sudden drop in his school grades. Now a certain amount of that is to be expected. But if these uncharacteristic behaviors go on for more than a couple of weeks and/or are fairly intense—in short, if your child shows a significant and profound change in his ability to function in major areas of his life—then he may need professional help.

What's more, adds psychiatrist Fassler, "It's not just the child who acts out who may need help; I'm just as concerned about the child who 'acts in,' that is, who becomes very depressed and withdrawn, no longer seems to enjoy the things he used to love, or no longer plays with his friends." Again, if this persists for more than a couple of weeks, consider some form of outside assistance.

Where do you find professional help? Try a referral from your clergyman, pediatrician, or family doctor. Another good source is a close friend whose judgment you respect, or a school guidance counselor. Or contact a professional association such as your local or state medical, psychiatric, or psychological society for the name of a qualified mental health professional.

If you've stayed with me throughout this quick course on child psychology, you're ready to move on. But whichever issues you choose to explore—in whatever order you choose to explore them—try and keep the information you've learned with you. It will serve you well as you and your child tackle the sensitive and complex issues that fill the pages of the chapters ahead.

Helpful Resources

ORGANIZATIONS

American Academy of Child and Adolescent Psychiatry
3615 Wisconsin Avenue, NW
Washington, DC 20016
(202) 966-7300

American Association for Marriage and Family
Therapists
1100 17th St., NW
10th Floor
Washington, DC 20036
(202) 452-0109
(800) 374-2638 (therapist referral only)

American Psychological Association
1200 Seventeenth St., NW
Washington, DC 20036
(202) 955-7710

American Psychiatric Association
Division of Public Affairs
1400 K Street, NW
Washington, DC 20005
(202) 682-6220

READINGS FOR PARENTS

Chess, Stella, and Thomas, Alexander. *Know Your Child: An Authoritative Guide for Today's Parents.* New York: Basic Books, 1989.

Elkind, David. *Child Development & Education: A Piagetian Perspective.* New York: Oxford University Press, 1976.

Faber, Adele, and Mazlish, Elaine. *How to Talk So Kids Will Listen & How to Listen So Kids Will Talk.* Mamaroneck, N.Y.: International Center for Creative Thinking, 1990.

Fraiberg, Selma. *The Magic Years.* New York: Charles Scribner's Sons, 1959.

Ginott, Haim G. *Between Parent & Child.* New York: Avon, 1976.

Leach, Penelope. *Your Baby & Child.*, rev. ed. New York: Knopf, 1989.

————. *Your Growing Child: From Babyhood to Adolescence.* New York: Knopf, 1986.

Spock, Benjamin. *Dr. Spock on Parenting: Sensible Advice for Today.* New York: Simon & Schuster, 1988.

————, with Rothenberg, Michael B. *Dr. Spock's Baby & Child Care.* New York: Dutton, 1985.

Special thanks to the following experts for their input into this chapter: Alan Cohen, M.D., medical director, Laurel Oaks Hospital; Nancy Cotton, Ph.D., instructor in psychology, Cambridge Hospital, Harvard Medical School; David Fassler, M.D., clinical director, Otter Creek Associates; Bill Rae, Ph.D., pediatric psychologist, associate professor, Texas A&M University College of Medicine.

Chapter Two

"MOMMY, WHY IS THAT MAN SLEEPING IN THE SNOW?"

Talking with Your Child About Homelessness

Seven-year-old Evan and his mom were picking up some last-minute Christmas gifts at Boston's Quincy Market. Despite the hectic pace, both mother and son were enjoying the best of holiday spirits—that is, until, arms loaded with gifts and heading happily home, they happened upon a homeless man. His bare feet were raw with sores and blisters; he was lying, eyes shut, on a tattered piece of cardboard that was barely visible underneath a layer of grime-stained snow.

Evan's mom, holding tightly to her son's hand, tried to hurry them past, but the youngster's pace slowed, his eyes riveted on the street person. Then, Evan looked up at his mother and asked, "Mom, why is that man sleeping in the snow?"

Queries such as this can throw even the most thoughtful and concerned parent for a loop. Why? Mostly because we don't know how we feel about the homeless ourselves. Typically we're conflicted: our sense of compassion mixes with disdain, disgust, and guilt. We resent the individual who becomes homeless and the system that seems unable or unwilling to help.

We honestly don't understand homelessness. We know that it exists and seems to be growing, but we don't really know why. We're not even certain who the homeless people are; the only thing we are sure of is that we want the sight of these heartbreaking and disturbing people to simply and magically disappear.

Parents have still another concern: the effect our kids' exposure to the homeless has on their view of themselves and the world. The tattered, pushy panhandler, filthy side-walk sleeper, and wild-eyed, raving unfortunate all upset us as adults: how, we worry, will they affect our children?

Understandably, parents want to be able to provide solutions for every problem their children face. But home-lessness seems to reject solutions and, therefore, to heighten our feelings of inadequacy. The ubiquitousness of street people won't let us shield our children from them, and images of homelessness constantly remind us that we can't make our kids' world a perfectly safe and wonderful place to be.

There is a way to discuss homelessness with children, however, and, in the process, to teach them important lessons in life. Talking about homelessness can help children realize that not everyone in this world is as lucky as they are. And it can teach them to be compassionate toward people who are different from and less fortunate than themselves.

Finding the best way to explain homelessness demands that we first understand the facts, clarify our own feelings, and learn how to communicate them honestly to our children. To begin, here's a brief synopsis of the issue of homelessness as it is understood today.

The Issue in Focus

Simply and accurately, to be "homeless" means to lack a permanent residence. Thus, people who live in shelters, or such emergency housing as hotels, bus terminals, subway stations, cars, caves, abandoned buildings, parks, tents, chicken coops, highway underpasses, and on sidewalks are homeless. And so are people who have "doubled up" in the homes of friends and relatives for a while—"but just for a while."

But in another sense, homelessness is a very complex issue that means a great deal more than not having a permanent place to live. "Homelessness in America: A Summary," a fact sheet put out by the National Coalition for the Homeless (NCH) in Washington, D.C., states it well: "Homeless means having no place to store the things that connect you to your past; it means losing contact with friends and family;

it means uprooting your kids from school; it means having to endure the shame of what is still perceived as personal failure. For some, it means breaking up the family just to find lodging for the night, since many 'family shelters' do not allow older boys to stay, and many homeless children are placed with relatives or put into foster care. Being homeless means . . . the frustration of not being able to provide for those who depend on you, the humiliation of having to rely on the kindness of strangers, the anonymity of government assistance. Being homeless means having no center in one's life, no haven to return to, no certainty about tomorrow."

It's hard to know just how many people in the U.S. currently suffer the indignity of homelessness; the peripatetic nature of the homeless makes them difficult to count. The National Coalition for the Homeless pegs their population at three million. The National Alliance to End Homelessness says that between 1.3 and 2 million people become homeless in any given year.

But all groups seem to agree that the number of homeless is growing. A study by Washington's Department of Housing and Urban Development (HUD), and reported in the NCH Fact Sheet, revealed that the number of people in shelters alone soared 155 percent between 1984 and 1988. And the U.S. Conference of Mayors (USCM) stated that requests for shelter by homeless families in 1989 increased an average of 23 percent in the twenty-seven major cities surveyed. (Keep in mind, though, that the homeless are not found only in cities, but in suburbs and rural areas as well.)

Who are the homeless? According to the USCM, 46 percent are single men. But the next largest segment of this population, and, sadly, the fastest growing, is families with children. They represent 36 percent of homeless people today. Single women account for 14 percent, and unaccompanied youth, 4 percent. And here's another fact that may surprise you: Nearly 25 percent of homeless people are employed—but don't earn enough to pay for housing. According to the USCM, about one-half of the urban homeless are black, over a third are white, and some 14 percent are categorized as "other."

The causes of homelessness are many. Primarily, people become homeless because they cannot find affordable housing. Not only isn't there enough low-income housing being built, but because of drastic cuts in federal housing programs, each year thousands of existing low-income units are being lost to conversion (into cooperatives and condominiums or other high-income housing), abandonment, fire, and demolition, says the NCH. Gentrification, the process by which landlords and developers upgrade neglected neighborhoods in order to attract higher-income tenants, and which raises the cost of housing enough to displace the original residents, has also made affordable housing scarce.

The state of our nation's current economy has fueled the increase in the homeless population. In short, the growing poor are growing poorer. Census Bureau statistics reveal that the number of Americans beneath the poverty line climbed from 26 million in 1979 to 32 million in 1988. The income of the average poor family dropped $4,851 *below* the poverty line in 1988. Add to that high unemployment and a minimum wage which, according to the Low Income Housing Information Service, does not allow a full-time worker (working for minimum wage) to earn enough to pay rent and utilities for a reasonably priced one-bedroom apartment in forty-four states, and you begin to understand why homelessness continues to climb.

But homelessness has even more causes. The NCH reports that federally funded programs to aid the poor suffered major cutbacks under the Reagan administration. Food-stamp programs as well as benefit levels for families in need of Aid to Families with Dependent Children (AFDC) monies have both been reduced.

Then there is "dumping," or, as it's sometimes called, "deinstitutionalization," the well-intentioned but ineptly enacted process by which thousands of mentally ill persons were released from, or not admitted to, mental-health-care facilities, and, almost literally, dumped on the streets. (Recent legislation is trying to alleviate this problem, but it is way too early to gauge its effects.) In addition, the lack of sufficient drug- and alcohol-treatment programs and facilities has also increased the numbers of homeless fending for themselves. After all, when poor people have a drug or alcohol problem, they rarely have the same resources as well-heeled drug and alcohol abusers to help them find a solution and keep off the streets.

Homeless advocates offer a variety of solutions to the homelessness dilemma, including providing more, and more affordable, housing and enacting federal legislation that will address homelessness seriously. But perhaps before any of these programs can be implemented successfully, each American must understand the problem and ask himself how much he is willing to help.

Housed parents of young children face an additional

predicament: how to help their children cope with the issue of homelessness. For, as Dr. Ellen Bassuk, president of The Better Homes Foundation, a nonprofit organization serving homeless families nationwide, says, "No matter where you live, whether Des Moines or New York City, your child probably has seen homeless people firsthand. If not, he has surely seen them on TV or in magazines, or perhaps even participated in discussions about homelessness at school. Or perhaps your child has a homeless classmate at school." Whatever the exposure, seeing the homeless can trigger some scary feelings in very young children—and it's up to us adults to help them cope. As Bassuk so eloquently puts it, "If we have a generation raised with compassion, a generation who understands that the homeless are not disgusting 'others' but human beings with a right to a decent quality of life, then we will take a big step toward eliminating the problem." And that would be a wonderful gift for our children and ourselves.

How to Talk to Your Kids About Homelessness

1. Confront the Issue.

Parents who try to sidestep the issue of homelessness in an attempt to shield their child from the harshness of this reality are being naive. What's more, they may be doing their kids a disservice. By refusing to discuss the topic, either changing the subject when it arises or being vague or dismissive when their children ask questions, they leave their children confused, unable to make sense of a reality they see.

Further, if you don't talk to your kids about homelessness, you can be sure that they'll take their questions elsewhere, and you'll miss out on an important opportunity to share your values and teach your beliefs to your own child. As your children mature and move into their teens and beyond, they will develop their own ideas and opinions. But for now they need to understand where your family stands on such issues as homelessness and what your family stands for. It's an essential part of learning their identity, of knowing who they and their family are.

2. Explain, in Simple Terms, What Homelessness Is.

Very young children don't need, nor can they understand, a long discussion of the social significance of homelessness. Instead, questions about what it means to be homeless merit a simple and straightforward explanation such as "When people don't have homes to live in, when they have no place to sleep at night and no place to cook their meals, they are homeless. Sometimes homeless people can go to a shelter to eat and sleep and wash. But sometimes not. Sometimes they have no place to go. That makes me feel sad."

3. Allay Their Fears.

Children, particularly kids under the age of ten, can feel anxious and frightened when they come face-to-face with a homeless person. You'll be walking down the street with your child, see a homeless person, and suddenly feel your youngster's hand grip yours more tightly. She may move closer to you; her face may reveal her anxiety. Your child may say something to you or ask a question about the situation. On the other hand, she may simply hang on tighter to communicate her distress.

Such a reaction is not at all surprising, says Harvard child psychiatrist Dr. Myron Belfer. "Kids see people who look dirty and disheveled and they don't understand how they got that way. Also, certain behavior by some homeless people—the begging, the intrusiveness—can be particularly disconcerting."

It's wise, therefore, to offer your children reassurance that they are safe and secure. You can explain that while some homeless people may look scary, they aren't really dangerous. Of course, if a homeless person *is* menacing, by all means assure your children that you will protect them, but also explain that the homeless person may be acting that way because he or she is ill.

Another aspect of homelessness that can frighten young kids is the makeshift cardboard box shelters some homeless people call home. Such images reminds kids of movie-style orphans who have no place to go and raise the notion of what life without a home can be like, an issue that is very frightening to a young child—almost as upsetting as fearing that a parent will die. Given that level of potential upset, then, you might want to reassure your child that not only is he safe now, but that he will continue to be safe and that he will not be homeless. To a four- to six-year-old you can say, "It's sad that that person has no home and has to live in a big box. We're lucky that we have a home where we can be happy and safe." To an older child you can talk about the specifics of your particular family to give the message more weight. For instance, you can say something like "I feel sad that this person has to live in a cardboard box. We're lucky that I have a job and Daddy has a job so that we have enough money to pay for our home. Also, we have family and friends to help us and to rely on in bad times, and that's something that homeless people often don't have."

4. Hear the Hidden Question.

When your child sees a homeless person on the street, it can prompt a plethora of questions, such as "Why is that woman so dirty?" "Why is she asking for money?" "Why are people stepping over that man lying on the sidewalk?" "Is he hungry?" "Is he cold?" "Why doesn't somebody help?" Each of these queries deserves a straightforward answer. But beware that underneath such questions may lie your youngster's more personal concerns.

"When young children ask about the homeless," says child and adolescent psychiatrist Dr. Bonnie Zima, "they are often really asking 'Will you let that happen to me?' 'Am I safe?' 'Could that happen to my Mommy and Daddy?' " Thus, you need not only to answer your children's spoken questions, but the unspoken ones as well. Such a response as "That woman is dirty because she doesn't have a place to wash" should also be followed by a statement like "We're very lucky that we will always have a nice place to live with a bathroom where we can wash and keep ourselves clean."

5. Don't Paint Too Rosy a Picture.

In an effort to reassure your child and to assuage her anxieties, you might explain that communities take care of the homeless and that there are shelters where homeless people can go to eat, sleep, and bathe. But you should take care not to paint too rosy a picture and to make any explanation about the homeless as realistic as possible. While you can explain that there are places for homeless people to go, you need to add that unfortunately, "these shelters don't always have enough room for everyone, so homeless people sometimes have to sleep outside in the cold. And that is very sad."

6. Show Compassion.

Many people in America believe that most homeless persons are alcoholics and drug addicts who choose to ruin their lives and thus deserve their fate. But such a lack of compassion can distort the reality of the homeless for both you and your child. While it's true that many homeless persons are addicted to drugs and/or alcohol, and some are, in fact, mentally ill, that does not mean that they deserve to live without a home. Having a decent quality of life that includes a safe and secure home is a basic human right that should not be denied anyone, no matter what the status of their physical or mental health.

Instead of blaming the victims of homelessness, then, it's important to explain to your children that homeless people are not bad, but unfortunate. They may not have jobs, so they don't have enough money to pay the rent. Their homes may have burned down and they did not have enough money to buy a new home. They may be dirty and smell because they have no place to wash; they are hungry because they don't have enough food to eat. Conveying a sense of compassion for the homeless is part and parcel of offering your children an honest explanation.

Of course, you cannot force your child to develop a social conscience immediately; that evolves over the years through the everyday experiences of a lifetime. Also, children under the age of seven may not be able to feel empathy for the homeless because putting oneself in someone else's shoes demands too sophisticated a level of emotional capability. Still, speaking empathetically about the homeless to even a very young child helps build a foundation for compassion that will blossom as your youngster matures.

7. Acknowledge Both Similarities and Differences.

Encouraging a sense of compassion involves helping your child understand that he is part of a world that not only includes himself, his parents, his siblings, other family members, teachers, and friends, but people from all walks of life—including homeless people.

Peter Rose runs Clear Pool Camp, a summer-day-camp program for poor and homeless kids living in New York City. Through that program, he has come to know homeless children and their families well, and he stresses that "in many ways, homeless people are no different from us, except that they are down on their luck and have no home. But they feel the same feelings, think the same thoughts, have hopes, dreams, aspirations. Homeless kids would like to play with toys if they had them; they'd like to live in a nice, clean home." Communicate this to your children; explain that both housed and homeless people are human beings and deserve to be treated with compassion and respect.

On the other hand, when your child sees a homeless person on the street, he sees that at least in some ways that person is very different from himself. As a parent, you need to acknowledge that difference and validate your child's observation. Thus, while explaining the fundamental similarities of all human beings, you should also explain some differences: for instance, that homeless people move around a good deal, so they don't have much stability and security—a warm, comfortable place to call home. Some homeless people are sick (though not the kind of sick that kids can catch—reassure them of that), so they may behave in strange ways. If your child responds to your explanations with "But it's not fair," as many young children do, you can say, "No, it's not fair. Homeless people deserve better and there are people in the world who are trying to help the homeless. But right now, homelessness is very unfair and unfortunate."

8. Encourage Firsthand Contact.

One of the best ways to show your children the similarities is to urge them to reach out to homeless people. If your child has a homeless classmate—an increasingly common occurrence these days—encourage her to befriend him. Invite the schoolmate to your home or to join you and your child at the playground after school.

But be prepared: sometimes peer pressure makes kids as young as six or seven balk at befriending a homeless youngster. Housed kids may ostracize their homeless classmates, teasing them because their clothes are tattered, worn, or unfashionable or because the homeless kid seems "dumb."

While you cannot force-feed friendships between kids, you can encourage your child not to withhold his friendship from a homeless classmate in order to remain "one of the guys." An effective technique is to take the time to discuss how homeless kids live. Explain that they don't have money for new clothes, and that rather than being "dumb," they are forced to move so much and subsequently may have missed so much school that they've fallen behind in their studies. Once your child begins to understand what it's like to be homeless, and gets the message that you don't approve of teasing or ostracizing the homeless child, he will be more likely to reach out to befriend his classmate.

Another way to foster understanding and compassion is to take your child to visit a shelter. But don't make it a "field trip" where you're only observing. As Lascelles Black, head of the Task Force on Homelessness of the American Orthopsychiatric Association, explained to me, "Homeless people are not objects in an exhibit. And you want to be careful about invading their personal space. There is already so little privacy in a shelter that you need to be careful not to violate it. If, however, you come with a purpose—for instance, you and your child volunteer to help prepare a meal at a local shelter—it's an excellent way for a housed youngster to see that the homeless are just human beings, but human beings who are very poor."

If going to a shelter is more than you're willing or able to do, you can encourage contact in other ways. One family in suburban New York City hosted a homeless child through the Fresh Air Fund. The experience enriched the lives not only of the homeless child, but of the family's own young children as well. Another possibility for a child of, say, age eight or older, is to suggest she become a pen pal with a homeless child. This won't work if you life in a big city where it's nearly impossible to keep track of a homeless family. But if you're in a small town where homeless families tend to stay within the same community, being a pen pal is a fun idea. The homeless child will be thrilled to get his own personal mail and your youngster will benefit from learning about homelessness on a more intimate level. (Be sure to explain to your child that since all homeless families move frequently, there may be long gaps between letters.)

9. Set an Example.

Young children learn as much from what their parents do as what they say. That's why it's important to show your child by your own actions that you care about the homeless. Bringing toys to a local family shelter, participating in food drives, collecting clothing for the Salvation Army, sending a check to an organization that helps the homeless, or supporting any community fund-raising events—in the Berkshires town of Great Barrington, Massachusetts, close to four hundred participants raised $19,000 in a fall walka-thon to help the homeless—can go a long way in showing your child what it means to care.

10. Watch Out for Mixed Messages.

Sometimes even a well-intentioned parent can confuse her child by sending out a double message about the home-less. Peter Rose recounts the story of one woman, "the president of a PTA, who tried to set a positive example by getting a group of kids together to paint and clean up our camp before the homeless kids got there. But that same woman was appalled at my suggestion that the children help to serve camp meals. 'No,' she said, 'twelve-year-olds are too young to have physical contact with *those* people.' How's that for a mixed message?" To avoid making a similar mistake, get your own thoughts and feelings straight before you approach your kids.

11. Explore Homelessness Via Play, TV, or Magazines.

A few years ago, Kay Taus, a teacher at Corrine A. Seeds University Elementary School at the University of California at Los Angeles, introduced homelessness as part of a curriculum for her four- and five-year-old students. "I've always been interested in how kids learn about values and how they develop prejudices and biases," Taus told me. "And I noticed that when I'd take the kids for walks and the little ones would see a homeless man, they'd call him a bum. I was concerned about their lack of compassion, but I knew that these street people could be scary."

As part of her "anti-bias" curriculum, Taus began using a doll to lead the kids into discussions of homelessness. She'd take the doll and say, "Mary [or whatever the children named the doll] took a trip downtown with her mother and she noticed that there were a lot of people there with shopping carts who looked dirty and unhappy. The doll said to her mom, 'Oh, look at those bums.' But her mom said, 'No, they are not bums. They are just people who have had some trouble in their lives and don't have a place to live. They probably feel bad about not having a place of their own to go. And they have feelings. They'd probably be hurt if you called them bums.' " And so on.

Explaining homelessness through doll play is a simple, fun way to explore this complex issue with very young kids. And it's nonthreatening. After all, a doll is once removed from a child, thus providing a safe psychological distance from which to discuss what can become an emotionally charged issue. But most important of all, it works. Says Taus, "I've had some great results. Kids really seem to understand more about homelessness and begin to develop some compassion."

Dolls offer just one opportunity to bring the homeless issue closer to home. Magazine articles, TV shows, and TV commercials also provide natural entrees for exploring homelessness with your child. Here's an example: Janice and her two sons, ages nine and ten, were watching the news when they saw a segment concerning the eviction of homeless people who were living at the Chicago airport. The newscast triggered a great many questions from the boys and gave Janice the perfect chance to discuss the issue. If you are alert to them, you'll find lots of opportunities, mostly provided by the media, to talk to your child about homelessness.

12. Talk About the Meaning of Home.

One of the best ways for kids to understand what it means to be homeless is to spend some time talking about what having a home really means. Unfortunately, this is one of the missing ingredients in most discussions of homelessness. Yet talking about what a home means—that it's a safe, comfortable place where everybody knows and loves you, and that it's somewhere you always belong—not only helps kids feel more secure, but gives them a context in which children as young as five or six can understand homelessness.

Sample Questions and Answers

Q: Mommy, why is that man sleeping in the snow?

A: The man is sleeping there because he has nowhere else to go. He does not have a home. He is very poor and doesn't have enough money to have a house or apartment. So he sleeps out on the street. We are very lucky to have a place to live, and Mommy and Daddy will always try their best to take care of you and make sure you have a nice, warm home. But some people, like this man, are not so lucky.

Q: Is he cold? Why doesn't someone help him?

A: Yes, he probably is very cold and that is very sad. Some people are trying to help him. They have set up shelters, places where people who have no homes can sleep during the night, and maybe the police will come and bring him to a shelter. But sometimes there is not enough room at the shelters, so he may have nowhere else to go.

Q: Why is that woman looking through the garbage can?

A: I think that she is hungry and looking for food, or maybe she is looking for bottles and cans she can return to the grocery store to get money to buy food. She is very poor and doesn't have enough to eat. Sometimes she can go to a shelter or a soup kitchen and get some food to eat for free. That's why we sometimes bring cans of food to the shelter. But sometimes there is not enough food. I feel bad about her, and at the same time I feel very lucky that we have enough food to eat every day.

Q: Why is that man so dirty?

A: That man doesn't have a home to live in. So he

doesn't have a bath or shower to clean himself. He spends a lot of time walking around the streets and the streets are very dirty. Just think how dirty you would be if you had no place to wash your hands and face and no place to take a bath.

Q: Daddy, why is that man on the street yelling and screaming? I'm scared of him. What's wrong with him?

A: That man may not feel so well and he's having a really hard time, so it's probably a good idea to stay away from him. Don't worry. Mommy and Daddy will take care of you. No one will hurt you. You just stay close to me.

Helpful Resources

ORGANIZATIONS

Children's Defense Fund
122 C Street, NW
Washington, DC 20001
(202) 628-8787

Homelessness Information Exchange
1830 Connecticut Avenue, NW, 4th floor
Washington, DC 20009

Interagency Council on the Homeless
Dept. of Housing and Urban Development
451 Seventh Street, SW, room 7274
Washington, DC 20410
(202) 708-1480

National Alliance to End Homelessness
1518 K Street, NW, Suite 206
Washington, DC 20005
(202) 638-1526

National Coalition for the Homeless
1621 Connecticut Ave., NW
Washington, DC 20009
(202) 265-2371
Hotline: (202) 265-2506

National Resource Center on Homelessness and Mental
Illness
c/o Policy Research Associates, Inc.
262 Delaware Avenue
Delmar, NY 12054
(800) 444-7415

National Student Campaign Against Hunger and
Homelessness
29 Temple Place
Boston, MA 02111
(617) 292-4823

The Better Homes Foundation
189 Wells Avenue
Newton Center, MA 02159-3320
(617) 964-3834

READINGS FOR PARENTS

Committee on Health Care for Homeless People, Institute
of Medicine. *Homelessness, Health and Human Needs,*
Washington, D.C.: National Academy Press, 1988.

Hombs, Mary Ellen. *American Homelessness: A Reference Handbook.* Santa Barbara, Calif.: ABC-CLIO, Inc., 1990.

Hope, Marjorie, and James Young. *The Faces of the Homeless.*
Lexington, Mass.: D.C. Heath and Company, 1986.

Kozol, Jonathan. *Rachel and Her Children: Homeless Families In
America.* New York: Fawcett Columbine, 1988.

Rossi, Peter. *Down and Out in America: The Origins of Homelessness.* Chicago: University of Chicago Press, 1989.

READINGS FOR CHILDREN

Carlson, Natalie. *The Family Under the Bridge.* New York:
Harper & Row, 1958. (Ages 8–11)

Kaufman, Curt, and Gita Kaufman. *Hotel Boy.* New York:
Atheneum, Macmillan Publishing, 1987. (Ages 5–10)

Maestro, Betsy. *Harriet at Home.* New York: Crown Publishers, 1984. (Ages 2–5)

Williams, Vera. *A Chair for My Mother.* New York: Greenwillow Books, 1982. (Ages 4–8)

Special thanks to the following experts for their input into
this chapter: Joan Alker, assistant director, National Coalition for the Homeless; Ellen Bassuk, M.D., president, The
Better Homes Foundation; Myron Belfer, M.D., professor
of psychiatry, Dept. of Social Medicine, Harvard Medical
School, and chief of psychiatry, Cambridge Hospital; Lascelles Black, head, Task Force on Homelessness, American

Orthopsychiatric Association; Mary Geigerich, teacher, Meade Heights Elementary School; Peggy Jackson-Jobe, coordinator of education for homeless children and youth, Maryland State Department of Education; Leanne Rivlin, Ph.D., professor of psychology, City University of New York Graduate School; Peter Rose, executive director, Clear Pool Camp; Jason Sachs, doctoral candidate, Tufts University; Kay Taus, early childhood teacher, Corrine A. Seeds University Elementary School at the University of California at Los Angeles; Bonnie Zima, M.D., Robert Wood Johnson Clinical Scholar, UCLA Neuro Psychiatric Institute.

Chapter Three

"WHY DID UNCLE TOMMY DIE?"

Talking with Your Child About AIDS

Tommy, a charismatic, athletic man with a special zest for life, was Alexandra's favorite uncle. And no wonder. He introduced her to the wonders of the zoo, taught her how to dance the jitterbug, and bought her her first two-wheeler. So when Tommy contracted AIDS and grew seriously ill, her parents, wanting to protect their eight-year-old daughter, did not tell Alexandra what was wrong. A happy, cheerful child, she went about her normal routine, but when Tommy died, the youngster tearfully asked the question her parents had been hoping to avoid: "Why did Uncle Tommy die?"

In the previous scenario, Alexandra's parents have a tough decision to make: Should they tell their daughter about Tommy's condition and expose her to its grim facts? Or should they continue to shield her with a vague statement like "Uncle Tommy died because he got very sick" and postpone the troubling questions and emotions any discussion of AIDS is likely to unleash?

Even when you're dealing with AIDS, being as honest as possible is still the best tack to take in talking to your kids. It keeps lines of communication open and builds a strong foundation of trust between parent and child. But there's something else to consider: Chances are Alexandra had already heard about AIDS at school, on TV, or in talks with friends—and who knows in what context? Rather than "contaminating" her with information about AIDS, then, Alexandra's parents would be helping her to understand what AIDS means.

Researchers say that despite what parents might think or wish, most young children have heard about AIDS. A recent University of Vermont study of children ages six to twelve showed that 62 percent of first-graders had heard of the illness; by the time they reached third grade, 93 percent had heard of it.

How? Overwhelmingly, via television, the study revealed. To a much lesser degree, parents, teachers, and schoolmates served as sources.

This same study showed that youngsters harbor misconceptions about AIDS. Many believed doctors could make people with AIDS well again, and that you could catch AIDS by giving blood. Another disturbing finding: AIDS made these kids both anxious and fearful. Among their most telling questions were "Will my mommy and daddy die of AIDS?" and "Will everyone get AIDS and die someday?"

This study underscores a difficult but important lesson for parents and caregivers: As upsetting and perplexing as it may be to broach the subject of AIDS with young children, it is essential to do so. Talking about this deadly disease gives you the opportunity to provide your child with accurate facts about it and to dispel any unsettling misconceptions. It also will allow you to reassure your children of their own, and their family's, safety. Finally, discussing AIDS will lay the groundwork for any future talks to encourage essential AIDS-preventive behavior.

But before you start talking to your child, you need to make sure you know the facts yourself. To that end, here's a quick look at the latest data.

The Issue in Focus

AIDS* stands for Acquired Immune Deficiency Syndrome: Acquired, because you acquire it from someone who already carries the virus; Immune Deficiency, because it weakens your immune system, making it ineffective in protecting your body from disease; and Syndrome, because it consists of a pattern of symptoms. AIDS is caused by a virus, usually referred to as HIV (Human Immunodefi-

*Unless otherwise indicated, the factual information in this section comes from the "Surgeon General's Report on Acquired Immune Deficiency Syndrome," published by the U.S. Department of Health and Human Services, Centers for Disease Control, 1987.

ciency virus), that attacks certain white blood cells (called T lymphocytes, or T cells) found in human blood. Since these white blood cells help guard against infection, their invasion by HIV weakens the body's ability to fight off any illness. (Actually, persons with AIDS do not die of AIDS per se, but of such illnesses as pneumonia or cancers which their weakened immune systems cannot combat.)

Once someone is infected with HIV, he may seem healthy for a while, even for as long as ten years or more; nonetheless, he is able to pass the virus along and infect others. Often, though, individuals infected with the AIDS virus do not feel well and develop AIDS related complex (ARC). Among ARC's symptoms are loss of appetite, weight loss, fever, night sweats, skin rashes, diarrhea, fatigue, and a weakened ability to fight off infection. ARC is often a precursor of full-blown AIDS.

If and when the HIV-infected individual develops AIDS, which means that his body's immune system is severely impaired, then bacteria, fungi, and other viruses and cancers can get into the system and cause a number of diseases. Most commonly, these are Kaposi's sarcoma, a form of cancer characterized by purplish blotches and bumps on the skin; pneumocystis carinii pneumonia; and tuberculosis. If the brain and nervous system are damaged, AIDS patients also may suffer from memory loss, poor coordination, paralysis, or dementia.

Clearly, AIDS paints a bleak picture for those it afflicts—and, sadly, the number of people with AIDS is on the rise. Today, some experts estimate that 1.5 million Americans are infected with the AIDS virus; American Foundation for AIDS Research (AMFAR) reports some twelve million cases worldwide. Scientists hesitate to predict how many of these individuals will develop full-blown AIDS, but by the end of 1991, an estimated 270,000 people will have AIDS; 179,000 deaths will have occurred since the disease was first recognized back in 1981.

Now, let's explode a few myths.

• *Myth:* AIDS is a big-city disease.

• *Fact:* While the majority of AIDS cases are clustered in such major cities as New York, Miami, Washington, San Francisco, Los Angeles, and the larger urban areas of New Jersey and Texas, AIDS cases have been reported from all fifty states.

• *Myth:* AIDS is a disease of homosexuals.

• *Fact:* No one is immune from AIDS. In the U.S., AIDS was first identified in the homosexual population; now, however, AIDS has reached well into the heterosexual population.

Even children can contract AIDS. Dr. Philip A. Pizzo, head of the Infectious Disease Section at the National Cancer Institute, is a pediatric AIDS specialist. And while official estimates of kids, age thirteen or under, with AIDS are only about 2,500, Dr. Pizzo told me he believes ten to twenty thousand children are infected with AIDS in the U.S. today. What's more, there has been a 38 percent increase each year since 1987 in children who have become infected with HIV.

How are so many kids getting AIDS? Mostly from infected mothers who are passing it along to their unborn children. Until 1985, when scientists discovered a way that is almost 100 percent effective to test for HIV and screen blood, children with hemophilia sometimes developed AIDS because they were transfused with infected blood.

• *Myth:* You can get AIDS easily.

• *Fact:* The AIDS virus is not transmitted by sneezing, coughing, or crying, by contact with dogs, cats, or other domestic animals, or by being bitten by a mosquito; there are no known cases of AIDS transmission by insects. You cannot get AIDS from toilet seats, doorknobs, or telephones. AIDS has also never been contracted from swimming, bathing in hot tubs, or from eating in restaurants. In short, you don't get AIDS from everyday living.

You do get AIDS if the HIV gets into your bloodstream, and that can happen through contact with infected blood or certain body fluids, including semen, vaginal secretions, menstrual blood and breast milk. Basically, HIV is transmitted in three main ways: (1) through unprotected sexual intercourse, either genital or anal, with an infected person, because of the risk of mixing blood and bodily fluids; (2) by sharing needles with infected individuals. Drug abusers who inject drugs into their veins are considered a high-risk group; (3) by receiving a transfusion of infected blood, though, as I mentioned before, today this is highly unlikely.

• *Myth:* Your children can catch AIDS from casual contact with an infected child.

• *Fact:* You cannot get AIDS through hand holding, casual kissing, hugging, eating from the same plate, or drinking from the same glass as someone with AIDS. That means that your children cannot catch AIDS by playing, touching, or hugging a playmate or classmate with AIDS. So relax.

• *Myth:* You can get AIDS by donating blood.

• *Fact:* You cannot get AIDS by giving blood because the equipment used for drawing blood is sterile. Also, it is unlikely that you could get infected by receiving blood, as long as the blood you're getting has been screened for HIV antibodies; since 1985, the current tests used to screen blood are almost 100 percent accurate.

While AIDS is, as pioneering AIDS researcher Mathilde Krim, founding co-chair of AMFAR, says, "inexorably fatal," there is some good news—it is preventable. By avoiding promiscuous sexual practices, by using a latex condom correctly whenever you have sex with someone who might carry the HIV, and by avoiding injecting illicit drugs or sharing any kind of needles with anyone, you can avoid contracting HIV and leaving yourself at risk for AIDS. Using general health precautions is also a wise idea.

Yet here's the critical question for parents: Since so few children under age eleven are having unprotected sex or using IV drugs, why do we need to talk to our kids about AIDS at all? Simple. Because they won't stay children forever. And because AIDS isn't going to go away. And because they've probably heard about AIDS and feel anxious about it. And, perhaps most important, because the best way to prevent the spread of AIDS is to educate our children so that they will know how to protect themselves in the future. We've spent a great deal of time and energy learning how we can die from AIDS. Now it's time to learn how to live with it.

How to Talk to Your Kids About AIDS

1. Start Early.

I've heard many parents of kids under age eleven say, "My child is so young; she doesn't need to know about

AIDS yet." But that's simply not true. Even kids as young as five or six live in the real world and many have not only heard about AIDS, they also have lots of questions about it. We do our kids a real disservice when we underestimate what they want and need to know.

Canadian family physician Margaret Merrifield, who authored a children's book about AIDS (see Readings for Children at the end of the chapter), told me that one of the reasons she wrote her book for four- to eight-year-olds was that she saw teenagers of thirteen to eighteen engaging in high-risk behavior—sleeping around and having unprotected sex. "But by then," says Dr. Merrifield, "it's too late to start talking to them about AIDS. To really prevent such behavior, you need to reach kids very early on." That way, you can lay the groundwork for AIDS prevention while there's still time.

2. Initiate AIDS Discussions.

Many parents tend to wait until their children ask questions before offering them information about any complex and sensitive subject. Sometimes that's okay. But when it comes to AIDS, I recommend initiating discussion. The reason is that while some children readily voice their fears about AIDS, other more reticent youngsters may keep their worries bottled up. To help them deal with their questions and concerns, you should bring the subject up at the earliest opportunity.

That doesn't mean you need to begin a discussion out of the blue. Instead, tie it into something your child sees or hears, such as a public service TV commercial about AIDS. After you watch it together, say something like "Have you heard about AIDS before? Well, what do you think AIDS is?" This way, you can ascertain what the child already understands and work from there. Additionally, this approach allows you to provide information easily and naturally, without putting your child off by a formal lecture.

3. Present the Facts.

No matter how young your child is, do your best to offer her the facts about AIDS. But be sure to tailor the information to your child's age and cognitive level. Information for kids four to eight, for instance, should be very basic. Explain what AIDS is and, in a general way, how you get it. Child psychiatrist David Fassler, who has also written a children's book about AIDS, suggests this sample script: "AIDS is a disease that makes people very sick. It's caused by a virus, which is a tiny germ. Chickenpox and some stomachaches are also caused by viruses, but these viruses are very different from the kind of virus that causes AIDS. The virus that causes AIDS is very, very hard to catch. You can't get it from playing with someone who has AIDS or by touching someone who has AIDS. People get AIDS from the blood of someone else who has AIDS. So you should always be very careful never to touch anyone's blood."

It's not necessary to discuss sexual transmission of AIDS with such young children unless they ask. Children need to be taught about sex and they need to be taught about AIDS. But it's not a good idea for a child's first information about sex to be associated with such a deadly disease. (For more information, see the sample questions and answers at the end of this chapter.)

In choosing your words, remember how literal young children's thought processes can be; otherwise, your explanations could backfire. I heard about one seven-year-old whose teacher had told him that AIDS is caused by a bug. Well, after that he became terrified when any insect came near him. Luckily, his father discovered what was wrong and explained that "AIDS is caused by a virus, which some people call a bug. But it's not the kind of bug that crawls around on the floor." After that, the youngster relaxed. But the anecdote points out how important it is to be accurate and factual when speaking with young children about AIDS.

Children over the age of, say, seven or eight, can be offered more detailed explanations, including a simple explanation of the immune system. You can say, "Your body is made up of billions of cells. Some of these cells help your body stay healthy by fighting off disease. These disease busters are called T cells. But if you get HIV, that virus kills the T cells. And when too many T cells get destroyed by HIV, your body cannot fight disease. People whose T cells are destroyed and whose bodies cannot fight disease have AIDS."

Most likely, you already have explained sexual intercourse to your older children; in that case, you should also explain to them that AIDS can be transmitted by body fluids during intercourse. You can explain that "during sexual intercourse, the semen from the man's body goes into the woman's body. That semen can carry HIV. Or a woman with the HIV could pass it along to the man." You might also want to tell them what condoms are and how they can protect people from getting AIDS. Older kids are ready to learn about the dangers of IV drug use, though whether or not you feel this is imperative may depend on the community in which you live. Many inner-city kids already know about IV drug use; in that case, it is essential that they also learn the connection between sharing needles and AIDS.

4. Stress Good Hygiene.

The first step in teaching your children about AIDS centers on laying a strong foundation of good health and grooming habits. Says AMFAR's Dr. Krim, "What young children need to be concerned about first and foremost is cleanliness and how to protect themselves against germs in general." And that means learning the importance of hand washing, teeth brushing, bathing, covering your mouth when sneezing or coughing, not drinking from other people's glasses, and, of course, never touching anyone else's blood. While only the last could help safeguard your child from AIDS, these good health practices present a context in which children can then learn about AIDS prevention.

5. Foster Self-esteem.

Successful AIDS education also depends upon helping your child develop strong self-esteem. By teaching children to take pride in themselves—in their bodies, their health, in their sense of self—it's easier to help them protect themselves against AIDS when they get older. If, for example, a child recognizes that her body is her own, if she takes pride in it and wants to keep it healthy, she is much more likely to be able to withstand peer pressure to have irresponsible sex or to do drugs when she gets older.

How can we build such self-esteem in our children? Offer consistent and frequent praise. You can always find something positive to say in what a child is doing. If he draws a picture, tell him how wonderful it is and, of course, explain why. If he masters the alphabet or goes out for the soccer team, tell him how and why you're so proud. Such positive feedback helps give your child a sense of competence. Setting realistic goals, praising their abilities, keeping up with their friends and interests, all communicate to your child that he is important and help to develop his self-esteem.

6. Create a Comfortable Setting.

Building a foundation for AIDS education also means establishing a relaxed atmosphere concerning sex. This begins very early on; parents should react calmly when infants and toddlers touch their genitals. In slightly older children, establishing a comfortable setting means naming the body parts, including the genitals, accurately, and answering questions about where babies come from without anxiety.

For the past fifteen years, William Fisher, Ph.D., professor of psychology at the University of Western Ontario in Canada, has studied the psychological factors that determine adolescents' sexual behavior. And when I spoke with him he said, "One of the things I see over and over again is that teens who grew up in a relaxed atmosphere where sensuality was not discouraged and sexuality was not taboo tend to be more comfortable about sex and ready to prevent high-risk behavior." What parents of very young kids can and should do, then, is to help set the stage, to approach discussions of sex with enough calm and equanimity that, as their children become teenagers, they will also approach sex calmly and wisely.

Creating a relaxed atmosphere is not just important when it comes to talking about sex; it's also critical in deflecting and assuaging kids' fears and worries about

AIDS. Because the disease is so closely tied to suffering and death, AIDS often makes children anxious and concerned about their own and their parents well-being. But unless your household is one in which kids' feelings are taken seriously, your child may hesitate to voice his concerns and that reticence will deny you the opportunity to calm his fears.

Parents who don't listen to their kids, or who try to dodge questions or certain topics, set up a barrier between themselves and their children. The kids learn that there are certain subjects, whether sex, death, or AIDS, that cannot be discussed. And that's not healthful; in the long run, it's better for children to voice their concerns out in the open and to have all their questions answered than it is for them to keep them bottled up inside. So if your child has a question about AIDS, no matter how silly or bizarre it may seem to you, answer it as clearly, accurately, and seriously as possible.

But be prepared for some pretty outlandish queries, because, says Paula Duncan, a pediatrician who teaches AIDS education in the Burlington, Vermont, school district, "Once you open the door, the questions get wild. I remember one eight-year-old who, after learning that AIDS is transmitted through the blood, asked me, 'Well, what if you had AIDS and were swimming in a lake and you cut your foot on a rock. Then I came by and cut my foot on the same rock at the same place where you cut your foot. Could I get AIDS then?' Usually, however, the questions are a little more down to earth, like 'Can I get AIDS from a mosquito bite?' or 'Can I get AIDS by drinking at a water fountain?'" Just remember that as long as you've boned up on your facts, kids' questions are not that hard to answer.

7. Set Them Straight.

Six-year-old Jason came home from school one day feeling anxious and agitated. When his mom asked him what was wrong, he said, "I fell down and scraped my knee in the schoolyard. It was bleeding, and Johnny said I was going to get AIDS and die." Then he started to cry.

As this anecdote illustrates, kids' misconceptions can be pretty scary, so it's important to correct them as soon as possible. Jason's mom needs to say something like "You do not have AIDS. You are fine. AIDS is a very hard disease to catch and you can't catch it when you scrape your knee in the schoolyard. The way it can get into your blood is if you mix your blood with the blood of someone who has AIDS. Do you understand?"

It's also smart to check back with the child a few days later by saying, "Do you remember what AIDS is?" That way, you'll be able to find out what the youngster understood and, if necessary, set the record straight. Understanding AIDS, particularly for young children, takes more than a single discussion.

8. Reassure Your Child of His Safety.

Young children view all issues on a very personal level; they are mostly concerned with how something affects them and their families, especially Mom and Dad. Children worry that their parents will contract AIDS and die, and that there will be no one to take care of them. Some children may worry that they will get AIDS and give it to their parents or brothers and sisters. So it's important to reassure them of their health and safety.

Several months ago, I read an article in *Parents* magazine that illustrates this point well. It concerned an eight-year-old girl whose uncle had died of AIDS. Soon after his death, the child began to refuse to play or to share food or sleeping quarters with her baby sister. After a few sessions with a psychologist, the reason for this behavior became clear. Apparently, the little girl once had eaten some cookies off her uncle's plate and was terrified that she had contracted AIDS. She was avoiding her baby sister to protect her: she did not want to give her AIDS.

Clearly, children can become extremely fearful about AIDS, which is why reassuring your kids of their safety is so important. Explain to your child that she doesn't have AIDS and that AIDS is mostly a disease of grown-ups. Also tell her that you don't have the HIV virus either (assuming, of course, that you don't), and that you will be there to take care of her.

9. Don't Let Your Prejudices Interfere.

One of the biggest obstacles to discussing AIDS with young children is the prejudices this disease highlights. Since AIDS was first detected in the homosexual community, many adults mistakenly believe AIDS is a homosexual illness; some feel that it is God's way of punishing gays for their "immoral and unnatural" behavior and communicate this belief to their children. Personally, I disagree. But wherever you stand on the subject, try not to let your feelings prevent you from giving your kids the information they'll need to insure their health and safety.

10. Be Prepared to Discuss Death.

Because AIDS is fatal, questions about death may surface in some discussions. So get ready to answer them. Bookstores and libraries are lined with publications that offer advice on how to explain death to children. (For a few suggested titles, see Readings for Children at the end of this chapter.) But let me offer just three key tips for talking with your child about AIDS and death.

First, be honest. Tell your child, in simple terms, what death means—that when someone dies, they don't breathe or eat or feel hungry or cold, and that they will never return. Remember, very young children won't be able to conceptualize such finality. But that's okay. Just be patient and repeat the message whenever such discussions arise.

Second, never explain death in terms of sleep. Such an explanation might result in your child's resisting going to bed at night for fear that he'll never wake up again. Third, reassure your child that you are not going to die from AIDS and that she won't either. Again, stress that while AIDS is a serious disease, it can be prevented.

11. Encourage Compassion.

AIDS provides an excellent opportunity to foster feelings of compassion. If, for instance, your child has a friend or classmate with AIDS, explain that "it's important to be nice to someone who has AIDS, just as you should be nice to anyone who is sick." Again, tell your child that he cannot get AIDS from playing with, or touching, or sitting next to someone with AIDS.

If your child has no immediate contact with anyone with AIDS, but has only heard about the disease, look for other occasions to encourage empathy and compassion. Psychologist Nancy Cotton took her eight- and eleven-year-old children to see the AIDS Quilt exhibition (each quilted square memorializes a person who died of AIDS) when it came to Boston. "We had discussed AIDS before and they knew the basics. But when they looked at the quilt, the emotional, human side of AIDS really hit home," she told me. "My eleven-year-old pointed to one square and said, 'This one loved horses, just like me.' My daughter, who wants to be a ballerina, said 'This person liked ballet, just like I do.' It brought tears to their eyes and really helped them understand that AIDS is a disease that can affect anyone. I think they think about AIDS more personally now than they did before. I hope that when they get older, and hear somewhere that AIDS is a punishment that happens to bad people, they'll remember what they saw and feel compassion rather than scorn."

When AIDS Hits Home

While most young children first learn of AIDS from a distance, more and more are experiencing the anguish of this disease much closer to home; they have a father, mother, sibling, uncle, other close relative, or classmate suffering from AIDS. One of the most touching and tragic incidences of young children being forced to cope with AIDS was told to me by Ellen Bukstel Segal, a young mother of three who lost her husband to this deadly disease. Here's the story she was kind enough to share.

"It all began in 1983 when my husband, Doug, who was a hemophiliac, learned that a batch of blood-clotting product he had used was contaminated with HIV. We were a little concerned, but since there was no test for AIDS then, and since our hematologist told us that Doug had more a chance of getting hepatitis than AIDS, we just didn't worry about it. We continued with our lives, including having a normal sex life. We already had a one-year-old named Brett; in 1984, we had Todd, and two years later, our daughter, Margo, was born.

"But in 1986, Doug started getting sick. He developed thrush [whitish spots that appear in the mouth], night sweats, fevers and overall malaise, all symptoms of AIDS. Since by that time there was a test for AIDS, Doug got himself tested. That's when we found out he had AIDS. (Fortunately, Ellen tested, and continues to test, negative for the disease.)

"We immediately went to our doctor, who advised us to 'make contingency plans and hope for the best.' There were lots of tears and certainly a sense of shock, but we followed our doctor's advice. Our children were so young at the time—our oldest was only four—that we didn't tell them much. We did put Doug's toothbrush out of their reach, but I still encouraged them to hug and kiss Daddy. And all they really knew was that 'Daddy has AIDS and doesn't feel so well sometimes.'

"That changed in mid-1987, when Doug's health really began to deteriorate. At that point, I started explaining to the kids that Daddy's immune system was broken because he got AIDS from contaminated blood. I told them that there was no cure for Daddy's disease and that he did not want to die, but he was probably going to."

At first, the kids would listen for three minutes, then run off and play. But as time passed, Brett, Ellen and Doug's oldest child, grew more concerned. Says Ellen, "He would ask me, 'What's going to happen to us if Daddy dies? Where will we go? What if you die, Mommy? Where will we go then?' I had made provisions for the kids, so I was able to give them very specific answers. And I always tried to reassure him, to reassure all of them, that I was fine and I would be here to take care of them.

"Doug and I went to the kids' school and told their teachers what was happening, and I must say we got overwhelming support and understanding. I know that isn't true for many people with AIDS, but the more honest and direct we were with people, the more positive response we received; people seemed to understand and to keep an open mind. Like everyone else, though, we were being torn apart by AIDS.

"Even at the very end, when Doug was home dying, I tried to keep things calm and relaxed. I never shooed the kids out of Doug's room, and while they felt sad, they seemed to accept things and didn't seem overly frightened. I remember seeing Brett climb up on Doug's bed one time, and say, 'I love you, Daddy. I wish you were not going to die.'" Brett's wish did not come true.

Life has not been easy for the Segal family without Doug, but they are managing, each person in his or her own way. Ellen says that "Todd, my younger son, initially had almost no reaction; he cried a couple of times, but that was it. But one night recently I was singing my daughter a song and Todd came in and put his hands over his ears. He said, 'Don't sing that song. It reminds me of Daddy.' Then he got real tearful. When I asked him why, he said, 'Because I just don't remember Daddy clearly. And I want to.'"

In contrast, little Margo talks about her Daddy all the time. "Once, when she had a bad dream at night, she told me that 'Daddy came into my room and chased the bad guys away.' She took comfort in that. But Brett, the oldest, is having the hardest time. He's gotten more aggressive and antagonistic since Doug died. He also talks about wanting his Daddy to come back. Given what they've been through, though, they're doing very well."

I hope that you and your children will never have to undergo such a heartbreaking experience. But in case you do have a relative or close friend who is dying of AIDS, here are some techniques to help you and your child cope:

• Don't be afraid to discuss what's happening. Interestingly, kids who are forced to confront the issues surrounding AIDS can become "developmentally accelerated," which means that they understand more than they should at their age. So don't be afraid to offer them as much information as they are willing to absorb.

• Try not to make AIDS a family secret. If you live in a very conservative community, you may feel hesitant to tell your child the truth about a relative with AIDS, for fear that he will talk about it outside of your home and incur the prejudices of the community. Still, it's best to be honest, because if you don't tell your child the truth, you run the risk of having him find out from someone else, which could be a lot more traumatic. And, if you tell your child but instruct him never to discuss it outside your home, he may feel caught in the middle between protecting your family secret and being honest with his friends and teachers. Unless there is a highly unusual set of circumstances, be truthful with your child. Then, you can help him deal with or fend off any of the hurts community prejudice might inflict.

• Calm your child's fears. Part of the horror of AIDS is that it has struck so many young people down. Most kids can accept that old people die, but when they lose someone that they know is young—say, a twenty-year-old uncle—that can be extremely upsetting. In these kinds of cases, you can and should broach the subject with your child by saying something like "Hey, you haven't said much about Uncle Bob's dying, but I want you to know that although sometimes younger people die, it's rare. I'm going to be around for a long time and so is Daddy. We'll be here to take care of you."

Sample Questions and Answers

Q: What is AIDS?

A: AIDS is a very serious sickness that is caused by a tiny germ called a virus. When you are healthy, your body can fight off diseases, like the Ninja Turtles fighting the bad guys. Even if you do get sick, your body can fight the germs and make you well again. But when you have AIDS, your body cannot protect you. That's why people with AIDS get very sick.

Q: How do you get AIDS?

A: You get it by mixing your blood or body fluids with the blood or body fluids of someone who has the HIV in his blood. But you can't get it just by touching or being near someone with AIDS. You can get it by sharing needles with someone who has AIDS; people who take drugs can get it by using the same needles. If their mothers have AIDS, babies can get it even before they're born. (NOTE: If you have already talked to your child about sex, you should also add, "You can also get AIDS by having sexual intercourse with someone who has HIV.")

Q: Can kids get AIDS?

A: Very few children get AIDS. But if they were born to a mommy who had AIDS, they could get AIDS when they were born. A long time ago, some kids who had hemophilia got AIDS when they got a transfusion. But since 1985, blood has been tested, so that is not likely to happen anymore. AIDS is usually a disease of grown-ups.

Q: What's a blood transfusion?

A: That's when a sick person gets the blood of a healthy person so that the sick person can get well again. But today, people usually don't get AIDS from blood transfusions because scientists have figured out a way to make sure any blood they give you is almost always safe.

Q: Can I get AIDS when I get a needle at the doctor's office?

A: No. The doctor always uses a clean needle. He uses it once, and then throws it away. So you can't get AIDS at the doctor's office.

Q: Does everybody who gets AIDS die?

A: Today, there is no cure for AIDS. Some people who get AIDS can live for years, and some for only a few weeks. But until doctors find a cure, everyone who gets AIDS will die.

Q: If you get just a little bit of the HIV in your blood, will you still get AIDS?

A: If your blood mixes with blood that is HIV-positive, you can develop AIDS.

Q: How can you tell if somebody has AIDS?

A: You can't tell. People with the HIV in their blood look just like you and me. Sometimes, though, people with AIDS become so sick that they get very thin and don't look well.

Q: How do you know if you have AIDS?

A: You have to go to the doctor and get a blood test. That's the only way to know for sure.

Helpful Resources

ORGANIZATIONS

AIDS Action Council
2033 M Street, NW, suite 801
Washington, DC 20036
(202) 293-2886

AIDS Action Committee
131 Clarendon Street
Boston, MA 02116
(800) 235-2331

American Foundation for AIDS Research (AMFAR)
1515 Broadway, suite 3601
New York, NY 10036
(212) 719-0033

American Red Cross
AIDS Education Office
1730 D Street, NW
Washington, DC 20006
(202) 737-8300

Association for the Care of Children's Health
3615 Wisconsin Ave., NW
Washington, DC 20016
(301) 654-6549

National AIDS Information Clearinghouse
P.O. Box 6003
Rockville, MD 20850
(800) 458-5231

National AIDS Hotline
(800) 342-2437

National Association of People with AIDS
2025 I Street, NW, suite 415
Washington, DC 20006
(202) 797-3708

National Childhood Grief Institute
300 Edinborough Way, suite 512
Minneapolis, MN 55435
(612) 832-9286

Pediatric AIDS Network
Children's Hospital of Los Angeles
4650 Sunset Blvd.
Box 55
Los Angeles, CA 90027
(213) 669-5616

READINGS FOR PARENTS

Alyson, Sasha, ed. *You Can Do Something About AIDS*. Boston: The Stop AIDS Project, 1988.

America Responds to AIDS. *AIDS Prevention Guide for Parents and Other Adults Concerned About Youth*. Washington, D.C.: Centers for Disease Control, 1989.

Shilts, Randy. *And the Band Played On: Politics, People and the AIDS Epidemic.* New York: Viking Penguin, 1987.

Quackenbush, Marcia, and Sylvia Villarreal. *Does AIDS Hurt?* Santa Cruz, CA: Network Publications, 1988.

————, and Mary Nelson with Kay Clark. *The AIDS Challenge.* Santa Cruz, CA: Network Publications, 1988.

READINGS FOR CHILDREN

Fassler, David, and Kelly McQueen. *What's a Virus Anyway?: The Kids' Book About AIDS.* Burlington, Vt.: Waterfront Books, 1990. (Ages 5–10)

Girard, Lina Walvoord. *Alex, the Kid with AIDS.* Morton Groves, Ill.: Albert Whitman & Co, 1991. (Ages 8–11)

Hausherr, R. *Children and the AIDS Virus.* New York: Clarion Books, 1989. (Ages 5–8)

Hyde, Margaret O., and Elizabeth Forsyth. *Know About AIDS,* 2d ed. New York: Walker and Co., 1990. (Ages 8–12)

Jordan, MaryKate. *Losing Uncle Tim.* Niles, Ill.: Albert Whitman & Co., 1989. (Ages 2–6)

Lerner, Ethan A. *Understanding AIDS.* Minneapolis: Lerner Publications, 1987. (Ages 8–13)

Merrifield, Margaret. *Come Sit by Me.* Toronto: Women's Press, 1990. (Ages 4–8)

Schilling, Sharon and Jonathan Swain. *My Name Is Jonathan (and I Have AIDS).* Denver: Prickly Pair Publishing, 1989. (Ages 5–11; contains somewhat graphic photographs)

READINGS FOR CHILDREN (ABOUT DEATH)

Keller, Holly. *Goodbye, Max*. New York: Greenwillow
    Books, 1987. (Ages 4–8)
Stiles, Norman. *I'll Miss You, Mr. Hooper*. New York: Ran-
    dom House/Children's Television Workshop, 1984.
    (Ages 4–8)
Varley, Susan. *Badger's Parting Gifts*. New York: Lothrop, Lee
    & Shepard Books, 1984. (Ages 5–8)
Viorst, Judith. *The Tenth Good Thing About Barney*. New York:
    Atheneum, 1971. (Ages 5–10)

Special thanks to the following experts for their input into
this chapter: Paula Duncan, M.D., health coordinator, Burlington School District; Clarence Crossman, M.Div., education coordinator, The AIDS Committee of London
Ontario; Jacqueline Etemad, M.D., associate clinical professor of psychiatry, University of California at San Francisco;
David Fassler, M.D., clinical director, Otter Creek Associates; William Fisher, Ph.D., associate professor of psychology, University of Western Ontario; Mathilde Krim,
founding co-chair, American Foundation for AIDS Research; Margaret Merrifield, M.D., associate physician, University of Western Ontario Health Services; Nancy Perez,
educational specialist, Dade County Public Schools; Philip
A. Pizzo, M.D., chief of pediatrics, and head of the Infectious Disease Section, National Cancer Institute; Sylvia Vil-
lareal, M.D., staff pediatrician, San Francisco General
Hospital.

Chapter Four

"WHAT MAKES SOME DRUGS GOOD AND SOME DRUGS BAD?"

Talking with Your Child About Drugs and Alcohol

When eight-year-old Stephan stepped off the bus from his Boy Scout camping trip, his father sensed something was wrong. Sure enough, as Stephan climbed into the family car, his first words confirmed these suspicions: "Dad," said the youngster in a small voice, "I don't feel so good." When they arrived home, Stephan dragged his duffel bag into his room and lay down on his bed; Dad took his temperature—102° F—and then hurried to the medicine chest to find some children's Tylenol. After giving his son the medication, Stephan's father called the doctor, who prescribed an antibiotic as well. Two days later, Stephan was back on his feet, thoughtfully devouring a stack of blueberry pancakes

at breakfast, when he said, "Dad, at the Boy Scout over-
night, the leader told us that drugs are bad for you. But
when I get sick, drugs make me better. What makes some
drugs good and some drugs bad?"

Stephan's question illustrates how confusing the issue of
drugs can be to young children. If drugs are so dangerous,
why is the family medicine cabinet chock full of them? If
alcohol is so bad for you, why does Dad drink a few beers
with dinner and Mom drink wine whenever she has guests?

And it's not just parents who send mixed messages
about drugs and alcohol: society does its share to muddy the
issue. On the one hand, public service announcements and
educational programs warn about the dangers of substance
use. On the other hand, movies, TV, and advertising frequently glamorize substance use, making it seem socially
desirable and just plain fun.

Now, very young children have a tough enough time
separating fact from fiction without having to deal with
such confusing contradictions, particularly when they center on such an important subject. It is up to parents, then,
and, to a more limited extent, teachers, to help children sort
out the facts by countering these inconsistencies and offering a more healthful path to follow. You can take a first step
by learning all *you* can about the matter at hand.

The Issue in Focus

Here's the good news: drug use in our country seems to be
declining. Between 1987 and 1988, the number of drug

users actually dropped some 37 percent. And consumption of liquor is at a new low. Don't be misled, though. Drug and alcohol use is still widespread in this country. According to the National Institute on Drug Abuse (NIDA), nearly 13 million people use illicit drugs in the U.S. today; more than 1.6 million of them are kids, ages twelve to seventeen. What's more, nearly 103 million people use alcohol, and just under 5 million users, again, are children under seventeen.

Get ready for even more disturbing data: the average age that a child initially tries alcohol is eleven; for marijuana, it's only twelve. According to a 1987 NIDA survey, 15 percent of eighth-graders already had tried marijuana, and 44 percent of those kids had tried it by the sixth grade! Children aren't limiting their drug experimentation to alcohol and pot, either. According to that NIDA survey, 21 percent of students had tried inhalants, and 61 percent of those kids had tried them by the sixth grade.

In fact, a wide range of substances pose a threat to our kids today. Parents, therefore, need to know as much as they can about these illicit drugs if they are to help keep their youngsters away from them. To help you get started, here's a thumbnail sketch of the most common culprits.

Marijuana.*

Also called pot, grass, weed, reefer, dope, Mary Jane, sinsemilla, Acapulco Gold, and Thai stick, marijuana looks like dried parsley. It's usually eaten or smoked in rolled cigarettes, known as joints, and has a pungent odor. It's a

---

*Much of the following data comes from "Learning to Live Drug Free, a Curriculum Model for Prevention" from the U.S. Department of Education.

second cousin to hashish, or "hash," which looks like brown or black cakes or balls and which is also eaten, or smoked in small pipes. The effects of such drugs include bloodshot eyes, a mellow and/or giggly feeling, hunger, and slight paranoia.

Cocaine.

Known as coke, snow, flake, white, blow, nose candy, Big C, snowbirds, or lady, cocaine is a white crystalline powder that can be inhaled, injected, or smoked. Cocaine can cause nasal problems, glassy eyes, a chronic cough, weight loss, and erratic changes in behavior. Its deadliest relative, crack, also called freebase or rock, comes in whitish or brownish crystals often packaged in small glass vials. Crack causes extreme mood and behavioral swings and is even more highly addictive. Both cocaine and crack have been known to cause heart and respiratory failure and consequent death.

Other Stimulants.

Amphetamines, also known as speed, uppers, black beauties, bennies (Benzedrine), hearts, or bumblebees, come in capsules and pills that can be swallowed, inhaled, or injected. Methamphetamines—a.k.a. crank, crystal, and speed—are usually in white powder or pill form and can be swallowed, injected, or inhaled. These stimulants bring symptomatic glassy eyes, loss of appetite, and, at times, severe depression. They can also increase heart and respiratory rates, cause headaches, dizziness, and anxiety. An amphetamine injection could result in death.

Depressants.

Barbiturates, including Nembutal and Seconal, are also known as downers, blue devils, yellow jackets, yellows, and barbs, and come in colorful capsules that are swallowed easily. Quaaludes, or "ludes," are also depressants and come in tablets that are also swallowed.

Tranquilizers—among the most common of which are Valium, Librium, and Equanil—come in swallowable tablets and capsules. Taken in small doses, they make users feel calm and relaxed, but larger amounts can cause slurred speech and drunken behavior; very large doses can induce coma and even death.

LSD.

LSD (lysergic acid diethylamide) is a hallucinogen or "mood-altering" drug that is usually dropped onto a sugar cube or brightly colored paper which is then then swallowed or licked. It can cause an elevated heart rate and body temperature, with accompanying feelings of panic, paranoia, anxiety, and confusion. Some users report "flashbacks," recurrences of the "trip" even after they stopped using the drug.

Inhalants.

A wide variety of inhalants exist, including amyl nitrite (called poppers or snappers) and butyl nitrite (Rush, Bolt, Bullet). Depending on the drug, inhalants can cause sneezing, coughing, fatigue, headache, and more. Repeated use of certain inhalants can damage the nervous system. What is particularly insidious about these drugs, particularly when it comes to children, is that they come in seemingly innocent-looking items you probably have around the house right now. For example, some aerosol cans of whipped cream contain nitrous oxide; chlorohydrocarbons are present in certain aerosol paint cans or cleaning fluid containers.

Alcohol.

Alcohol *is* a drug and can be addictive; repeated use can lead to dependence and, over time, higher and higher doses are needed to achieve the same "high." Effects of alcohol use can range from temporarily impaired judgment and coordination to damage to vital organs, including the brain and liver, and in very high doses, respiratory depression and death.

Happily, few kids under age eleven get involved with illicit drugs or alcohol. But that doesn't mean they're home free. Studies of teens point to several factors, many of which begin well before adolescence, that increase young people's chances of abusing drugs or alcohol. These include a lack of communication between parent and child, a weak sense of self-esteem, depression, family (particularly parental) misuse of substances, peer substance abuse, poor academic performance, and lack of spiritual values.

Parental attitudes toward substance abuse is also a major influence. Specifically, moms and dads who convey a permissive attitude, who believe there's nothing wrong with teenagers smoking marijuana or drinking alcohol "as long as they learn how" or "as long as they do it in moderation," may up the odds that their children will use illicit substances. As for adults who indulge their kids with sips of beer or wine even in their early teenage years or younger— or who feel that "experimenting" with drugs and alcohol is a normal part of growing up—they, too, may well be endangering their children's future. Research has shown that the use of alcohol or other drugs before age fifteen *doubles* the risk of those children developing substance-abuse problems later in life.

Some parents who came of age in the sixties have said to me, "Well, I tried drugs when I was younger, and I'm okay. What's wrong if my kids play around a bit?" My answer to that is "A great deal." First of all, just because you were lucky enough to come away unscathed doesn't mean your child will. Second, drugs are different than they were years ago. Marijuana is a great deal stronger. And crack, which is more powerful than cocaine and more highly addictive, wasn't even around in the sixties. Finally, kids' exposure to the media, when coupled with the easy accessibility of drugs these days, forces today's children to confront drug issues at a much earlier age, when their judgment is not yet developed and their life experiences are few. Enough said?

Let's consider a few more risk factors. University of Washington's Dr. David Hawkins, who has done an intensive review of the research involving substance abuse, believes that poor family management also can hurt kids' chances of remaining drug-free. "Parents who fail to convey clear expectations for their family's behavior, who don't set clear limits on behavior and enforce those limits," may be leaving their children vulnerable to drug use.

Genetics may also play a role in determining an individual's risk for substance abuse. Dr. Norman Hoffman, who has been evaluating alcohol- and drug-treatment programs for a decade, explains that "recent research shows that there may be some genetic predisposition to addictive behavior, at least for some people. Apparently, kids who were adopted but whose biological parents were alcoholics seem to have the same risk of becoming alcoholic as kids raised in alcoholic families." But, Dr. Hoffman hastens to add, "just because something may be genetic does not mean it's immutable."

In fact, some "high-risk" kids don't take drugs, just as some "low-risk" kids do. So what moves a youngster to action? Why do kids actually start taking drugs?

The main reason appears to be peer pressure. According to a much-heralded survey of fourth- to sixth-graders by *Weekly Reader,* kids take drugs to fit in with their friends. But it's not the only reason. Dr. Hoffman's work leads him to believe that kids also take drugs to flee from life's pressures. When youngsters feel overwhelmed by the stresses of adolescence—including familial, social, and educational stress—and haven't learned the skills they need to cope effectively, they may turn to drugs to escape their problems.

So how can parents help? I know that many moms and dads shy away from discussing alcohol and drugs with their kids, either because they believe that their child could not possibly get involved with illicit substances—the "not my child" syndrome—or because they simply don't know what to say or how to say it. Others may steer clear because they are afraid that talking about such subjects will put unwelcome ideas into their kids heads. Well, let me set the record straight: first, any child, no matter his race, religion, intelligence, or economic background, can get into trouble with drugs. Second, talking about drugs and alcohol and explaining why they are harmful will not push your children into using these substances; instead, it will increase the likelihood that they'll stay away from dangerous drugs. And it's not too early to start. Even if your child is just a pre-schooler, you can begin to lay a strong antidrug foundation for your kids.

How to Talk with Your Child About Drugs and Alcohol.

1. Listen Carefully.

Student surveys reveal that when parents are accessible to their children, and when children feel comfortable talking to their parents about anything, including drugs and alcohol, kids are less likely to develop a use problem. Listening to your kids' questions, concerns, and, *equally important,* feelings, and then responding in a calm, supportive, nonjudgmental manner will go a long way toward establishing the kind of open communication that can help keep your kids away from drugs.

2. Let Kids Know It's Okay to Act Independently.

Since peer pressure is so enormous—and the main reason kids try drugs—we need to teach our children that it's okay to be different and to act independently of others.

Stuart Copans, the director of Brattleboro Retreat's adolescent substance-abuse program, makes this important point: "We have found that the family is the model for relationships with peers. So ask yourself this: Is it acceptable for people in your family to do things differently from one another? If everyone in the family but your eight-year-old daughter wants to go on the roller coaster, do you force her to go—or do you insist the entire family not ride the coaster?"

If the answer to any of these questions is yes, you may be neglecting to send your child an important message: that it's okay to act independently from the group. It's a life lesson that will serve your child well if and when he is pressured to smoke marijuana or drink a beer because "everybody else is doing it."

3. Role-play How to Say No.

Spend some time role-playing ways in which your child can refuse to go along with his friends without becoming a social outcast. For instance, you can try saying something like this with your eleven- or even twelve-year-old: "Let's play a game. Suppose you and your friends are at Andy's house after school and they find some beer in the refrigerator. Now, the rule in our family is children are not allowed to drink any alcohol. What could you say?" If your child comes up with a good response, commend him and encourage him to brainstorm some more. If he can't think of anything, you can offer a few suggestions like "No, thanks. Let's play Nintendo instead" or "No, thanks. I don't drink beer. I need to keep in shape for soccer practice" or even "No, thanks. My parents would kill me if I drank a beer. Let's do something else instead." Explain that each of these responses not only gets your child off the hook but lets his friend know that it's the beer, not the friendship, that is being refused.

4. Encourage Choice.

Most of the time children are told what to do by the adults in their lives. But it's important to allow your child plenty of opportunity to make choices on her own and thus become more confident in her ability to do so.

You can ask even a four-year-old, "Which color sweat-shirt do you want to wear today, the green or the yellow?" Then let the child choose, and commend her selection. A ten-year-old is certainly capable of deciding if he wants to join the soccer team or the karate club. Later, as your child becomes skilled at making good choices, both you and she can feel more confident in her ability to make the right choice when the stakes become higher—that is, when it concerns drugs and alcohol.

5. Provide Basic, Age-appropriate Information.

As I already mentioned, offering accurate, honest infor-mation is essential in helping to keep kids away from drugs and alcohol. Don't leave it up to your child's school; take the initiative—and the opportunity—to teach your child what you want him to know about drugs. Even if your youngster is involved in a classroom program, at-home talks can serve to reinforce any antidrug messages and make a stronger impression on your young one.

It is important, though, to make sure that any informa-tion you offer is appropriate to your child's age and cogni-tive level. "Drug talk" for a very young child—perhaps between ages four and seven—might best be presented in the context of good health. For instance, while you're help-ing your child brush his teeth, you can say, "There are lots of things we need to do to keep our bodies strong and healthy, like brushing our teeth and washing our hands before we eat. But there are also some things that we shouldn't do because they can hurt our bodies, like smok-ing, or taking any medicines when we are not really sick."

Another good approach is to talk about drugs and safety, particularly in terms of the medicine cabinet. You might want to explain to your children that "the medicines, or drugs, in the medicine cabinet are very strong. If you're sick, they can help you make you better. But if you take them when you're not sick, those same drugs can make you feel awful. That's why you may never take anything from the medicine cabinet unless Mommy or Daddy tells you it's okay. That's an important rule."

Kids around six or seven years old also can understand simple lessons about marijuana or alcohol. When you are watching TV and an antidrug public service message appears, take advantage of the moment to bring the subject up. Try saying something like "Do you know what marijuana is? It's a very bad drug that can hurt your body." If your child pops out with questions or comments, follow his lead and see where the discussion will take you. If not, let it go. Short, simple comments, if repeated often enough, will get the message through to your child.

You can offer somewhat older children, ages eight to eleven, the same message but with the addition of more drug-specific information. You can explain what marijuana is—what it looks like, its street names, what it smells like, how it can affect their bodies—and that it is against the law. (For some facts about marijuana, refer back to the Issue in Focus section in the first part of this chapter.) You might also want to talk to your child about cocaine and crack. Again, explain what these drugs look like and what they can do to your body. Don't be afraid to talk tough. You can say something like "Cocaine and crack are very dangerous and illegal drugs that could kill you even if you take them just once. It's very foolish to try any of these drugs even one time. And remember: If you have any questions about these or any other drugs, please come and ask me. I'm always here to listen to you and to try to answer any questions you might have. Okay?"

Don't forget to include alcohol in your drug discussions. You can perhaps say, "You know, even though in that movie we just saw, people look like they're having a good time drinking, it's just a make-believe story. In real life, alcohol—and that includes beer and wine coolers—can hurt your body's chances of growing big and strong." If your child is ten or older, you can add a bit more detail, like "Alcohol can hurt your liver and make you sick and weak. What's more, drinking alcohol is against the law for young people."

6. Establish a Clear Family Stand on Drugs.

You need to have a family position on drugs and to communicate it clearly to your kids. You can simply say, "We don't allow any drug use in this family and children in this family are not allowed to drink alcohol. The only time you can take any drugs is when the doctor or Mommy and Daddy give you medicine because you are sick. But you are not allowed to take medicine yourself or to take any other drugs. We made that rule because we love you very much and know that drugs can hurt your body and make you very sick, maybe even kill you. Does anyone have any questions? Does everyone understand?"

7. Teach Children to Follow Rules.

Establishing a clear family policy toward drugs won't do much good unless your children learn from a very early age how to obey rules. Whatever your family "laws" may be, just be sure to state them simply and clearly and explain why you made then. For a four- or five-year-old, the rule may be as simple as "You must always hold Mommy's hand when you cross the street. That's because there is lots of traffic there and I don't want you to get hit by a car." For an eight- or nine-year-old it might be "no throwing balls in the living room. There are too many things in there that could break." For a ten- or eleven-year-old, "No TV until after all homework is done. To do well in school, it's important that you be able to concentrate clearly on your assignment. The TV is too much of a distraction."

Children should also know the consequences for breaking a rule. Suppose, for example, that your son and his buddy decide to play a quick game of catch in the living room, and they break a lamp. Your child should know beforehand that he will be punished—perhaps no television for a certain period of time. If your children grow up knowing that when a rule is set, you expect it to be followed, and that there will be a price to pay if they break it, they will be more likely to know you mean business when you set down rules about drug taking or drinking even in their preteen and teenage years.

8. Become a Role Model.

Lee Dogoloff has been concerned about drugs and kids for many years. He was President Carter's "drug czar" and now serves as a member of President Bush's drug advisory council. Today he is also the executive director of The American Council for Drug Education. When I interviewed him for this chapter, he asked me to emphasize one piece of advice: "No matter what words parents may say, if their kids see them drinking to excess or taking drugs irresponsibly, it undercuts all of their well-intentioned messages. Kids follow the example their parents set involving drugs and alcohol."

Be sure, then, to set the right example for them. After an exhausting day at the office, try not to reach for the martini pitcher; it only conveys the message that drinking is the best way to unwind. If you're throwing a dinner party, offer nonalcoholic beverages to your guest in addition to wine and spirits. Also, take care not to pop pills, even over-the-counter remedies, indiscriminately. In addition to your words, your behavior needs to reflect your belief that drugs and alcohol are potent substances that must be used both responsibly and sparingly.

9. Brainstorm a List of Trustworthy Adults.

Most young children believe that an adult—any adult—always knows better than they do. But since parents know that some adults don't show good judgment when it comes to kids, we need to help children identify trustworthy adults (in addition to you) to whom they can bring their questions and problems. One day, maybe when you're driving in the car or when the family is eating dinner at the local pizza place, you can say, "I have a question. Suppose you had a question or a problem and neither Daddy nor Mommy were around to help. Who else could you go to?" Then make a list of the actual people—Mrs. Jones, Uncle Andrew, Coach Al—to whom the kids could turn.

Keep in mind that you'll probably need to repeat this list again and again, until the names become second nature to your children. But be patient. Eventually the message will sink in—and it's important enough to warrant the extra effort.

10. Discuss What Makes a Good Friend.

Again, since peer pressure is such an important factor when it comes to kids' involvement with drugs and alcohol, it makes sense to discuss with children, from a very early age, what makes a good friend. To a four-year-old, you can explain that "a good friend is someone who makes you feel good and who you like to play with." To a nine-year-old you might say, "A good friend is someone who thinks the same way you do, who likes the same kinds of games and who's fun to be around." Eleven-year-olds can participate in a more sophisticated discussion in which you explain that a friend is someone who shares your values and experiences, someone who respects your decisions (and whose decisions you respect) and listens to your feelings. Once you've gotten the concept of friendship across, you've an excellent basis for explaining, when your child gets a little older, that "friends" who pressure him to drink or smoke pot aren't really friends at all.

11. Encourage Interpersonal Skills.

Kids who aren't able to get along well with peers, and who find themselves without good friends in their teenage years, are more likely to get involved with drugs and alcohol when they're older than kids whose interpersonal skills enables them to enjoy the camaraderie of close companions. You're already working on such skills whenever you explain to your four-year-old that "we don't grab toys from friends, but instead try to share them." Encouraging sharing and cooperation among peers now will help your children make and maintain good friendships as they mature.

12. Build Self-esteem.

Encouraging a healthy sense of self-esteem is one of the most important parenting tactics you can learn, particularly when it comes to drugs and alcohol. That's because when kids feel good about themselves, they are much less likely to turn to illicit substances to feel high than if they feel they're worthless.

As parents, you can do many things to enhance your child's self-image. First, you can offer lots of praise, both for goals that your child accomplishes and for the effort he puts into them. Applauding a six-year-old for the wonderful painting she did at school or for trying so hard to learn how to roller skate can help your daughter feel very worthwhile. So can telling your eight-year-old how proud you are that he tried out for the soccer team, even though he didn't get a starting position. Do take care not to offer empty praise, however; instead, explain why your child's accomplishment is so terrific. In praising your child's finger painting, you can say, "Oh, what a pretty picture. You chose such beautiful colors—how creative you are!"

Another important tactic is to correct your child in a supportive way; that is, to criticize the action, not the person. Suppose, for instance, you are helping your ten-year-old with a math problem and he gets the answer wrong. It's much more constructive to say, "Look, you added wrong. Let's try it again," rather than tearing him down by exclaiming, "What's the matter with you? Are you stupid?"

You can also help build self-esteem by assigning your child a manageable, age-appropriate chore—a four-year-old can bring her plate to the sink herself when she's finished eating; a ten-year-old can water the plants every week. Performing such duties and being praised for mastering them well lets your children know they are valued and valuable members of the family.

Another effective tactic: help your child set her sights realistically. When you or your child set goals that are too high, it becomes too easy to fail. Be sure, then, to keep goals appropriate to your child's level and abilities and to help your youngster figure out what steps he'll need to take to achieve those goals. And *always* stress that it is the effort, not the end result, that really counts.

Finally, say "I love you." Nothing will make a child feel better about himself than knowing that he is loved by Mom and Dad.

13. Stress Critical-assessment Skills.

Movies and TV advertisements barrage kids with distorted messages about drugs and alcohol. Beer commercials—of which your kids will see some 100,000 before they graduate from high school—are a case in point. They usually feature healthy, perfect-bodied young men and women having a fabulous time on the beach, in a sailboat, or at a party. The central idea: drinking beer makes you popular and sexy.

Fortunately, parents can help counteract these messages and, in the process, help teach children how to assess critically what they view. To help kids learn how ads distort the truth, try pointing it out the next time you and your child see a toy commercial. You can say to your seven-year-old, "Boy, that commercial makes that toy look like fun. But I'm not so sure it will be so much fun without all that great music and special effects. They don't come with the toy; the advertiser put that into the commercial so kids will want to buy it."

If you and your eleven-year-old are watching TV together and a beer commercial comes on the air, you can make an "offhanded" comment like "Hmm, those people look like they're having a good time. After all, the company who made the commercial wants you to buy their beer. But what they don't show you is how sick those people might feel after spending all day in the hot sun and drinking so much beer." Soon your kids will get the hang of it and will start pointing out such discrepancies to you!

14. Spend Quality Time with Your Children.

I know, I know. You're sick and tired of hearing about "quality time." But it's impossible to build a meaningful, open relationship unless you are willing and able to spend some dedicated time with your youngster. I realize that this is particularly difficult for parents who work outside the home, but making the effort is essential. Even if you just set aside fifteen uninterrupted minutes per child per day to talk, play a game, or take a walk, you will be letting your child know that you care and that she is a cherished individual.

15. Foster Your Child's Involvement in Fun, Healthful Activities.

Children who are very involved in wholesome activities they enjoy are more likely to make friends and develop interests that will keep them away from drugs. It's wise, then, to encourage your child's participation in such groups as Scouts, community- or religiously sponsored youth organizations, or sports teams. Just make sure your child doesn't become overextended so that every minute of her day is programmed: kids also need time out simply to relax and play.

16. If You Suspect a Problem, Seek Help.

It's relatively uncommon for kids under the age of eleven to become involved in drug and alcohol use. But it can—and does—happen. If you notice that your child (or more possibly, his older brother or sister) has become unusually withdrawn, loses weight, starts doing poorly in school, turns extremely moody, has glassy eyes—or if you find that the drugs in your medicine chest seem to be disappearing too quickly—don't close your eyes. Instead, take note and seek help. Talk to your child and reach out to any one of the helpful organizations listed at the end of this chapter. You'll be helping your youngster find a healthful, happy future.

Sample Questions and Answers

Q: Why are some drugs good and some drugs bad for you?

A: When you get sick, some drugs that the doctor gives you will help you get better. That's why some drugs are good for you. But if you take these drugs when you're healthy, they can make you sick. Also, there are some drugs, like marijuana or crack, that are never good for you. To be safe, never ever take any drugs unless Mommy or Daddy or the doctor gives them to you. Okay?

Q: Why do people take bad drugs?

A: There are lots of reasons. Maybe they don't know much about how dangerous drugs are, or they do it to be one of the guys. Or maybe because they feel bad about themselves or don't know how to handle their problems. Or maybe because they don't have parents they can talk to. Why do *you* think they do?

Q: You and Dad drink beer and wine. Why can't I?

A: Because beer and wine contain alcohol. When you're young and your body is still growing, alcohol can keep you from growing up big and strong. That's why you are not allowed to drink anything that has alcohol in it until you are an adult. When you are big and grown up like Mommy and Daddy, you can have some wine or beer if you still want to and if you are careful about it. Understand?

Helpful Resources

ORGANIZATIONS

The American Council for Drug Education
204 Monroe Street, suite 110
Rockville, MD 20850
(301) 294-0600
(800) 488-DRUG

"Just Say No" International
1777 North California Boulevard, suite 210
Walnut Creek, CA 94596
(800) 258-2766

National Clearinghouse for Alcohol and Drug
Information
P.O. Box 2345
Rockville, MD 20852
(800) 729-6686

National Council on Alcoholism and Drug Dependence
Inc.
12 West 21st Street
New York, NY 10010
(800) NCA-CALL (for referral to local affiliate)

National Institute on Drug Abuse Information &
Treatment
Referral Helpline
(800) 662-HELP

PRIDE (National Parents' Resource Institute for Drug
Education)
50 Hurt Plaza, suite 210
Atlanta, GA 30303
(404) 577-4500

Readings for Parents

"The Fact Is . . . You Can Prevent Alcohol and Other Drug
    Problems Among Elementary School Children." Rock-
    ville, Md.: National Clearinghouse for Alcohol and
    Drug Information, 1988.
Gold, Mark S. *The Facts About Drugs and Alcohol,* 3rd ed.
    Washington, D.C.: The PIA Press, 1988.

―――――. *The Good News About Drugs and Alcohol.* New York: Villard Books, 1991.

Growing Up Drug Free: A Parent's Guide to Prevention. Washington, D.C.: U.S. Dept. of Education, 1990.

Hawkins, J. David., et al. *Preparing for the Drug-Free Years: A Family Activity Book.* Seattle: Developmental Research and Programs, 1988.

What Works: Schools Without Drugs. Washington, D.C.: U.S. Dept. of Education, 1989.

Tobias, Joyce. *Kids and Drugs: A Handbook for Parents and Professionals,* 2d rev. ed. Annandale, Va.: Panda Press, 1989.

Readings for Children

Gilson, Henry. *Purple Turtles Say No, No to Drugs.* Edmonds, Wash.: Purple Turtle Books, 1987. (Ages 3–4)

Hemming, Judith. *Why Do People Take Drugs?* New York: Franklin Watts, 1988. (Ages 7–10)

Mann, Peggy. *The Sad Story of Mary Wanna or How Marijuana Harms You.* New York: Woodmere Press, 1988. (Ages 6–10)

Sanders, Pete. *Why Do People Drink Alcohol?* New York: Franklin Watts, 1989. (Ages 7–10)

Super, Gretchen. *You Can Say "No" to Drugs!* Frederick, Md.: Twenty-First Century Books, 1990. (Ages 5–8)

―――――. *Drugs and Our World.* Frederick, Md.: Twenty-First Century Books, 1990. (Ages 5–8)

―――――. *What Are Drugs?* Frederick, Md.: Twenty-First Century Books, 1990. (Ages 5–8)

Vigna, Judith. *I Wish Daddy Didn't Drink So Much*. Niles, Ill.: Albert Whitman & Co., 1988. (Ages 4–8).

———. *My Big Sister Takes Drugs*. Niles, Ill.: Albert Whitman & Co., 1990. (Ages 5–9)

Whiskers Says No to Drugs. Middletown, Conn.: Field Publications, 1987. (Ages 7–9)

Special thanks to the following experts for their input into this chapter: Stuart A. Copans, M.D., associate professor of clinical psychiatry, Dartmouth Medical School, and director of the Adolescent Substance Abuse Division at Brattleboro Retreat; Lee Dogoloff, CSW, executive director, The American Council for Drug Education; David Hawkins, Ph.D., director of The Social Development Research Group, and professor, School of Social Work, University of Washington; Norman Hoffman, Ph.D., assistant professor of psychiatry, University of Minnesota; Sharon Rose, director of marketing, The National Federation of Parents for Drug Free Use; Rob Simmons, PRPH, program director, "Just Say No" International.

Chapter Five

"MOMMY, WHY ARE THOSE PEOPLE SO ANGRY?"

Talking with Your Child About Racism and Prejudice

Samantha, six years old, was stretched out on the living room floor, drawing in her favorite coloring book, when her mom flipped on the TV news. At first the youngster paid little attention to the broadcast, but when the screen showed four white, handcuffed teenagers being led to police cars, Samantha looked up from her book. She watched intently as the reporter interviewed the distraught black mother whose son had apparently been beaten by the teenagers, and as a group of adults held up protest signs and shouted angrily behind the reporter, who struggled to make his closing comments. When the segment ended, Samantha's blue eyes seemed troubled as she asked, "Mom, why were those people so angry? Did they make the lady cry?"

As young Samantha is beginning to discover, incidences of racism and prejudice are a sad fact of American life. And as Samantha's mother is beginning to realize, she cannot protect her daughter from witnessing them. Samantha will see all kinds of prejudice as a member of our real and troubling world. Although blond and blue-eyed, she may herself become a victim of bias as she confronts sexism in education, social relations, sports and the workplace. And the way she deals with life's bigotries will affect the extent to which she fulfills her seemingly unlimited potential.

Since minority groups represent a growing segment of our society, Samantha and others of her generation will be a part of one of the most culturally diverse populations of students our nation's educational system has ever known. As adults, they will work alongside the most broadly diverse group of colleagues. And unless Samantha and her contemporaries, no matter what their ethnicity, are raised to understand and appreciate people whose cultures and heritages are different from their own, they may well have trouble thriving in this ever more ethnically varied environment.

In an interview published by the Anti-Defamation League, renowned pediatrician Dr. Benjamin Spock explains why. "The young child who is being taught by parents to look down or shun any group is given the impression that these others are somehow dangerous. . . . This impairs his trust in people and, more seriously, his trust in his own ability to deal with people." In short, children who fear and distrust people who are different from themselves, and who therefore narrow their own world and range of life experience, have a serious handicap in our rapidly shrinking world. Today, raising your child to be as prejudice-free as possible is not only morally right, but psychologically and practically sound.

How then do you raise unbiased children in our prejudice-ridden world? With a great deal of effort and care—and with a keen understanding of racism and bigotry as it affects you and your child. Let's take a closer look.

The Issue in Focus

Most of us realize that race consciousness, and indeed prejudice, are deeply embedded in American culture. Despite the passage of such protective legislation as the Civil Rights Act of 1964, which forbade discrimination in "public accommodations" and threatened to withhold federal monies from communities that maintained segregated schools, people of color face bigotry in both job and housing markets. On average, their incomes still fall below those of the white majority.

What's more, prejudice exists not only between whites and blacks, but among people of the same race or heritage as well. You may see tension, for instance, between light- and dark-skinned blacks. And I remember teaching English as a second language to a class of Hispanic adults in which Mexican students regularly snubbed their Puerto Rican classmates.

TV news chronicles our society's bigotry every day. In 1989, newscasters vigorously reported New York City's

Bensonhurst case, in which a group of white youths surrounded a sixteen-year-old black teenager who was shot in the ensuing incident. I would bet that whenever and wherever you are reading this, your local TV news will be reporting another racially motivated crime tonight.

Currently, no conclusive numbers show racially motivated incidents to be increasing, but the public perception is that they are on the rise—so much so, in fact, that only last year the United States passed the Hate Crime Statistics Act of 1990. This act requires the attorney general to collect data on crimes that are based on race, religion, sexual orientation, or ethnicity. But whether or not the tally will eventually reveal an increase in hate crimes isn't important; even if one or two occur per year, that is still too many. Our best bet in ridding our country of such behavior lies in trying to raise a generation of prejudice-free kids.

How do children become prejudiced in the first place? Most people believe kids are blissfully ignorant of any such differences as skin color or hair texture until adults point them out. The popular thinking is that without adult interference, children would naturally develop into bias-free adults.

But this simply isn't true. Research shows that children notice physical differences a lot earlier than ever suspected—actually, when they're around two or three years of age. While that may seem like a startling fact to some, it really shouldn't. After all, young children are constantly trying to make sense of the world around them; they identify and categorize people, places, and things all the time. Two-year-olds, for example, are beginning to recognize their own sexes and the sexes of those around them. They're also learning to identify colors. Three- to five-year-olds are fascinated by what makes them the same as and different from others and often raise such questions as "Will I always be a girl?" or "Will I always have this color skin?"

Clearly, then, children recognize differences. The trouble surfaces if and when they form negative mental and emotional associations with people of different colors or cultural heritages.

How is this most likely to occur? In large part, that depends upon the extent of the children's contact with people of different cultures. A white child who lives in an all-white neighborhood and attends an all-white preschool and/or primary school is likely to feel a lot less comfortable with black people than the child who has regular and frequent associations with African-Americans.

Children's levels of comfort will also depend on the messages, both direct and indirect, they receive from their parents and caretakers. The parent who grabs hold of his child's hand the minute they pass someone of another race in the street or who always tells her kids to roll up the windows of the car while driving through a particular ethnic neighborhood is teaching that youngster a powerful lesson in racism.

Television, too, plays a role in teaching children to attach negative significance to differences. Sitcoms often stereotype minorities; most cartoon enemies speak with a foreign accent; television news tells us that most criminals are dark skinned. All combine to teach children bigotry.

The way to combat this prejudiced "cultural curriculum" is to send your kids frequent and consistent antibias messages. Parents who want to rear prejudice-free kids need to proactively intervene so that their children grow up understanding and appreciating not only their own cultures, but the cultures of a wide range of people whose world they increasingly share. Here follow some proven techniques in achieving this worthy goal.

How to Talk with Your Child About Racism and Prejudice

1. Face Up to Your Own Prejudices.

Admitting to and scrutinizing your own racial and cultural biases is an essential first step in trying to raise your child to be prejudice-free. The reason, says Dr. Alvin Poussaint, a psychiatrist at the Judge Baker Children's Center in Boston and script consultant to TV's "The Cosby Show" and "A Different World," is that if you don't acknowledge your own prejudices and become keenly aware of them, they are likely to slip out unconsciously when you talk with your kids about racial issues.

To discover your biases, ask yourself a few key questions:

• Does one group of people "all look alike" to you?

• Do you tend to generalize about a particular group? (For example, do you think "all white people are racist," or "all Asians are smart"?)

• Would you be upset if your child attended a school in which your cultural group did not comprise the vast majority of students?

If you answered yes to any of these queries, you're probably harboring some prejudices toward one or a number of different groups and need to make an effort to work through your feelings. It's not all that difficult: a simple starting point is to become more familiar, through reading and personal contact, with that cultural or racial group. Information and understanding go a long way in overcoming fear and prejudice.

2. Encourage Self- and Group Identity

Most parents are adept at helping their children learn who they are as individuals—you help your daughter understand that she's a girl, that she is smart, athletic, Catholic, and more. But just as important as self-identity is your child's cultural identity. Talk to her about her heritage; trace your cultural roots. If you are African-American, for example, find some books about the African culture and explain to your child how rich her racial background is. Try to display African art in your home. Pull out the family photo albums; try to reconstruct your family tree. Knowing who they are both as individuals and as members of a particular cultural group helps kids develop a sense of security and self-esteem.

3. Don't Deflect Racial or Cultural Questions.

Noticing differences between people doesn't cause prejudice; avoiding questions and discussions about them may. A typical four-year-old white child may publically ask, "Mommy, how come that boy's skin is brown? Is he dirty?"—much to the dismay of his mortified parent, who generally responds with "Shh! You'll hurt that boy's feelings." But such a response implies that the curious child has said something wrong—that there's something *wrong* with having dark skin.

Even when a well-meaning parent answers with "We

don't talk about the color of people's skin. All people are
the same," he confuses his child. Children *see* striking differences in skin color. Telling them they don't exist is like
trying to tell them that sexual differences don't exist. You
would not tell your child that all boys and girls are the same;
why try to tell them that all races are the same?

A much better answer would be "That boy is not dirty.
He just has brown skin. You have white skin because your
mommy and daddy have white skin; he has brown skin
because his mommy and daddy have brown skin." For a
four-year-old, that's usually enough. An older child may be
told that dark-skinned people have a chemical called melanin in their bodies that makes their skin darker.

A nine- or ten-year-old can understand that skin color
signifies a cultural difference as well; classmate Jamal has
dark skin because he is African-American; Myoko has different shaped eyes because she is Japanese; Janie has white
skin because her family came from Europe. What you want
to do is acknowledge your child's correct observation of
difference and explain it simply and objectively, without
attaching any pejorative connotations.

The same holds true when your child asks a question
about something he's seen on the TV news. Don't turn the
set off or in any way try to silence his questions. Instead, try
to help him understand what he's seeing. Here's an example. Nine-year-old Tony happened to catch a news report
on the Bensonhurst incident. After it was over, he asked,
"Why did that black guy get shot? What did he do?" Trying
to avoid such an uncomfortable topic, Tony's father said,
"It's too complicated to explain. Anyway, it happened in
New York and doesn't concern us here in Michigan. Now
go out and play." But young Tony would have been better

served if his father had simply answered his son's question, saying, "That teenager got shot because he was black. There are people in this world who don't like people because of the color of their skin, or because of their religion. But people like that are ignorant. I'm glad that most people don't feel like that and that there are lots of people in this world working to make sure that terrible things like the incident on the news don't keep happening."

4. Celebrate Diversity.

While confronting the issues of racism directly and answering your child's questions openly and honestly are important, they are not enough. You also need to help your child recognize and celebrate diversity. Columbia University's Dr. Ian Canino, a child and adolescent psychiatrist who specializes in cultural diversity issues, likes to tell kids that the world they live in is like "a beautiful animal park. There are giraffes, zebras, and lions in this park, and even though they all look different and each is very special in his own way, they are all animals who can talk to each other, and can share lots of things with each other, like a pond to drink out of and the grass to roam in. In the same way, every child is different and special. But all children also can share and play together and be very good friends."

Another way to help your child understand the richness of diversity is to bring him into contact with children from other cultures. If your child's school is fairly homogeneous, try getting him into a more diverse play group, sports team, club, or community program. Trips to museums are another relaxed and enjoyable way to introduce your children to the richness of other cultures.

Try to create a multicultural atmosphere in your home

as well. When reading to your child, choose books that include characters of all different races (and avoid stories in which white is clean and good and dark is dirty and bad). If your child is black, try to expose her to positive black images through books, magazines, art, theater, or dance in order to balance the "white is best" message mainstream American culture conveys. Both black and white parents should give their children dolls with different skin colors; a superhero brown-skinned doll like "Sunman" may be particularly appealing to any young boy.

Teach your children crafts and games from different cultures; origami is a particularly good choice for children with sufficient manual dexterity to control paper folding. Discourage kids from watching TV programs that stereotype others by race, gender, or sexual orientation and encourage them to watch shows like "Sesame Street," "Electric Company," and, for slightly older kids, "Life Goes On" (where a Down's syndrome youth is the star), that show all kinds of people doing normal and entertaining things.

Introduce your kids to different foods and use them as springboards to learn about other cultures. I remember one six-year-old telling me that he liked only "American food." But when I told him that pizza (his absolute favorite) was Italian and that egg rolls (another winner) were Chinese, we got into a discussion of those cultures. After that, he started announcing to anyone who would listen, "I eat foods from all over the world!"

5. Intervene in Any Discriminatory Behavior.

Do not permit your child to make racist comments, tell racist jokes, or engage in any bigoted behavior. School-age children may, unfortunately, pick up racist terms and use them. But if Johnny says "Mom, a new girl came to school today. Tommy said she's a nigger," don't pretend you didn't hear. Instead, immediately say something like "Johnny, 'nigger' is a very bad word and will hurt the new girl's feelings. I don't want you to ever use that word again." Then, offer your child an alternative: "The new girl is named Keshia and she is African-American. That is the term you should use."

Parents also may need to teach their children how to respond if others call them racist names. Even four- and five-year-olds can be taught to say, "I don't like you calling me bad names and I want you to stop." Often, such a direct approach brings about a simple and immediate end to the problem.

6. Explore the Source of Bigoted Behavior.

If your child displays any prejudiced behavior—suppose, for instance, that he consistently refuses to play with a classmate of another race—you need to explore the source of such bias. Sometimes children can develop negative attitudes if and when they've had a bad experience with someone of another culture and have generalized that experience to the entire race. Just ask your youngster why he is refusing to play with the other child. An answer like "Because Rami is Indian just like my old baby-sitter and I *hated* her" will give you more information to help you deal with the situation. In that case you might say, "I know that you didn't like that baby-sitter. You thought she was mean. And she *was* Indian. But that doesn't mean that all Indian people are mean. There are nice Indian people and Indian people who are not nice, just like there are nice black people like us and black people who are not nice. You really have to get to know somebody before you can decide whether you like him or not. I think if you start to play with Rami, and get to know him, you might like him very much."

Here's another problem. White parents sometimes ask what they can do to prevent their children from becoming bigoted when their kids have had negative experiences— particularly fights—with black youngsters who behaved belligerently towards them. There are no conditions under which parents should allow their children to accept abuse from other children, even if the white parents (and, to an extent, the kids) feel guilty about being white in a world that has discriminated against blacks. "Good friendships," says Poussaint, "are based on mutual respect and equality and not on one person feeling superior to or subjugated by another."

But it's also important to explain that while the black children who picked on the white child are wrong, there are good and bad people in all races. Additionally, these white parents need to make an effort to help their kids enjoy positive encounters with black youngsters in order to counteract the negative experience.

Exploring the source of bigoted behavior will also keep you from jumping to the wrong conclusion, and may reveal that an apparently bigoted remark or action was nothing of the kind.

Here's what I mean. One black mom told me that her five-year-old son is having a problem at preschool because he refuses to sit next to a Korean classmate at lunch. The teacher assumed it was because the youngster was prejudiced, but when the mother talked with her son, she learned the real reason—the Korean girl always eats pickles at lunch, and her son detests pickles. "So," his mom told me, "we're having some talks about the idea that what someone eats is not something upon which to base a relationship."

One further point: Sometimes what may seem a racist remark, particularly in children under the age of eight, may reveal a misconception. While shopping with her mom in a department store, for example, four-year-old Carmen pointed to a black man and shouted, "Look, Mom. Bill Cosby!" Though the knee-jerk response of many parents might be to pull the child away in a paroxysm of parental embarrassment, Carmen's mom reacted differently. She said, "No, Carmen. That man is not Bill Cosby. But he does have the same color skin. He is a black man and so is Bill Cosby." Here, then, lies another lesson: explain, don't reprimand. It's a much more productive response.

7. Foster Self-esteem.

Individuals with a poor self-image are more likely to devalue others in an effort to boost their own sagging self-esteem. By contrast, people who feel good about themselves are more likely to tolerate and appreciate differences in others. In order to discourage prejudice and encourage antibias attitudes, it is necessary to help our children develop a strong and positive sense of self-esteem.

Promoting self-esteem is achieved over the course of time. It begins in infancy when you respond to your child's cries and coos, and extends into childhood as you praise your child frequently and encourage her to feel good about herself—her physical traits ("You have such beautiful brown skin," or "You have such lovely blue eyes"); her intelligence ("Look how quickly you put that puzzle together. How smart you are!"); her talents ("What a lovely picture you drew. You're a wonderful artist"); and her character ("You are very generous to share your toys with your friend"). As your child gets older, your praise should remain ample.

8. Encourage Empathy.

Individuals who can understand how the victim of prejudice might feel are much less likely to participate in bigoted, biased behavior than people without a sense of compassion. Very young children may not be emotionally ready to be fully empathetic toward others, but even kids as young as five or six can understand something about how another might feel if you explain a situation in very concrete, personal terms. For instance, six-year-old Clarissa, a black child who had limited exposure to children of different races, joined her playmates in making fun of a new Korean neighbor, calling the little girl "slanty eyes." An effective response to this situation would be for Clarissa's parent or caretaker to take her aside and say, "It's not nice to call the new girl names. It will hurt her feelings. Remember last month when you got your hair cut and the kids called you a boy and you felt so bad you cried? Well, that is how this new girl must feel when you call her names. I'm sure if you call her by her real name—Kim—and ask her to play with you, you would like her very much."

9. Help Your Child Handle Anger.

Sometimes, children displace their anger onto an inappropriate subject—a situation which might manifest itself in racist or prejudiced behavior. Suppose a youngster gets angry at his mom because she won't let him watch a certain TV show; he may then take his anger out on a vulnerable classmate, such as a minority child who is already the object of some students' ridicule. To forestall the possibility of such behavior, allow your child to ventilate his anger and to blow off steam in a way that won't hurt anyone—maybe swatting a punching bag or kicking a ball around the backyard. Such activity permits him to release his aggression appropriately and reduces the chance that his anger will manifest itself in biased actions.

10. Point Out Role Models.

Kids of all races and nationalities need positive role models if they are to become productive, competent adults. White American children are lucky to have an abundance of models to emulate, from Mr. Rogers to President Bush. They learn about white heroes on TV, at school, in the news, and at home.

Children of color are not as fortunate, mostly because their heroes are not as visible in American society. I remember a seven-year-old black girl who told me she wished to be white. When I asked her why, she said "Because I want to be a teacher, like you." As it turned out, the youngster had never had a black teacher, so her parents and I made an effort to introduce her to educators who shared her racial heritage.

The lesson, then, is clear: Parents must make a concerted effort to identify positive role models within their own race or heritage. They should talk about important figures in their cultural history; find appropriate books, movies, and videos. Try to point out politicians, entertainers, athletes, educators, doctors, lawyers, writers, policemen, and others who share your child's heritage. The goal is to show your kids that there are no limits on who or what they can become.

11. Set an Example.

While offering verbal explanations can help your child overcome the prejudices around him, setting an example is equally important. Your own racist remarks, which may be as offhanded and well intentioned as "Black people make the best athletes," can cancel out much of the antibias talks you've had with your kids.

It's not that hard to set a good example. Here are a few easy rules of thumb:

• Watch your own language. Don't use any epithets when talking about people of other races or nationalities. Ever.

• Don't stereotype. To say "all blacks are good dancers" is as racist as saying "all blacks are lazy." Expose children to all kinds of people and allow them to make their own judgments.

• Behave in a proactively nonprejudiced manner. If, for instance, you're white and you see a taxi driver refuse to pick up a black couple but offer to give you a ride instead, turn him down and tell your child why. That gesture will go deeper than any classroom lesson in brotherhood.

• Don't go overboard in "being nice" to people of other cultures. As Dr. Leonard E. Lawrence, an adolescent psychiatrist at the University of Texas Medical School, explains, "Some parents make extreme overtures of friendliness toward people of another race—overtures that they don't make to people of their own race—and kids pick up on that phoniness. Kids ask themselves, 'What is there about this person that makes my parent act so differently toward him?' And that can lead to prejudice as much as anything can. Let your child see that you treat all people with respect and dignity."

• Take a public stand. From making sure your child's school teaches the history of other races and nationalities to joining organizations whose mission is to fight for equality for all, going public in efforts to stamp out bigotry teaches your child a valuable lesson about your family's values.

Sample Questions and Answers

Q: Lee Ling has funny eyes. Can she see?

A: Lee Ling's eyes are shaped like her mommy's and daddy's eyes, just like your eyes are shaped like your mommy's and daddy's eyes. She can see just as well as you can.

Q: Will the brown on Carmello's skin wash off?

A: No. Carmello's skin is brown because his mommy's and daddy's skin is brown. It has something in it (called melanin) that makes it brown and it will be brown forever. Your skin will always be white because my skin is white. And Carmello's skin will always be brown.

Q: Why am I called black if my skin is brown?

A: That's a good question because your skin is a beautiful brown color, not black. But "black" is a term grown-ups use for people whose ancestors—that means their grandpa's or grandpa's grandpa—came from Africa. Sometimes black people are also called African-American.

Q: Why am I called white if my skin is pink?

A: You're right. Your skin isn't white like the snow, but more of a pretty pinkish color. But grown-ups use the word "white" for people whose ancestors came from Europe. Your great-great-grandma and grandpa came from Ireland, which is in Europe, so you are called white.

Q: Why is Kareem's hair so curly?

A: His hair is curly because his mom and dad's hair is curly. Some people have curly hair, some people have straight hair, or kinky hair or wavy hair. But all of them are pretty in their own special way.

Q: Why does Hong talk so weird?

A: Hong doesn't talk weird, although it may sound a little funny to you. He is just learning English, so he speaks with a little accent. He comes from Vietnam, where they don't speak English; they speak Vietnamese. Would you like to learn how to say something in Vietnamese? Let's ask Hong (or Hong's mom) to teach us a word.

Q: Why did they call me a nigger?

A: Some people are sad and angry and don't like themselves. So they pick on other people and call them bad names. But that's not a nice thing to do. They don't understand how nice and interesting black people are, and they certainly don't know how nice you are. No matter what any person calls you, though, remember you are very special and that I love you very much.

Helpful Resources

ORGANIZATIONS

Anti-Defamation League of B'nai B'rith
823 United Nations Plaza
New York, NY 10017
(212) 490-2525

Council on Interracial Books for Children
1841 Broadway
New York, NY 10023
(212) 757-5339

National Association for the Advancement of Colored
People (NAACP)
4805 Mt. Hope Drive
Baltimore, MD 21215
(301) 358-8900

National Association for the Education of Young
Children
1834 Connecticut Avenue, NW
Washington, D.C. 20009-5786
(800) 424-2460

National Conference of Christians and Jews
71 Fifth Avenue, suite 1100
New York, NY 10003
(212) 206-0006

National Institute Against Prejudice and Violence
31 South Greene Street
Baltimore, MD 21201
(301) 328-5170

READINGS FOR PARENTS

Allport, Gordon W. *The Nature of Prejudice.* New York: Doubleday, 1958.
Blauner, Bob. *Black Lives, White Lives: Three Decades of Race*

Relations in America. Berkeley: University of California Press, 1989.

Clark, Kenneth B. *Prejudice and Your Child.* Boston: Beacon Press, 1955.

Comer, James P., and Alvin Poussaint. *Black Child Care: How to Bring Up a Healthy Black Child in America.* New York: Pocket Books, 1975.

Derman-Sparks, Louise, et al. "Teaching Young Children to Resist Bias." Washington: National Association for the Education of Young Children, 1989.

Gould, Stephen J. *The Mismeasure of Man.* New York: W. W. Norton, 1981.

Hopkins, Susan, and Jeffry Winters, eds. *Discover the World: Empowering Children to Value Themselves, Others and the Earth.* Philadelphia: New Society Publishers, 1990.

Hopson, Derek and Darlene. *Different and Wonderful: Raising Black Children in a Race Conscious Society.* New York: Prentice Hall Press, 1990.

McGinnis, Kathleen and James. *Parenting for Peace and Justice.* Maryknoll, N.Y.: Orbis Books, 1981.

Rothenberg, Paula. *Racism and Sexism: An Integrated Study.* New York: St. Martins, 1988.

Stone, John. *Racial Conflict in Contemporary Society.* Cambridge: Harvard University Press, 1986.

READINGS FOR CHILDREN

Berridge, Celia. *Going Swimming.* New York: Random House, 1987. (Ages 2–5)

Berry, Joy. *Every Kid's Guide to Overcoming Prejudice and Discrimination.* Chicago: Children's Press, 1987. (Ages 8–13)

Carlson, Natalie Savage. *The Empty Schoolhouse,* New York: Harper & Row, 1965. (Ages 8–11)

Carlstrom, Nancy White. *Wild Wild Sunflower Child Anna.* New York: Macmillan, 1987. (Ages 2–5)

Curtis, Gavin. *Grandma's Baseball.* New York: Crown, 1990. (Ages 5–8)

Feeney, Stephanie. *Hawaii Is a Rainbow.* Honolulu: University of Hawaii Press, 1985. (Ages 1–5)

Gilson, Jamie. *Hello, My Name is Scrambled Eggs.* New York: Lothrop, Lee & Shepard, 1985. (Ages 10–13)

Harmeyer, Barbara. *My Very Own Puppy.* New York: St. Martins, 1987. (Ages 2–5)

Jenness, Aylette. *Families: A Celebration of Diversity, Commitment, and Love.* Boston: Houghton Mifflin, 1990. (Ages 10 and up)

Johnson, Angela. *Tell Me a Story, Mama.* New York: Orchard Books, 1989. (Ages 5–8)

Levine, Ellen. *I Hate English!* New York: Scholastic, 1989. (Ages 6–9)

Mendez, Phil. *The Black Snowman.* New York: Scholastic Hardcover, 1989. (Ages 7–10)

Naidoo, Beverly. *Chain of Fire.* New York: Lippincott, 1990. (Ages 10 and up)

Phillips, Tamara. *Daycare ABC's.* Niles, Ill.: Albert Whitman, 1989. (Ages 2–4)

Simon, Norma. *All Kinds of Families.* Niles, Ill.: Albert Whitman, 1976. (Ages 4–7)

Yarbrough, Camille. *Cornrows.* New York: Coward, McCann & Geoghegan, 1979. (Ages 2–5)

Special thanks to the following experts for their input into this chapter: Angela Antenore, Western States Director for Special Training, Anti-Defamation League; ReGena Booze, Master Teacher of Preschool Three's, faculty at Pacific Oaks College; Ian Canino, M.D., deputy director of training, Division of Child and Adolescent Psychiatry, College of Physicians and Surgeons, Columbia University; Ruth Fuller, M.D., associate professor, Department of Psychiatry, University of Colorado Health Sciences Center; Phyllis A. Katz, Ph.D., director, Institute for Research on Social Problems; Leonard E. Lawrence, M.D., child and adolescent psychiatrist, associate dean for student affairs, University of Texas Medical School at San Antonio; Alvin F. Poussaint, M.D., associate professor of psychiatry at Harvard Medical School and senior associate in psychiatry, Judge Baker Children's Center; Eliot Sorel, M.D., medical director, Washington, D.C.'s Trans Cultural Psychiatry Center; Beverly Tatum, Ph.D., associate professor, Dept. of Psychology and Education, Mount Holyoke College; Nikola Trumbo, child development specialist.

Chapter Six

"WHY ARE ALL THESE
GROWN-UPS FIGHTING?"

Talking with Your Child About War
and the Nuclear Threat

In the heat of the war in the Persian Gulf, a group of first-graders sat in a semicircle around their teacher as she tried to answer their questions about the conflict. One query, however, left her at a loss. "How come," asked nine-year-old Adrianna, "you're always telling us not to fight on the playground, and my mom and dad tell me not to fight with my baby brother at home, but all these grown-ups are allowed to fight?"

"Yeah," piped up Stephen. "How come kids aren't allowed to fight but countries are?"

Why *are* countries allowed to fight? It's one of those "out of the mouths of babes" questions that leaves more than a few parents and teachers groping for a sound response. A part of us wants to say, "You're absolutely right. Countries shouldn't be allowed to fight," but our world-weary selves know that in the adult world, the answers just aren't that simple.

War is a tricky subject to address with young kids because our own feelings and thoughts are often conflicted. Most of us dislike war, but few believe it is never warranted. Further, since both the concept and reality of war are so complicated, colored in shades of gray, we wonder if our children, who view the world in black and white, can possibly understand. Finally, we worry that any mention of war will upset our children. We fool ourselves into believing that if we don't talk about it, then they won't think about it, and if we're lucky, we won't ever have to discuss it.

Then some military conflict breaks out and we are jolted out of our silence. Our children begin to flood us with questions and we struggle to find an adequate response. Even after the crisis ends and we all let out a collective sigh of relief, we know that it will not be our nation's last conflict and that the questions will someday begin again.

Children's television also plays a key role in keeping war in youngsters' minds. From Ninja Turtles to G.I. Joe, images of violent conflict abound. Experts like Peggy Charren, former president of ACT (Action for Children's Television), worry that the messages of kids' cartoons can lead our children down an anxious path, for they tell our children that the world is forever unsafe and the enemy could be lurking anywhere, ready to harm us even without provocation. Some of the cartoons seem so real to very young children, who are not quite adept at keeping fantasy and reality separate, that kids can find it difficult to distinguish between the animated fantasies and the six o'clock news.

Clearly, parents have their work cut out for them in trying to explain war and the nuclear threat to young children—as well as to themselves. It's important, then, to reflect on war, to understand how it has evolved, and to consider where it might lead us.

The Issue in Focus

The wars that we face today, and the wars of our future, are immeasurably different from the battles of the past. One of the most startling differences is the extent of civilian involvement. Hundreds of years ago, professional soldiers fought professional soldiers; civilians were largely uninvolved. Citizens were pillaged and raped, but as a terrible byproduct, not a spoil, of war and thus not as an integral part of the conflict itself. In the years after the French Revolution, however, when many countries were attacking France, the French launched the first draft of civilians ever. From then on, "the people" joined professional soldiers in making war.

When the Industrial Revolution allowed weaponry to be made on a mass scale, civilians, who manufactured the weapons, became part of the war effort; during World War II, military productions plants in which ordinary citizens worked became a "legitimate" target of war. Cities went on warring nations' hit lists, the most egregious example being the atomic bombing of Hiroshima and Nagasaki. Today, terrorists attack civilian sites as their primary targets, making each and every one of us more involved in and frightened by contemporary war.

War has also changed in its increasing numbers of casualties. Early skirmishes counted deaths in the hundreds; later ones listed thousands of victims. Forty million people died in the Second World War, five times as many as in the First World War. Seventy thousand people died in Hiroshima alone—*all* within five minutes.

Still another way in which war has changed, in particular for Americans, is in its growing danger of reaching our shores. Psychologically, the media has already brought war closer to us than ever before; we didn't watch World War II on TV, but Vietnam was beamed into our homes every night.

Furthermore, the improvement in high-tech weaponry has taken away the protection our bordering oceans once offered. Some missiles, like the Intercontinental Ballistic Missiles, move so fast that they could reach the U.S. from the USSR in about thirty minutes. And these missiles can be armed with nuclear warheads.

That fact brings up another touchy area in today's troubling world—the nuclear threat. I remember the "duck and cover" drills from my own childhood in the fifties. When the bell rang, my classmates and I had to get under our desks, turn our heads away from the windows, and keep our eyes covered. I was terrified that our school would be blown away when "the bomb" dropped. I remember trying to calculate how quickly I could get home before it landed. Somehow, my seven-year-old self believed that I could endure the end of the world if I was with my family.

In the years following WW II, many researchers grew

interested in studying the impact of the nuclear age on the children of my generation. One of the most respected and well known of those scientists was Milton Schwebel, who today is the senior research scholar at Harvard's Center for Psychological Studies in the Nuclear Age. Schwebel and his colleagues found that young children born in the post-Hiroshima period did indeed worry about nuclear war; the issue of the nuclear threat negatively affected how they felt about themselves and their future.

When I asked Schwebel if today's kids still feel that threat, he said, "The extent of a child's concern depends on what was going on when he or she reached real consciousness. That is, kids who became seven or eight after WW II or in the fifties perceived nuclear war as a real threat. And many kids who reached that age around 1979 or early eighties, the days of 'The Evil Empire' and the massive arms buildup, had a similar experience. However, children who turned eight or nine around 1987 or so, during the Gorbachev years, when some important disarmament treaties were signed, probably felt less threatened."

That's a comforting thought—until you consider another. While there is no conclusive evidence as yet, the Gulf War, with its talk of chemical and nuclear warfare, awakened similar fears even in children of the relatively peaceful Gorbachev years. Thus it is still important to understand how young children perceive the images and realities of war and the nuclear threat.

What Kids Think

Studies have shown that preschoolers have heard about nuclear bombs but have no real comprehension of what threat they pose. Any war images—bombs, big airplanes, grown-up men carrying heavy guns and wearing gas masks—equal something big, very powerful, and very bad in a preschooler's mind, not unlike the mean and wicked witches and monsters that appear in children's fairy tales. Preschoolers also pick up their parents' anxieties and fears of war, without Mom and Dad having said one word. Their magical thinking, their egocentrism and inability to think very abstractly, can leave them confused about the realities of war. I learned of one four-year-old who saw her Marine daddy, then stationed overseas, on TV. She ran up to the screen, hugged the TV, and demanded that Daddy come out from there and return home.

Children between five and seven often become more concretely concerned with their own safety and the safety of their family and friends. They may worry that a bomb from a hostile country will fall on and blow up their school or their house. It doesn't matter how far away the enemy country may be; any enemy is a clear and present danger.

Kids between seven and eleven are the most at risk for emotional problems brought on by fears of the nuclear threat and, indeed, of war overall, believes Dr. Schwebel, because they are able to recognize the real dangers of both. They know that nuclear bombs can kill many people and that war results in casualties on both sides. But psychologically, they are in a no-win situation, because while they understand the problems of war, they have difficulty comprehending the more abstract strategies that bring about an end to war.

Concepts like nuclear deterrence, for example, are beyond their ken; so is the idea that there are thousands of people worldwide who are trying to bring about an end to war and the nuclear threat. The only "solutions" kids in this age group understand are simplistic and concrete.

Psychologist Steven Zeitlin told me a story recently that illustrates this point. An eleven-year-old girl asked her dad why the man who invented "the bomb" can't just get rid of it. When her father tried to explain—"You can't do that, actually. Once the cat is out of the bag you can't put it back"—the youngster said impatiently, "Sure you can. Tie his paws."

Age is not the only factor that affects how children think about war and the nuclear threat. Gender, too, plays a role. Dr. Petra Hesse, well known for her studies of how children form concepts of "the enemy," says that time and again, young girls show more concern about the victims of a particular conflict than the conflict itself. When Hesse and her colleagues asked girls to draw what war looks like, they drew people bleeding, people hurt, pictures of graveyards. Boys, on the other hand, drew scenes of warfare. They seem enamored of weapons and arms. A 1990 survey of 110,000 students in grades one through twelve, conducted by Scholastic Inc., supports Hesse's findings. Specifically, nearly twice as many girls (34 percent) as boys (19 percent) said they believed that there's no good reason for going to war.

It's hard to know how much of this gender difference springs from how we raise our children—giving toy guns and trucks to boys, dolls and stuffed animals to girls—and how much is innate. But one pertinent point made to me by psychiatrist John Mack, a respected researcher and founding director of the Center for Psychological Studies in the Nuclear Age, is that boys' fascination with the accoutrements of warfare does not preclude their fears when a real war breaks out.

Mack explains that "for this generation of kids, war has been fun and games—all computers, video games, and movies. But once we got into the Persian Gulf War, things changed; the real threat stood side by side with fantasy and the fears often eclipsed the excitement." Many young children, and particularly boys, became confused. The only wars they had known before were those fought in cartoons and movies, and the all-good hero always triumphed over the evil enemy. As one nine-year-old asked, "Where is Rambo? Why doesn't he come and save all the Americans?"

Clearly, both boys and girls today are frightened and confused about war and the nuclear threat. And as always, the best way to diffuse such fears and anxiety is to talk about them.

How to Talk with Your Child About War and the Nuclear Threat

1. Get Your Own Feelings Straight.

No matter where you stand on war and nuclear weapons, you'll make your kids much less anxious and a good deal more secure if you sort out your own feelings first. The child of a career soldier or a peace activist is in a sense better off than the child of parents who are vague and confused about their own emotions. That's because both the soldier and the "dove" can respond to their children's questions with clarity and confidence and help them sort out their own confusing array of reactions. Even if you have mixed feelings about war—as many of us do—identifying those thoughts and then sharing them with your children teaches them that some issues are complicated, and that having mixed emotions about them is perfectly acceptable.

2. Encourage Kids to Talk It Out.

No matter how scary an issue is for kids—and war is certainly among the scariest—children feel better when they can talk about their feelings. It lifts the burden of having to face this frightening issue all by themselves. Talking to their parents assures kids that they are not alone in their concerns and that their parents are there to help. As one eleven-year-old expressed it, "I'm glad my parents talked about war with me. For a while I thought I was the only one who was scared. But I felt much better knowing that, well, my family cared as much as me and that other people did, too. Plus I found out that lots of people were trying to stop war."

Talking about their fears also offers children a kind of emotional release. As adults, we've all had the experience of being very worried about something, and feeling much better after discussing the problem with a trusted friend. Young children view their parents as trusted friends and feel that same sense of relief when they can talk about what frightens them—in this case, war and the nuclear threat. Research has shown again and again that kids are *not* traumatized by talking about a subject, but can be harmed if and when that topic becomes taboo.

3. Find the Opportunity.

Some child-rearing experts believe parents should not initiate conversations about war unless their children ask specific questions. I don't agree, at least not in all cases. While some kids may not ask questions or discuss issues of war because they are honestly not concerned, others may keep quiet to protect their parents; that is, they sense that any discussion of war may upset their mom or dad. (This is particularly true during an ongoing war when parents have other children or close relatives stationed overseas.) Other children may be so overwhelmed by their fears that they cannot find the words to express how they feel.

So find an opportunity to check out how your youngster is feeling. If he's watching a pertinent newscast, ask him, "Do you understand what's going on in that country? What do you think about it?" or "How does it make you feel?" If you know the war was discussed at school, you can say "Did you talk about the war today? What did your teacher say? How do you feel about what you learned?" Another good technique is to encourage your child to draw a picture, and to notice what she is depicting. If images of war planes, bombs, or dead soldiers dominate her pictures, she may be telling you that she is indeed worried about war.

If your efforts don't lead anywhere and your child makes it clear that he doesn't want to talk about this issue, drop it. You can't force a child into greater awareness; pushing a discussion might make the youngster more anxious. But if a dialogue begins, by all means encourage it to continue.

4. Acknowledge Their Fears and Offer Reassurances.

Young children always need support, reassurance, and a sense of security, and this is especially true when dealing with issues of war. During any ongoing conflict, parents need to reassure their children that their personal world will remain safe. (This advice is particularly valid for American families, who happily have not had to face war in their backyards; families in many other countries cannot offer this kind of reassurance.) For children under the age of ten or so, you can say something like "I know that you feel a little scared by the war, but you'll be fine. Mommy and Daddy are here to protect you and take care of you just as they always have." A special "I love you" and frequent and reassuring hugs can go a long way in allaying a young child's fears.

Older children need to receive the same message, but you might want to offer a few more details. You can say, "I know that you feel a little frightened by the war. So do I sometimes, because wars are very serious events. But your life will go on as usual—you'll go to school, take your piano lessons, play with your friends just like you always have. And Mom and Dad will always be here to care for you and to answer any questions you have."

Children whose mothers or fathers are involved in a military engagement need special reassurance, not only about their own safety but about the safety of the parent overseas. The fears are tied into worries of abandonment—pretty scary notions for a young child. It is up to the caretaker to provide reassurance to that child, but not to make any false promises. You cannot assure the child that his parent will come home safe and sound; if you do, you risk adding betrayal to his fears. But you *can* say something like "I know you worry about Daddy. I do, too, because it's dangerous where he is. But Daddy is not alone; there are lots of people with him who are taking care of him. And Daddy is very good at taking care of himself, so chances are he'll be just fine. I know he misses you and wants to come home as soon as he can. But in the meantime, I will take care of you and you'll keep right on doing the things you always do—going to school, playing with your friends. And we'll write to Daddy and tell him that we love him, because he and I love you very much."

5. Monitor Any News Watching.

Children under eleven rarely watch TV news, but if you're viewing, they may listen in, particularly if something like a bombing catches their attention. Be careful, though, to monitor their reactions to what they are seeing.

This tactic is important because many young children won't be able to express their reactions verbally, but may signal their discomfort by squirming or looking away. In that case, you can respond by saying, "Boy, that looked pretty scary. I'm glad we're safe at home and that all that is going on so very far away." Then be prepared to answer any questions or respond to any comments your child may have.

One more point: During many international conflicts, some adults become so concerned that they keep the news on almost all day long. If you have very young children, try to resist this impulse. Continuously tuning in to the war may convey the message that you are extremely upset and concerned, and that in itself may frighten your child. I'm not suggesting that you abstain from TV news. But until the kids are in bed, let moderation be your guide.

It's also a good idea to control kids' cartoon watching.

According to Harvard's Center for Psychological Studies in the Nuclear Age, preschoolers and school-age kids watch more than twenty-seven hours of TV per week. Much of that time is spent viewing cartoons in which kids learn that conflicts are usually resolved by force. Given this, it makes sense not only to monitor the kind of cartoons your children are watching, but also to set limits on the time they spend tuned in. My sister-in-law tried this with great success, declaring "electronics-free" days during which the entire family, including her eight- and eleven-year-old sons, are forbidden to use any electronic entertainment—including Nintendo and TV. Believe it or not, the kids readily took up the challenge, and happily turned their attention to sports, crafts, books, and other family games to amuse themselves.

6. Make War Understandable.

Young children don't need to know the many whys and wherefores of war. But they do need to know what war is. The task for parents is to make any explanation understandable, no matter what the age of the child. As one nine-year-old said at the start of a recent international conflict, "I watch the news with my parents, but I don't think the people who write the news know that there are little kids watching. They use really hard words that I don't understand, so I get confused." Take a tip from this astute youngster: use simple words and offer basic information, and don't deluge kids with more than they want to know.

Here's a sample explanation suitable for four- to seven-year-olds: "War is not like when people fight with each other. It's not like when you fight with your sister or even when Mommy and Daddy fight. War is much bigger and

much more serious. It means when whole countries fight."
With kids eight and over, you might want to explain why a
particular war is going—or has gone—on. Since kids of this
age often understand the concept of the enemy as bully, you
might begin to talk about WW II by saying that "the leader
of Germany was a man named Hitler and he went into
many other countries and tried to claim them for his own.
Many countries, including our own, went to war to stand up
to this bully and to make sure he stopped hurting other
countries and their people."

Since young children better understand what they can
see, it's a good idea to follow such explanations with a quick
map lesson in which you point out the countries you have
been discussing. Seeing how distant the site of the war is
from the U.S. will also help to allay kids' anxieties over their
immediate safety. And be prepared to emphasize it over and
over again. Young children need a great deal of reassurance
that their home, family, and immediate environment are
safe.

7. Get on Your Child's Wavelength.

Sometimes even the most elementary explanations can
get distorted in a young child's mind. I'm reminded of the
four-year-old whose mother told her not to worry about the
war because it was "very far away." But the youngster began
to cry and when her mother asked why, she answered that
she was worried about Grandma, who also lived "very far
away." The child didn't relax until her mom took out a map
and showed her how far her grandmother was from the
fighting.

This anecdote underscores the importance of not assuming that your child has clearly understood what you

have explained. Try to figure out what your child is really thinking, saying, or asking before you plunge ahead with more discussion.

8. Balance Boys' Titillation with War.

As I mentioned earlier, studies show that war and military weaponry often fascinate young boys, and adults can find that upsetting. Many parents worry that their child will become too "hawkish" or violent without understanding the cost war has on human lives. Some mental health experts share this concern and recommend that parents offer the other side of war to their sons. For instance, if a youngster seems excited by a TV newscast showing a bomb that's exploded a building in a war, these pundits recommend saying, "Gee, I wonder how many people were hurt or even killed by that bomb."

That approach is fine with kids of around age nine, ten, or older. They are able to understand two sides of an issue simultaneously; that is, that war can be both exciting and devastating. But stressing the human sacrifice in war may be too confusing and upsetting to younger kids. They'll come to appreciate war's downside as they develop their cognitive ability to think and conceptualize all the many sides of an issue. For now, though, I recommend balancing their feelings by showing them that they can feel just as excited by more constructive activities. As Dr. Barry Garfinkel, head of child and adolescent psychiatry at the University of Minnesota, explains, "You can validate your kids' feelings by saying, 'Yes, this war stuff can seem exciting. But you know what? I think playing soccer is just as exciting, so why don't we try to spend more time doing that.' "

9. Don't Get Upset by Your Child's Overly Hawkish Statements or Military Games.

Sometimes parents and teachers get upset by statements like "We should nuke that country" or "kill" that leader coming from their usually gentle children. While such concerns are understandable, you have to keep in mind that children tend to see the world as black or white. To a child who has watched the enemy get killed on countless cartoons, such hawkish statements make perfect sense and are, in fact, commonplace. Children don't understand the moral implications of killing or the devastating ramifications of dropping nuclear bombs. It's just a kid's way of expressing a simple, effective way to stop the war.

While I don't suggest drawing too much attention to these statements, you might want to say, "Well, I'm not sure I agree with you. I think it would be better if the countries' leaders figured out a peaceful way to solve the problem, like you and Jackie did yesterday when you both wanted the same toy and shared it rather than fighting about it. But I do agree that I wish this conflict would end as soon as possible."

During an ongoing war, parents also may want to ease up on allowing their children to play war-oriented games. Kids express their concerns and work out many problems through play. As one nine-year-old girl explained, "Me and my friends liked to play war during the Gulf War. When we played, Hussein always got killed and the war came to an end. After we finished playing, I always felt so much better."

There is also something to be said for permitting "war play" even when our country is not embroiled in a conflict. Fantasy play with such items as toy guns or soldiers, as well as a certain degree of roughhousing, offers children an acceptable outlet for their aggressive tendencies. If your child gets angry at his new baby sister for usurping the parental attention that was once his alone, better to have him release his anger through a rough-and-tumble game of war than to take a swipe at the infant.

Again, though, if your child plays with aggressive toys and games to the *exclusion* of everything else, you might say, "Well, these games seem like fun. But I know other things to do that are just as much fun." Then, encourage your child to participate in such alternative (and vigorous) activities as soccer, karate, or bicycling, both with you and with his buddies.

10. Become More Politically Active.

Studies have shown that political activism doesn't make children more anxious about war and the nuclear threat; rather, it lessens their anxiety by fostering a feeling of empowerment, a sense that their actions can make a difference. That's why it's a good idea to set an example for your child by becoming active yourself—donate money to a relief fund or political campaign, get involved in a political action group, write letters to your politicians. Explain to your youngster that you are doing these things because each person can help change things he or she doesn't like.

You can also encourage your child to follow suit. Suppose, for instance, that your son says he doesn't want there to be any more bombs. You can suggest that he write to the president about his concerns. You can also include your child in political marches. Making it a family event fosters feelings of closeness, and again, conveys the message that everyone can make a difference. Even doing something as simple as tying a yellow ribbon around a tree, a particularly popular act during wartime, can give your child a sense that he can do something to help.

11. Encourage Cross-cultural Understanding.

My brother, Jeff, a political economist at the University of Texas at Dallas, recently gave me food for thought when he said, "You know, for decades the British and French have had the ability to destroy much of the U.S. in a nuclear attack, but we spend no time worrying about this because our relationships with these countries are so good. On the other hand, we spend, or at least have spent, a lot of time worrying about the nuclear capability of the Soviet Union because our relationships with it are, or at least have been, so poor."

What we can learn from that information is this: Good, positive cross-cultural relationships based on a real understanding among the peoples of different countries can go a long way in removing the threat of war and nuclear attack. And a wonderful way to begin developing these healthy international relationships is with our children. Through books, movies, TV shows, visits to museums, contact with people from various cultures, and a good deal of open talk, we can help them grow to understand people of other countries. Such cross-cultural understanding can make our world, and the world our children will inherit, a safer and less troubling place to be.

12. Watch Out for Marked Stress.

Many healthy children will show some concern about war, especially if our country is embroiled in one at the moment. They may ask lots of questions, seem somewhat preoccupied with war news or draw lots of pictures of war images—missiles, fighter planes, soldiers, even cemeteries. This behavior is perfectly normal and to be expected during times of crisis.

Some children, however, particularly those who have lost a parent or close relative in a war, may show a great deal of anxiety. Their concerns may manifest themselves in sleep disturbances, including nightmares, a change in eating habits, a desire to spend more time alone and a turning away from social interaction, or even regressive behavior—a return to bed-wetting in a child who is well toilet trained, for example. If such uncharacteristic behavior persists more than a few weeks, you may want to seek professional help. Talk to your pediatrician for a recommendation to a mental health practitioner and/or call a local mental health association (see the Helpful Resources section at the end of Chapter 1) for a referral.

Considering Terrorism

One of the most frightening aspects of today's world is terrorism. The threat of bombs exploding in public places such as banks or train stations, and on airplanes worries all of us because their seeming randomness and unpredictability take away our sense of security.

Children, even as young as four or five, pick up adults' nervousness over terrorist acts; even the most offhanded comment made by a parent—"Gee, I'm a little worried about flying these days"—may be pounced on by a youngster sensing his mom or dad's concern.

If your child expresses any fears about terrorism—they usually won't use that word; instead their fears come out in such questions as "Could a bomb explode at the mall and hurt everybody?"—your best move is to reassure your child without making any false promises. To a four- or five-year-old you can say, "I know that sometimes you worry about that. Sometimes I do, too. But there are lots of people, like the police, who work hard to make sure that every place you go is safe. And Mommy and Daddy will always try to be there to protect you. So don't worry about that. Let's just do what we always do and have a really good time."

To reassure an older child, use a more concrete example. For instance, you could say, "I understand you're feeling scared. Sometimes I feel a little scared too. But there's really no reason for that. Our government works hard to make sure all its people are safe from terrorist attacks. Remember when we went to visit Grandma in Florida and we had to walk through a special machine? And our bags went through another machine? That was to make sure that we had no bombs or guns, and that's how they make sure the planes are safe. So there are lots of people whose job it is to keep us all safe. And the best thing we can do is to live our lives just as we always do and not worry. And remember that Mommy and Daddy will always try to be there to take care of you as best we can."

Sample Questions and Answers

Q: You told us not to fight; how come adults are allowed to fight in wars?

A: I know it's hard to understand; sometimes I even have a hard time understanding why the leaders of our countries can't solve their problems by talking them out. But sometimes the problems are so hard to solve that they just can't. So they go to war. But the problems in our house or in your school are never so big that they can't be solved by talking them out. That's why Daddy and I and your teacher never want you to fight.

Q: How do you know when somebody wins a war?

A: Well, one side usually gives up, so then the other side wins. But sometimes, the leaders of the countries in a war sit down together and talk things out even while the war is going on. Then, when they find an answer to their problems, the fighting stops and the war is over.

Q: Will the whole world die if a nuclear bomb goes off?

A: No, the whole world won't die. And Mommy and I will do whatever we can to try to keep you safe. But many people will die and many animals and plants, too. So we have to work hard to make sure that no one ever uses a bomb like that.

Q: Why can't we get rid of the bombs?

A: Maybe someday we can. That's why Mommy and Daddy write letters to the president and go on marches. When we do that, we are saying we want everyone to get rid of the bombs. You can help, too. Why don't we sit down and write a letter to the president and ask him to work hard to get rid of all the bombs.

Helpful Resources

ORGANIZATIONS

Action for Children's Television
20 University Road
Cambridge, MA 02138
(617) 876-6620

American Friends Service Committee
1501 Cherry Street
Philadelphia, PA 19102
(215) 241-7000

Center for Psychological Studies in the Nuclear Age
1493 Cambridge Street
Cambridge, MA 02139
(617) 497-1553

Concerned Educators Allied for a Safe Environment
c/o Peggy Schirmer
17 Gerry Street
Cambridge, MA 02138

Educators for Social Responsibility
23 Garden Street
Cambridge, MA 02138
(617) 492-1764

National Coalition on Television Violence
P.O. Box 2157
Champaign, IL 61820

READINGS FOR PARENTS

Carlsson-Paige, Nancy, and Diane E. Levin. *Helping Young Children Understand Peace, War and the Nuclear Threat.* Washington, D.C.: National Association for the Education of Young Children, 1985.

——————. *Who's Calling the Shots?: How to Respond Effectively to Children's Fascination with War Play and War Toys.* Philadelphia: New Society Publishers, 1990.

Cloud, K., E. Deegan, A. Evens, H. Imam, B. Signer. *Watermelons Not War! A Support Book for Parenting in the Nuclear Age.* Philadelphia: New Society Publishers, 1984.

Dyer, Gwynne. *War.* New York: Crown Publishers, 1985.

Greenwald, David S. and Steven J. Zeitlin. *No Reason to Talk About It.* New York: W. W. Norton & Co., 1987.

Hopkins, Susan, and Jeffry Winters, eds. *Discover the World: Empowering Children to Value Themselves, Others and the Earth.* Philadelphia: New Society Publishers, 1990.

La Farge, Phyllis. *The Strangelove Legacy: Children, Parents, and Teachers in the Nuclear Age.* New York: Harper & Row, 1987.

Schell, Jonathan. *The Fate of the Earth.* New York: Alfred A. Knopf, 1982.

Tolley, Howard. *Children and War: Political Socialization to International Conflict.* New York: Teacher's College Press, 1973.

Van Ornum, W., and M. W. Van Ornum. *Talking to Children About Nuclear War.* New York: Continuum, 1984.

READINGS FOR CHILDREN

(NOTE: It's particularly difficult to specify age ranges for books on war; parental guidance, therefore, is strongly recommended.)

Baker, Betty. *The Pig War.* New York: Harper & Row, 1969. (Ages 5–10)

Bunting, Eve. *The Wall.* New York: Clarion, 1990. (Ages 5–8)

Donnelly, Judy. *A Wall of Names: The Story of the Vietnam Veterans Memorial.* New York: Random House, 1991. (Ages 8–11)

Durell, Ann, and Marily Sachs, eds. *The Big Book for Peace.* New York: Dutton Children's Books, 1990. (Ages 8–12)

Needle, Jan. *A Game of Soldiers.* London: William Collins & Sons, 1985. (Ages 10–12)

Dr. Seuss *The Butter Battle Book.* New York: Random House, 1984. (Ages 6–12)

Vigna, Judith. *Nobody Wants a Nuclear War.* Niles, Ill.: Albert Whitman, 1986. (Ages 5–9)

Winthrop, Elizabeth. *That's Mine!* New York: Holiday House, 1977. (Ages 4–7)

Zeifert, Harriet. *A New Coat for Anna.* New York: Alfred A. Knopf, 1986. (Ages 5–9)

Special thanks to the following experts for their input into this chapter: William Beardslee, M.D., clinical director, Dept. of Psychiatry, Boston Children's Hospital; Harry Croft, M.D., diplomate, American Board of Psychiatry;

Lloyd Jeffry Dumas, Ph.D., professor of political economy, University of Texas at Dallas; Ernest Fleishman, Ph.D., director of education, Scholastic, Inc.; Barry Garfinkel, M.D., head of child and adolescent psychiatry, University of Minnesota; David Greenwald, Ph.D., clinical director, Family & Psychological Services; Petra Hesse, Ph.D., research associate, Center for Psychological Studies in the Nuclear Age, Harvard Medical School; Edmund Levin, M.D., psychiatrist and former chairman of the American Psychiatric Association's Committee on Developmental and Clinical Aspects of the Nuclear Threat; John Mack, M.D., professor of psychiatry, The Cambridge Hospital/Harvard Medical School, and founding director of the Center for Psychological Studies in the Nuclear Age; Milton Schwebel, professor emeritus, Rutgers University, and senior research scholar, Center for Psychological Studies in the Nuclear Age; Larry Shapiro, Ph.D., president, The Center for Applied Psychology; Morley Shaw, Ph.D., psychotherapist; Steven J. Zeitlin, Ph.D., research associate, Center for Psychological Studies in the Nuclear Age.

Chapter Seven

"WHY CAN'T WE BE
A FAMILY?"

Talking with Your Child About
Divorce

Casey loved Father's Day. It was special. He and his dad would go to a ball game or the zoo, then meet up with Mom for dinner at a favorite restaurant. But when his parents began fighting all the time, the celebration stopped. And once his folks got divorced, eight-year-old Casey hardly ever saw his father. Now, two years later, Casey dreads Father's Day. At school, when the teacher asks the children to make cards for their dads, the youngster sits in the back of the room, feeling sad, angry, and very much alone. "Why," Casey wonders bitterly, "can't we be a family?"

Young Casey is experiencing what hundreds of thousands of youngsters go through each year: the pain of divorce. Children are the innocent victims of a marriage gone awry; they didn't make the decision to break up their family and have little to say about the divorce's consequences. They are left to cope as best they can with the lifelong trauma that divorce can impose.

I use the phrase "lifelong trauma" advisedly: "lifelong" because recent research, particularly findings cited in Dr. Judith Wallerstein's landmark book, *Second Chances* (see the Readings for Parents section at this chapter's end), has shown that the effect of divorce on kids reaches well past the immediate breakup and into adulthood. Even children who initially appear to come though divorce quite well may have trouble with intimacy as they reach adolescence and beyond. I use the term "trauma" because nearly every divorce has a major impact on the psychological and emotional life of its youngest victims.

But not all marital dissolutions devastate the children. Many kids do just fine, both in the short and long terms. To understand how and why some children do so well while others suffer tragically, it's helpful to take a closer look at the status of divorce in America today.

The Issue in Focus

Each year approximately two million couples marry in the U.S., according to the National Center for Health Statistics. And each year, more than one million marriages end in divorce. These failed couplings affect more than the husbands and wives involved; they touch their children as well.

According to recent data from the National Center for Health Statistics, for example, more than one half of couples who divorced in 1988 had children under the age of eighteen. This means that over the years, millions of our nation's children have endured—and will continue to endure—the pain of their parents' divorces.

But children are more than statistics, and the impact of divorce on these youngsters is hard to quantify. Fortunately, though, reams of research offer good insight as to divorce's effect on young kids.

In general, we know that most children feel a strong sense of abandonment when confronted with the realities of separation and divorce. A young, egocentric child does not perceive a marital breakup as two adults not being able to live together anymore, but as "Daddy [or Mommy] left *me*." His fears, anxiety, and sadness often center not only on the parent who left but also on the parent who remains, causing the child to worry, "If Daddy left me, will Mom leave me, too?"

Anger is another emotion common to children of divorce. The child becomes angry at the parent who left *and* at the custodial parent, whom she may blame for "driving Daddy away." Often, however, kids do not voice their outrage for fear that releasing such powerful feelings may chase the custodial parent away. So they express their resentment obliquely, either by acting out—getting into schoolyard brawls, talking back to teachers, or, in the case of younger kids, pinching, biting, or kicking playmates—or by acting in, that is keeping their anguish inside, which can lead to feelings of depression and diminished self-esteem. Typically, kids of divorce feel caught in the middle of a tug of war between two belligerent parents, and this, too, can lead to anger, resentment, anxiety, and confusion.

The age of a child also influences how he or she feels about and reacts to divorce. Egocentric three- to five-year-olds who have limited cognitive understanding of what's going on may believe that Daddy left because they were bad—they didn't pick up their toys or refused to go to bed on time. Because they may not be able to verbalize their anxiety, it often manifests itself in behavioral regressions; that is, there may be a lapse in toilet training, or the child may stop sleeping through the night. Fears of abandonment and feelings of self-blame may make even a normally outgoing, carefree child more clingy and withdrawn.

At ages six to eight, children have a greater understanding of divorce; at the very least, they've heard about it on TV or from other children at school. Their own parents' divorce may trigger feelings of intense sadness and an acute sense of loss. Since children in this age range also tend to engage in magical thinking, they may entertain strong fantasies that their parents will reconcile—"If I wish it really hard enough, Mom and Dad will get back together again"—that may go on for years. These frightened, sad, and frequently irritable kids often display their upset at school: grades drop and discipline problems emerge.

Slightly older children, ages nine to eleven, share the feelings of many of their younger counterparts, but since they have a more sophisticated understanding of what divorce means in the long term, their reactions may be more extreme. For instance, these youngsters can become very angry and may act out their anger by becoming sullen, uncooperative, belligerent, or, at the other extreme, withdrawn at home and in school. Because they are strongly oriented toward their peer group, children in this age group

often feel embarrassed and ashamed in front of their
friends, believing that they are the only ones who've ever
gone through divorce. Anxiety about their uncertain futures
may show up in sleep difficulties, eating problems, and a
decreased sense of self-worth.

Interestingly, though not surprisingly, experts often observe a distinct difference in how girls and boys, particularly
in this age range, react to divorce. As clinical psychologist
and divorce researcher Robert Emery explained to me,
"With boys, there's a lot of denial and acting out. They try
to relieve the pressure they feel by getting their parents to
shift their energy from fighting with each other to attending
to their kids. But girls try to make things better between
parents by being perfect little ladies. In short, boys often
become devils while girls tend to become angels."

While it is obvious that divorce takes its toll on children's emotional health and well-being, it's wrong to as-
sume that every divorced kid suffers long-term damage.
Actually, many youngster weather divorce well and gain
certain benefits in the process. If parents have negotiated an
amicable, rational separation and divorce, children can learn
how to resolve life's emotionally charged conflicts reason-
ably. Additionally, children of divorce can become more
resilient and self-reliant as a result of their experience.

The extent to which children will be affected by divorce, either positively or negatively, depends upon a great
many factors. First and foremost is the degree to which they
are exposed to fighting between parents both before and
after the marriage. When divorce brings an end to the
feuding, it may offer some sort of relief from the tension
and bitterness and, as I mentioned before, a lesson in conflict resolution. But when arguing continues or intensifies

after the breakup, so does its negative impact on the children.

Another factor that determines the degree to which kids are hurt by divorce, at least in the short term, is the extent to which the child's routines change. Clearly, severe disruptions in daily living, such as moving to a new home, losing a beloved nanny, or changing schools can heighten children's anxiety, insecurity, and feelings of loss. Since financial realities often precipitate many of these disruptions—divorced families usually experience a dramatic decrease in income, particularly if the primary breadwinner is the parent who moves out—economics is another factor that can complicate kids' lives.

While researching her book, *A Hole in My Heart: Adult Children of Divorce Speak Out,* my friend and fellow journalist, Claire Berman, talked with many now-grown divorced kids. One of the things she discovered was that divorced parents' ability to continue to co-parent also had a major influence on the impact of divorce. Berman observed that "when the noncustodial parent remained in contact with the child, when both parents continued to be involved in the child's life—when they both went to the Little League games or to parents' night at school—the children seemed to do better than when contact with and involvement of the noncustodial parent ended." She also noted that when divorced kids had other support systems, such as those offered by siblings, involved grandparents, or even concerned neighbors and friends, it mitigated the potentially devastating effect of divorce.

Finally, children's temperaments and personalities influence how they react and adjust to divorce. A withdrawn, anxious child who had problems with self-esteem and social

interaction before the divorce is at greater risk for emotional and behavioral problems after the breakup than is an
even-tempered, outgoing, socially confident child. Clearly,
the latter will show more natural resilience and be better
able to snap back, at least after the immediate trauma of
divorce has passed.

Actually, there are three stages to every divorce, says
Dr. Neil Kalter in his book, *Growing Up With Divorce*. The
first, the "immediate crisis," begins as soon as the parents
separate; the second, the "short-term aftermath," starts
once the immediate crisis has passed and ends up to two
years later, when economic supports, custody, and visitation
schedules are fairly well in place. Finally comes Kalter's
third stage, the "long-range period," which consists of the
many years that follow.

Since this chapter is intended as a starting-off point for
parents, the information and advice that follows focuses on
the immediate crisis period, the first stage of divorce. Hopefully, the advice that follows will set you and your youngsters on the right course as you navigate divorce's troubling
waters.

How to Talk with Your Child About Divorce

1. Alert Them to the Upcoming Separation.

When I started researching this book, I was astounded
to learn how many parents don't tell their children about an
impending separation. I've heard story upon story of children who woke up one morning to hear suddenly that

"Daddy has left and he's not coming back. We're getting a divorce." While I'm sure that these parents feel they are doing the best thing for their children by not upsetting them in advance, such poor judgment can cause enduring damage to any child's sense of security and trust.

A much better tactic is to inform your child of the upcoming separation in advance. Don't do it if you're still undecided; if you change your minds and stay together, you've caused your child undo anxiety. But once you've made a *final* decision to separate, sit down with your youngster and explain what is going to happen. A week's notice might be sufficient for a four- or five-year-old to start processing the information; a couple of weeks is probably a good idea for a ten- or eleven-year-old. (Don't be surprised, however, if your kids already have an inkling that a separation is being considered; kids are quite adept at picking up all sorts of cues concerning their parents' distress.)

It's best if Mom and Dad can tell the child together; that way, you can assure your youngster that both parents will remain in his life. But even if that's not possible, make sure at least one parent has a heart-to-heart with the child, telling him what will happen, validating his feelings, and reaffirming his parents' love for him.

For example, you might explain to a four- or six-year-old, "You know how Mommy and Daddy have been fighting a lot lately? Well, we've been talking, and we decided it would be best if Mommy and Daddy didn't live together anymore. This is a grown-up decision and it's not because of anything that you did. You are a wonderful daughter and we both love you very much. But now Daddy will be living in a new apartment and you and Mommy will stay here. You'll still see Daddy every weekend and you can talk to him on the phone whenever you want. We'll still be your Mommy and Daddy and we'll always love you."

You can present the same information, but at a slightly more sophisticated level, to a ten- or eleven-year-old by saying something like, "Mom and I are having a hard time getting along. We are trying to sort things out, but we're having trouble doing that. So we are going to separate and live apart from each other. I'm going to move out and get an apartment and Mom is going to stay here with you and your sister. You will come visit me a lot though, and we'll talk on the phone, too. I feel really bad about this because I know it's not going to be easy for you. It's not going to be easy for us, either. But in the long run, we think this is the best thing to do. Just remember that we both love you as much as always and we'll always be your parents, no matter what."

2. Try to Offer a Positive, Though Always Honest, Explanation.

Telling your child about your breakup can be a wrenching experience, but if you can, try to add a positive note to the news. You can say something like "I know you feel bad about this and so do I. But I think living apart will help things calm down around here—there won't be so much fighting, and that will be better for all of us. Also, I'll be able to spend even more time with you alone—just the two of us."

3. Explain the Major Causes of the Breakup.

Children are entitled to know why Mom and Dad are splitting up; besides, if you don't tell them, they're likely to conjure up their own inaccurate and possibly hurtful reasons, like "Mommy left me because I was bad." Offering your children a reason for your divorce can preclude such misconceptions.

You don't need to go into all the sordid details; just as kids deserve an explanation, you are entitled to some privacy. But to, say, a nine-year-old you can offer something like "Mommy and Daddy are fighting so much that we're making each other unhappy" or "Daddy has a drinking problem and we both feel that he needs to be living apart from us until he can get some help."

Even if Dad's moving in with another woman, you can say, "When you were born, Mommy and Daddy loved each other very much. But we both changed too much and now we are having a hard time living together. Daddy has found another lady who he wants to live with and so he is moving out of our house and into a house with her. This makes me very sad and angry at Daddy. But I'm not angry at you. And I want you to know that no matter what has happened between Mommy and Daddy, nothing can ever stop us from loving you. We'll always be your parents and we'll always love you very much."

4. Be Specific.

As you may have noticed from the previous sample scripts, it is important to be specific about how the separation and divorce will affect your child's daily life. Take care, then, to make sure your explanations include as much detail as possible, particularly about where the child and the non-custodial parent will be living. After you explain that Dad (or Mom) is moving out, you can say, "Daddy is going to take his own apartment. It's on Rumsey Road, right near the big pizza restaurant. This is his phone number and you can call him there whenever you want. And you will see him every Tuesday night and every Saturday for the whole day. You'll still live with Mommy in our house; that's where your toys will be and that's where your bed will be. You'll go to the same school, have your same friends, take your piano and karate lessons. That won't change. What will change is that Daddy won't be living in our house anymore."

5. Anticipate Several Discussions.

Telling a child that his parents are about to separate packs a powerful emotional punch, no matter how carefully you couch your explanations. Children won't be able to absorb all the information and its many ramifications in one neat discussion. That's why you'll need to give your child permission to engage in several talks about the divorce, even if it means repeating what you have already explained over and over again. A good way to let your child know she can always come back for more is to say, "I know that this is a lot to hear and think about right now. We'll talk more about it soon. In fact, we can talk about it as much as—and whenever—you want. Okay?"

Even if your child doesn't take the initiative and ask you more about the divorce, you should broach the subject several times over the course of the next few days, weeks, and months. Children, particularly very young children caught up in magical thinking, often deny the reality of divorce and need to be reminded several times that the separation or divorce is actually taking place.

Having many talks about the divorce will also enable you to identify and correct any misconceptions your child may have. I remember reading about one preschooler who believed that getting "lavorced," as he put it, meant that his

parents would be using a certain brand of mouthwash together. Don't nag the child with constant "divorce talk," but
do repeat the information until you feel your youngster
understands.

6. Encourage Children to Express Their Feelings.

It's best if children can express their feelings about the
divorce. Getting their emotions out can help ward off such
somatic problems as stomachaches and headaches that tend
to appear when kids deny powerful feelings or shut them up
inside. But don't expect all children to welcome the opportunity to reveal their emotions. As Kalter points out in his
book, "Children generally hate looking squarely at and talking about their emotional distress. The preferred modes for
coping with internal turmoil are not to think about it, to act
as if nothing was wrong, and to admit to no upset feelings."
All the more reason, I believe, to encourage your child to
air what's on his mind.

You can try this verbally by asking such open-ended
questions as "You haven't said much about Mom and Dad's
divorce. What have you been thinking about it?" and then
letting the child speak freely, without him having to worry
about incurring your anger or upset. Another approach is to
encourage your child to express his feelings through drawings. You can ask the youngster to "draw a picture of
divorce" and use his finished creation to trigger some discussion. Putting on a puppet show in which one of the
puppets—perhaps the one your child is manipulating—
learns his parents are getting a divorce is another way you
can prompt your child to communicate feelings. Still another tactic is to find some children's books on divorce and
spend time reading them together. You'll find the titles

suggested at the end of this chapter are particularly appropriate.

When your child is able to communicate his emotions, make sure you acknowledge them no matter how you may be feeling. Suppose, for example, your five-year-old says, "I don't think Daddy loves me anymore, that's why he moved away and I only see him on weekends." Even if you're very angry with your ex-spouse, don't fuel these negative feelings with statements like "You're right. Daddy is so selfish he doesn't love any of us anymore." Instead, help your child to feel better with a response like "I know it feels as if Daddy doesn't love you anymore. But it's not true. Daddy does love you and tries to see you as much as he can." Even if your child's words hurt you—"I hate you, Mommy! You made Daddy go away"—try to stay calm, validate his feelings, and correct his misconceptions. You might say, "I know that you are angry at me, but I didn't make Daddy go away. Daddy and I both decided that we couldn't live together anymore and that's why he went away. And I want you to know that no matter how angry you get at me, I'm staying right here. I will always love you." What you want to do, as psychologist Judith Wallerstein says, is "give your child the right to express his own feelings and the right *not* to express yours."

Another note on feelings: Most parenting books on divorce advise you never to let your children see how upset you are. While it's true that getting hysterical in front of the kids serves no one well, I believe that letting your child see that you're sad is perfectly okay. If your youngster notices a few of your tears, you can simply say, "Mommy is very sad that she and Daddy are getting a divorce. I know that someday I'll feel better, but right now I feel sad." And don't be surprised if your child responds with "I feel sad, too." Seeing you express your emotions may well draw your child out and help him understand that it's okay to express his feelings, too.

7. Do More Than *Say* "I Love You."

While it's important to tell your children you love them, it's equally critical to *demonstrate* how much you care. If you're a noncustodial parent, make sure to spend as much time as possible with your child. When you say you'll pick your daughter up on Tuesday night, be there Tuesday night. If you have to change those plans, contact your child directly, explain what happened, and make alternate arrangements. The father or mother who says "Oh, I really love my kids" and never shows up after the divorce may be doing their children a great deal of harm.

Custodial parents also need to show their love by devoting some quality time to their children. Try to spend at least fifteen uninterrupted minutes (and hopefully more) with each child, each night. Read a book together, take a walk, play a game—it doesn't really matter what you do as long as you let your child know that during this time, she is the sole object of your attention.

Ideally, both parents should make an effort to show up for parents' night at school (you can work out a mutually agreeable schedule in the event that you don't want to appear at the same time), sporting events, or other occasions that you know are important to your child. But if you both can't be there, at least one parent should make it his/her business to participate.

8. Explain That the Divorce Is Not Your Child's Fault.

Sometimes, though not always, young children believe that they caused their parents' divorce. The four-year-old may say, "Daddy left because I didn't eat my spinach." The nine-year-old may feel his poor math grades drove his mathematician father from home. That's why it's important to reassure your children that the divorce is not their fault. Each conversation about your divorce—and especially the one in which you break the news—should carry the message that "Mom and Dad made the decision to get a divorce because . . ." and give the reason. Then add, "It has nothing to do with you. You didn't do anything wrong. Nothing you did or said caused this to happen. This is a decision grownups sometimes have to make, and it has nothing to do with their children."

9. Don't Overburden Your Child.

A child psychologist I know told me of a four-year-old patient whose divorced father had made him a confidant. The father, a successful contractor, would boast, "I tell my son everything—about my love life, my career, my hopes, my plans. And he understands." But when the therapist saw the youngster in session, the child played out games in which he was being hit by a truck over and over again. "It became more and more apparent," the therapist told me, "that this child was feeling overburdened by his dad."

As this brief example illustrates, children need to be children. They do not have the emotional or cognitive abilities to cope with the stresses and strains of adulthood. Having been divorced once myself, I understand how the breakup of a marriage can make any adult feel isolated, emotionally shaky, and vulnerable—and a loving child can offer great comfort. But be careful that your child doesn't start to "replace" your spouse. Children have a tendency to try to "make things all better" by taking care of their parents. And while that's okay to a point—for example, there's no harm in allowing your child to help you prepare breakfast like your ex used to—burdening your youngster with too many caretaking responsibilities and/or leaning too heavily on him for emotional support during this time can overtax your kid and hinder his normal, healthy development.

10. Permit a Positive Relationship with the Other Parent.

Sustaining a positive relationship with both parents, including the noncustodial one, is to any divorced child's advantage. But in order for this to occur, not only does the noncustodial parent have to be willing and available, but the custodial parent has to cooperate as well. That is, she (or he) must make an effort not to put the other parent down or to make custodial visits difficult. She (or he) must be able to listen to the child relate stories of what happened during the last visit, and be willing to say, "I'm glad you're having so much fun with Dad," or "I'm so proud of your improved math grade. Let's call Dad and tell him the good news." No matter how angry you are at your ex-mate, you need to try and separate your role as spouse from your role as parent.

Permitting your child to have a good relationship with the other parent, however, does not mean that you need to idealize that parent. If, for instance, the child's father rarely shows up for his scheduled visits and continuously disappoints the youngster, you might say something like "I know you feel like Daddy doesn't love you anymore. But try to understand that sometimes your Daddy has trouble doing the things he says he's going to do. Even though he says he'll call on Sunday and doesn't, it doesn't mean he doesn't love you. It means he has a problem about keeping his word. It really has nothing to do with you. You're a terrific kid."

11. Keep Life as Predictable as Possible.

Divorce throws everyone's emotional life into confusion. To dilute some of this tumult and counteract any threat to your children's sense of security and safety, try hard to keep their everyday lives as predictable as you can. Maintain such routines as mealtimes and bedtimes. If possible, keep child-care arrangements intact. Don't dismiss the nanny, change baby-sitters, or pull your preschooler out of day care unless it is absolutely necessary.

Additionally, make room for happy rituals. I know that throwing a birthday party for your eight-year-old is the last thing on your mind when you're slogging through a divorce, but try to do it anyway. It's important for your child (and you) to remember that happy times will continue even in the wake of a painful divorce.

12. Effect Your Divorce as Quickly as Possible.

Once you and your spouse have decided to end your marriage in the courts, don't drag out the process. Instead, effect a rapid resolution as quickly as possible. Kids have difficulty coping with uncertainty and it will help them to know where and with whom they are going to live, how often they will see both parents, where they will go to school, and so on.

13. Don't Suspend Household Rules or Punishments.

Parents often feel so guilty over getting divorced that they let their kids run wild, totally suspending household decorum. But you'll be helping your child to maintain a sense of stability and security if you stick to your regular rules and regulations. Keep bedtimes consistent, let your child know she still has to do her chores, and convey the message that "no running in the living room" still applies.

14. Encourage Consistent Relationships with Other Adults.

Divorce causes so much disruption in a child's relationship with his parents, particularly with the noncustodial parent, that the youngster can lose faith in the stability of child-adult connections. He can also be thrown off if he does not have enough positive adult role models. To offset this possibility, encourage dependable relationships with other adults. Make an effort to permit consistent contact with grandparents, aunts, uncles, teachers, or even parents of your child's friends. Just make sure to monitor your child's contact with these adults to insure that the relationship is a healthy, positive one.

15. Allow Children to Adjust at Their Own Pace.

Some children seem to handle their parents' divorce quite well; they may spend the initial few months feeling sad and upset, but soon return to their normally happy selves. Others seem to take a much longer time to come to terms with what has happened. As one youngster said, "My parents told me about their divorce in February but I had to wait till my summer vacation to believe it."

Still others have an even longer delayed reaction to

divorce. They may deny it for as much as a year or so—drawings during this time may show Mommy and Daddy in bed or at home watching TV together—and then suddenly one day they may start crying. Another set of young children seems to do fine after divorce; later on, when they reach adolescence and begin to experiment with more sophisticated interpersonal relationships, they have problems with intimacy.

It's helpful to remember that divorce is not a discrete event, but an emotional and psychological process that may go on for many, many years after the court has given its ruling. Each child adjusts to divorce at his own pace and in his own way. Parents need to stay calm and permit that individualized adjustment to occur.

Certain warning signs, however, may indicate your child is having more than the usual difficulties and needs special attention. Specifically, if your youngster withdraws, becomes clingy and fearful, has an abrupt change in appetite or sleeping habits, begins wetting the bed or regressing in other ways, or if your child starts acting out in school or at home—and if this new behavior continues for more than a few weeks—you should probably consult a mental health professional. (See chapter 1, page 25, for how to find the best expert for you and your child.)

16. Inform Other People in Your Child's Life.

Sometimes parents are so embarrassed by their "failed" marriage that they try to keep it a family secret. Bad idea. First of all, divorce is so commonplace these days that no one need feel ashamed. Second, your child will get more and better support if you let others in his life know what he's going through. So inform teachers, coaches, doctors, religious leaders, the parents of your child's closest friends, anyone who has frequent contact with your child and anyone who might be able to offer your youngster a supportive and sympathetic shoulder.

17. Take Care of Yourself.

A depressed, withdrawn, and upset parent isn't able to effectively nurture her child, which is why it's essential for you to take care of yourself in the aftermath of a divorce. Pamper yourself every now and then—splurge on a sitter and go out to a movie. If finances permit, go away for a relaxing weekend. Also, find some more mature shoulders than your child's to lean on for emotional support. Self-help groups for divorced parents have proliferated around the country; check with your local Y, church, or synagogue, or look in the Yellow Pages for a group near you. Turn to adult family members or friends, or try professional counseling. Your local medical or mental health society may be able to refer you to a therapist who can help you, and, indirectly, your child, through what can be one of life's most stressful times.

Sample Questions and Answers

Q: Did Daddy (or Mommy) leave because I was bad?

A: No. Daddy and Mommy haven't been getting along well and we decided that it would be best if we didn't live together anymore. That's why Daddy left. Daddy and Mommy are grown-ups and this was a grown-up decision. It has nothing to do with anything you did. You are our special child and we both love you very much.

Q: Will Daddy (or Mommy) ever come back?

A: I don't think that Daddy will ever come back to live with us again. But that doesn't mean he will stop being your daddy. He will always be your daddy and I will always be your mommy. Daddy and I have made arrangements for you to visit him every other weekend in his new house. Then you and Daddy can have special time together, just the two of you.

Q: Are you going away, too?

A: No, I am never going to leave you. I can understand that you may feel scared about that, but I want you to know that I'm going to stay right here and take care of you.

Q: Will Daddy (or Mommy) be okay?

A: Both Mommy and Daddy are going to be sad for a while and maybe we'll even act a little different for a while. But we're all going to be okay. I'm going to stay right here with you in our house and Daddy is going to live in another house not too far from here. And we're all going to be just fine.

Helpful Resources

ORGANIZATIONS

The Divorce Resource Center
P.O. Box 98
Flushing, NY 11361
(718) 224-5947

National Childhood Grief Institute
3300 Edinborough Way, Suite 512
Minneapolis, MN 55435
(612) 832-9286

Rainbows for All God's Children, Inc.
1111 Tower Road
Schaumburg, IL 60173
(708) 310-1880

The Stepfamily Foundation, Inc.
333 West End Avenue
New York, NY 10023
(212) 877-3244

READINGS FOR PARENTS

Adler, Allan J., and Christine Archambault. *Divorce Recovery: Healing the Hurt Through Self-Help and Professional Support.* Summit, N.J.: The PIA Press, 1990.

Berman, Claire. *A Hole in My Heart: Adult Children of Divorce Speak Out.* New York: Fireside Books, 1992.

Diamond, S. *Helping Children of Divorce: A Handbook for Parents and Teachers.* New York: Schocken Books, 1985.

Emery, Robert. *Marriage, Divorce & Children's Readjustment.* Newbury Park, Calif.: Sage Publications, 1988.

Goldstein, S., and A. Solnit. *Divorce and Your Child: Practical Suggestions for Parents.* New Haven, Conn.: Yale University Press, 1984.

Herman, Stephen P. *Parent vs. Parent: How You & Your Child Can Survive the Custody Battle.* New York: Pantheon, 1990.

Johnson, Laurene, and Georglyn Rosenfeld. *Divorced Kids: What You Need to Know to Help Kids Survive a Divorce.* Nashville: Thomas Nelson Publishers, 1990.

Jong, Erica. *Megan's Book of Divorce—A Kid's Book for Adults.* New York: New American Library, 1984.

Kalter, Neil. *Growing Up With Divorce: Helping Your Child Avoid Immediate and Later Emotional Problems.* New York: The Free Press, 1990.

Rogers, Fred, and Clare O'Brien. *Mister Rogers Talks with Families About Divorce.* New York: Berkley Books, 1987.

Salk, Lee, Sonja Goldstein, and Albert Solnit. *Divorce and Your Child.* New Haven, Conn.: Yale University Press, 1985.

Wallerstein, Judith S., and Sandra Blakeslee. *Second Chances: Men, Women & Children a Decade After Divorce.* New York: Ticknor & Fields, 1989.

READINGS FOR CHILDREN

Adams, Florence. *Mushy Eggs.* New York: G. P. Putnam's Sons, 1973. (Ages 4–11)

Bienenfeld, Florence. *My Mom and Dad Are Getting a Divorce.* St. Paul, Minn.: EMC Corp., 1980. (Ages 4–11)

Brown, Laurene Krasny, and Marc Brown. *Dinosaurs Divorce: A Guide for Changing Families.* Boston: Joy Street Books, 1986. (Ages 4–8)

Fassler, David, Michele Lash, and Sally B. Ives. *Changing Families: A Guide for Kids and Grown-ups.* Burlington, Vt.: Waterfront Books, 1988. (Ages 4–12)

Girard, Linda Walvoord. *At Daddy's on Saturdays.* Niles, Ill.: Albert Whitman & Co., 1987. (Ages 7–10)

Hazen, Barbara. *Two Homes to Live In: A Child's Eye View of Divorce.* New York: Human Sciences Press, 1978. (Ages 4–8)

Ives, Sally Blakeslee, David Fassler, and Michele Lash. *The Divorce Workbook: A Guide for Kids and Families.* Burlington, Vt.: Waterfront Books, 1985. (Ages 4–12)

Simon, Norma. *All Kinds of Families.* Niles, Ill.: Albert Whitman & Co., 1976. (Ages 7–9)

———. *I Wish I Had My Father.* Niles, Ill.: Albert Whitman & Co., 1983. (Ages 7–9)

Sinberg, Janet. *Divorce Is a Grownup Problem: A Book About Divorce for Young Children and Their Parents.* New York: Avon Books, 1978. (Ages 4–6)

Special thanks to the following experts for their input into this chapter: Claire Berman, author, *A Hole in My Heart: Adult Children of Divorce Speak Out;* Robert Emery, Ph.D., clinical psychologist, Dept. of Psychology, University of Virginia; David Fassler, M.D., clinical director, Otter Creek Associates; Sally Ives Loughridge, Ph.D., clinician, Otter Creek Associates; Edy Nathan, psychotherapist; Judith Wallerstein, Ph.D., executive director, Center for the Family in Transition.

Chapter Eight

"WHY CAN'T GRANDPA REMEMBER MY NAME?"

Talking with Your Child About Aging and the Elderly

Last summer, Raul's grandfather came for a long visit. The five-year-old had a great time palling around with his "grampy"—they got up early and gathered seashells along the beach, went fishing, told each other silly jokes. In fact, young Raul had such a terrific time that he cried when his grandad went home. A few months later, though, Raul's father explained that Grampy had been sick and was coming to stay with them again, this time to recuperate. At first Raul was thrilled at the chance to see his grandfather again. But the day after he arrived and Raul bounded into his grandfather's room to show him his latest baseball-card acquisition, the elderly man looked perplexed and a little frightened. And when his grandfather called him by the wrong name, Raul felt anxious and confused. "Mommy," the youngster asked his mother before bed that night, "why can't Grandpa remember my name?"

No one likes to think about growing old, particularly in our Western culture, where youth is so highly prized. We associate old age with diminished physical, emotional, and intellectual capacity, a time when we become burnt out, useless, and worst of all, dependent. Consequently, we spend a great deal of time, money, and energy trying to stave off the onset of wrinkles, liver spots, or any other symbol of our own aging process.

Children, too, can have difficulties coping with aging; they may feel curious, confused, or even anxious when they confront an individual who bears physical signs of aging. We see it in the child who clutches her mom's hand as an elderly, humpbacked lady slowly passes them in the street, and hear it when a youngster like Raul asks why an aging grandfather can no longer remember his grandchild's name.

As parents and caretakers, however, you can do a great deal to alleviate your children's anxiety, to help kids appreciate the patience, wisdom, and maturity of the elderly, and to teach them that each stage of life, including old age, offers its own special promise. And there's another benefit: by helping to raise a generation of children who are comfortable with older persons, we might eventually put an end to the ageism that has become so much a part of our troubled world. The first step, however, lies in furthering our own understanding of society's seniors, and in becoming more aware of how children at different developmental stages view the elderly.

The Issue in Focus

Today, persons over sixty-five account for 12.5 percent of the U.S. population, and their numbers continue to grow.* Demographers predict that within the next forty years, people over the age of sixty-five will represent nearly 22 percent of our population. (Individuals over fifty-five will constitute 25 percent of Americans within the next twenty years!) Much of this dramatic increase will be caused by the "baby boomers" hitting age sixty-five, which will occur somewhere between the years 2010 and 2030.

Aging is a natural part of life and the aging process takes its toll on older bodies; frequently, seniors experience ongoing (though often minor) ailments that require them to go a little easier, to take more medications, or to restrict their diets more than they did when they were young. Nonetheless, advances in medicine and a general increase in health education and awareness have made today's elderly more vital and fit than any earlier generation. Many contemporary seniors lead full, active, and productive lives. Unfortunately, however, myths about older persons still abound. Let me explode a few of the most common:

- *Myth:* All old people eventually become senile.
- *Fact:* In many cases, what we used to call "senility" is

*Statistics on the elderly provided by the American Association of Retired Persons.

now known as Alzheimer's, a form of brain disease. Yet according to the National Institute on Aging, even among individuals age eighty and over, only 20 to 25 percent develop this or other incurable brain ailments.

• *Myth:* Mental confusion and intellectual decline are inevitable consequences of old age.

• *Fact:* While many elderly people do suffer some memory loss, their mental and intellectual capacity does not necessarily diminish with age. Most seniors maintain or even improve at least some of their intellectual skills.

• *Myth:* Personality changes with age; people become more crotchety after age sixty-five.

• *Fact:* Personality does not necessarily change with age. Sometimes, when older persons live with illness and pain, they can become more irritable and edgy, but the same is true of younger people. It is chronic discomfort or psychological distress, such as loneliness or depression, rather than aging that can sour an individual's disposition.

• *Myth:* Interest and participation in sex ends with old age.

• *Fact:* Most persons over sixty-five can lead satisfying and active sexual lives.

Despite the absurdity of some of these myths, it isn't surprising that they still exist. From the time we are babies, we hear stories about wicked *old* witches and mean *old* men. We still see the elderly stereotyped as dotty or cantankerous in movies, television shows, and books. Happily, though, such ageism is beginning to change. As more and more Americans reach the second half of their lives, they are realizing that the most accurate statement about older persons is that they are a diverse group of individuals that includes the healthy and the sick, the rich and the poor, the independent and the dependent. Nonetheless, we still have a long way to go before we find ourselves living in an unbiased, non-ageist society.

Even children seem to have conflicting attitudes toward older persons. They adore Grandma and Grandpa and cherish the time they spend with them—as one youngster put it, "I love to be with my grandpa 'cause he never says 'hurry up!' "—but they don't want to be like them. Studies show that young children are frightened by the physical aspects of aging. Time and again, kids will tell you that they, like Peter Pan, "will never grow old."

Dr. Carol Seefeldt, co-author of an excellent book on children and aging called *Young and Old Together* (see the Readings for Parents section at the end of this chapter), has spent years researching intergenerational issues and talked to me at length one afternoon about how children in two key age groups view aging and older persons. Here's a summary of her findings:

• Ages three to five—As we might expect, very young children are puzzled by aging. Many preschoolers equate older with bigger and often believe they can "catch up" in age to an older brother or sister if and when they "get bigger." And here's a surprise: while preschoolers may love specific older persons, like a grandparent or older caretaker, in general they harbor very negative views of the elderly, often describing them as "sick," "ugly," or "bad." Young kids also worry that if they do something bad, they could suddenly "turn old" and can "catch" wrinkles and that might be painful to them.

• Ages six to eight—At this stage, children are still somewhat confused about aging. They know that everybody gets older—even grandparents have birthdays—but they can't grasp such concepts as the relationship between birth order and age. For instance, "Aunt Joan is younger than Daddy because she was born after him" is far too sophisticated an idea for a child in this age range.

Like their younger counterparts, these children don't seem to have a completely positive view of the elderly. Their descriptions do become a bit more gentle, however, moving away from "mean" or "bad" and toward such phrases as "older people need help" or "they walk with canes." Significantly, the most derogatory comments—like "old people chew funny"—center on the physical aspects of being old. Attitudinally, kids in this age group often describe the elderly as "wonderful" and "good."

Seefeldt's work also shows that as children themselves grow older, they develop more realistic concepts of the elderly. Not surprisingly, though, most kids still insist that they themselves do not want to grow old and die.

As with any kind of prejudice, our best chance to create an unbiased world lies in teaching children the truth about older persons and in helping them to understand their diversity. Hopefully, the advice that follows will head you and your kids in the right direction.

How to Talk with Your Child About Aging and the Elderly

1. Encourage Children to Share Their Feelings About Older Persons.

Young children don't always communicate their feelings. Preschoolers and early-elementary-school-aged kids may not have the vocabulary to express themselves; some older children tend to keep their emotions to themselves, particularly when it comes to such sensitive areas as loss, death, and aging.

It's up to parents, then, to help draw children out. For instance, if you're in the park with your six-year-old and you feel him huddle close to you when a wrinkled, elderly man, cane in hand, walks slowly by, take note. Once the man is out of earshot, you might say, "That man was walking very slowly. What did you think about him?" Depending on how your child responds, you might say, "Sometimes older people can seem a little scary, especially if they have lots of wrinkles and walk with a cane. But there's really nothing to be afraid of. He was using a cane because his legs don't work that well and he needs the cane to help him walk; that happens to some people when they grow old and their muscles grow weaker. Not *all* old people walk with canes; Grandpa Joe doesn't. But I guess this man needs to." Such an explanation provides several benefits: It validates your child's distressing feelings and encourages him to air his emotions while providing an objective, simple, and reality-based explanation which helps to allay any anxiety and dispel any frightening fantasies.

2. Convey a Positive, Though Realistic, Attitude.

In her work with children, intergenerational expert Carol Seefeldt has found that when children are presented with positive aspects of older persons—that many are healthy, active, productive individuals—kids' attitudes toward them become much less negative. Additionally, hearing positive messages about older persons can help youngsters develop an appreciation for the diversity of the elderly.

You can influence your own kids in this way by actively conveying an upbeat, though realistic, attitude toward older persons. If possible, start with your own family. While you can acknowledge that Grandma or Grandpa may move a little slower than they used to when they were young, try to highlight all the things that they still do—play golf, cook up a storm, travel to Australia. When your child comes into contact with an older person who is very frail or ill, offer a more balanced picture by saying something like this to your five- or six-year-old: "I know you saw a lot of old people at the hospital when we went to visit Grandpa Frank today. But you know, while older people do get sick sometimes— and that may make us feel sad—not *all* old people are sick. Nana is old, too, but she's healthy and has lots of energy. Just like there are all kinds of young people in the world, there are all kinds of old people in the world."

To your slightly older and more sophisticated ten- or eleven-year-old you might add, "You know, each stage of life—being a kid, a teenager, an adult, or an older person like Grandpa—has good and bad things about it. What's most important is to enjoy each day and each phase of life as we live it."

3. Tune Into Your Own Stereotyping.

How often have you said something like this to your youngster: "Oh, pick that up for me, honey. My bones are too old." You know you're kidding, but your children may not. They hear such statements and believe them. Too, if you're overly concerned about growing older—if your kids overhear such comments as "Gee, didn't so-and-so look terrible? She looked so *old*," or watch you panic at the arrival of each new gray hair—they may well begin to develop negative ideas about aging.

So become aware of your own ageist thinking and take care not to communicate it to your child. Kids can "catch" fear of aging just as they can fear of a different ethnic or racial group.

4. Challenge Your Child's Beliefs.

As we have already discussed, many young children harbor at least some negative feelings about older persons. Occasionally, you may even hear your youngster say something like "I hate old people. They're always sick and tired." If you do, don't be afraid to gently challenge your child's mistaken assumptions. You can simply say something like "I know that you might think that because Grandma Alice is very old, and because she is sick a lot, that all old people are sick. And it's true that many older people aren't as strong and healthy as they were when they were young. But not all old people are like Grandma Alice. Grandpa is old; he's eighty, and he helped you build your tree house last summer. Dr. Smith, your dentist, is old; but he's not sick and tired. Can you think of some other older people we know that are active and healthy?" If you can help your child figure out for himself that all old people don't conform to any particular standard, you will have offered him a valuable anti-ageist lesson.

5. Initiate Contact with Active Older Persons.

One of the best ways to counter children's negative attitudes toward the elderly is to bring them into contact with older persons who are vigorous, fit, and productive. Spending time with such vital seniors allows children to see firsthand the happier aspects of aging—to appreciate that older persons can still do lots of things, that they have learned a good deal through their years of experience, and that they often have more time and patience to play with and talk to young children than do the other adults in your kids' lives.

Consider the experience of one eleven-year-old with whom Dr. David Pelcovitz, chief child and adolescent psychiatrist at North Shore/Cornell University Hospital in New York, worked: the boy was doing terribly in school. "Then," Pelcovitz told me, "his grandfather started to tutor him. Not only did he have the patience to get through to this child, but the older man offered a long-term view, explaining to his grandson that his own son (the youngster's father) had had trouble in school when he was a boy and now had a Ph.D. This gave the child hope that he, too, would be okay, and soon his grades started to improve."

Of course, a generation ago when families weren't so geographically splintered it was easier for children to have frequent contact with older relatives. But contemporary families still can insure a healthy intergenerational connection through letter writing, phone calling and, best of all, visiting older relatives who may live in distant towns. Once a year my young nephews visit their grandparents in Florida.

In addition to spending a good deal of concentrated time with Grandma and Grandpa, they get to see other seniors, some of whom are disabled and even wheelchair bound, but most of whom live full, active lives playing tennis, swimming, dancing, and enjoying movies and concerts. So the kids not only grow closer to their grandparents, but learn about the diversity of older persons overall.

Outside of the family, you can initiate contact with the elderly and help your children appreciate older persons' diversity by reaching out to community-based programs. Many senior citizens' centers sponsor projects in which older people work together with children; if your town has one, get your child involved.

6. Underscore That Life Has Continuity.

You can help children become less confused about the aging process if you show them that life goes on, and that it has both continuity and richness at different stages. Encourage Grandpa to tell your children stories about what life was like when he was young; show your children family albums that feature photos of Grandma as a young girl, bride, young mother, and as she is today. These kinds of activities teach children that people don't suddenly become "old" and that, instead, aging is a gradual process. It also underscores the idea that life offers opportunity and challenge at every stage.

7. Offer Simple, Factual Explanations About Illness, Physical Change, and Death.

When children have contact with older persons, some of whom may be ill (even gravely so), questions about sickness and death may arise. By offering simple, factual, and compassionate answers, you can help your children begin to accept these circumstances as a natural part of life.

Suppose, for instance, that a beloved older person, such as a grandmother, has a sudden stroke that causes some kind of physical or mental dysfunction. Your youngster may well become anxious, confused, and frightened. He may worry about several things: that he somehow caused the physical change or illness; that it could happen to him or to you, his parents; and/or that his grandmother could die.

One of the most effective ways to ease his anxiety and eliminate his confusion is to offer a simple, age-appropriate explanation in a calm tone of voice. To a five-year-old you might say, "Grandma got very sick and now her legs don't work right so she can't walk. She also can't talk well. It didn't happen because of anything anybody said or did; it just happened. But for a while at least, she won't be able to play with you. Even though her outside looks a little different, I want you to remember that inside she's the same grandma and she loves you very much."

To a ten-year-old you could say, "Grandma has had a stroke. That means that the blood couldn't get to her brain and now the brain isn't working so well. So Grandma can't talk very well or walk very well; she may not even be able to remember your name. We don't know what will happen—the doctors say Grandma is very sick and because she is very old, she may not ever be able to do the things she used to do. But they are doing everything they can to make her feel better. I want you to know that what happened to Grandma didn't happen because of anything anybody said or did; it just happened. But inside, Grandma loves you very much and I love you very much. And we'll just have to see what happens."

(If Grandma dies, you also will need to talk with your child about death. For practical advice on how to do that effectively, see the chapters on talking with your children about AIDS and cancer. You may also want to refer to the chapter on cancer for more insight into how to talk to your kids about an ill relative.)

One more point: When a sudden and serious illness strikes someone in the family, particularly your aging parent, it places great demands on your time and energy. But try not to get so caught up in caring for the ill person that you neglect your child. Your kids need you to remain available emotionally and physically. Make a real effort, then, to spend at least fifteen or twenty minutes a day with each child and to keep lines of communication open. It will help your child—and you—to cope more effectively and easily during this stressful time.

8. Control Visits to the Nursing Home or Hospital.

When a relative is in a nursing home or hospital setting, many parents wonder whether it is advisable to take their young child to visit. Well, the answer is a qualified yes. But there are two prerequisites for such a visit: first, that your child has expressed a desire to see this relative; and second, that you take the time to prepare the youngster for what she'll find during that visit. For example, you might explain to your four-year-old that "Grandpa has been very sick. He doesn't feel well and he's gotten very thin, so you can't jump all over him and sit in his lap like you used to. But he still loves you and will be happy to see you, so we'll go visit him. We'll just stay for a little while and then we'll go home."

To a nine-year-old you could say, "Grandpa may seem a little different from the last time you saw him. He's gotten very thin and he has trouble speaking; sometimes he can't remember things and he might not recognize you. But that's because he has been sick. I'm sure it will make him happy to see you, although we'll have to make our visit short."

Actually, there is one more important aspect to consider before taking your child to visit a nursing home or hospital—whether or not a positive relationship between the elderly person and the child already exists. As Dr. Clarice Kestenbaum at the Columbia University College of Physicians and Surgeons says, "You would not take a child to see a relative or anyone else he's never met before. It's not the time to start a relationship. But if there's a relationship already going with the older person, and the child wants to visit and is prepared beforehand, then by all means take the child with you." Be sure, however, to carry crayons, a book, or some other quiet activity with you to keep your child busy. And, of course, always keep visits short.

9. Encourage, but Don't Force, a Positive Relationship.

For all the reasons we've already discussed, helping your children develop positive relationships with older persons can be enormously beneficial in helping kids mature into tolerant, unbiased, and confident adults. But you cannot force such a relationship. In some cases, the older person may reject your youngster, communicating in words or actions that he or she simply doesn't want to be bothered. If that's the case, you can only insist that your child (and the older person) be respectful and polite—and that's it. Love cannot be forced; it will grow only where it is welcome. Just make sure that your child understands that many older people love to be around children. I'm sure you won't have any trouble at all finding an elderly individual who will be delighted with—and who will delight—your young child.

Sample Questions and Answers

Q: Do I have to grow old?

A: Yes. As the years go by, we all grow old. And old age can be a wonderful, happy time, like it is for Grandma and Grandpa. But what's important now is that you enjoy every single day and realize that each day of your life is special.

Q: Will I always stay the same even when I get older?

A: Your inside stays the same but your outside changes. You will always be Janie, but you'll grow taller and bigger and stronger, and you will be able to do more and more things all by yourself.

Q: Do wrinkles hurt?

A: No, they don't hurt. They just happen when your skin gets older and a little softer.

Q: Does it hurt to be old?

A: No, it doesn't hurt to be old. Sometimes, if people get sick when they are old, they may not feel well and may feel very uncomfortable. But being old doesn't mean you *have* to be sick and being old doesn't mean you *have* to hurt. Lots of old people are very healthy and happy.

Helpful Resources

ORGANIZATIONS

Administration on Aging
Dept. of Health and Human Services
300 Independence Avenue, SW
Washington, DC 20201

American Association of Retired Persons (AARP)
601 East Street, NW
Washington, DC 20049

The National Council on the Aging, Inc.
409 Third Street, SW
Washington, DC 20024
(202) 479-1200

The National Institute on Aging
Information Center
P.O. Box 8057
Gaithersburg, MD 20898-8057
(301) 495-3455

READINGS FOR PARENTS

Butler, Robert N. *Why Survive? Being Old in America.* New
    York: Harper & Row, 1975.
Dodson, Fitzhugh, with Paula Reuben. *How to Grandparent.*
    New York: Harper & Row, 1981.

Dychtwald, Ken and Joe Flower. *The Age Wave: The Challenges and Opportunities of an Aging America.* Los Angeles: Jeremy P. Tarcher, 1989.

Erikson, Erik H., Joan M. Erikson, and Helen Kivnick. *Vital Involvement in Old Age.* New York: Norton, 1986.

Kingson, Eric R., Barbara Hirshorn, and John M. Cornman. *Ties That Bind: The Interdependence of Generations.* Washington, D.C.: Seven Locks Press, 1986.

Kornhaber, Arthur, and K. Woodward. *Grandparents, Grandchildren: The Vital Connection.* Garden City, N.Y.: Anchor Press/Doubleday, 1981.

Kornhaber, Arthur. *Between Parents and Grandparents.* New York: St. Martin's, 1986.

Seefeldt, Carol, and Barbara Warman, with Richard K. Jantz and Alice Galper. *Young and Old Together.* Washington, D.C.: National Association for the Education of Young People, 1990.

U.S. Senate Special Committee. *Aging in America: Trends and Projections.* Washington: U.S. Senate Special Committee, January 1988.

READINGS FOR CHILDREN

Ancona, George. *Growing Older.* Boston: Little Brown, 1971. (Ages 6–10)

de Paola, Tomie. *Nana Upstairs and Nana Downstairs.* New York: G. P. Putnam's Sons, 1973. (Ages 5–8)

Farber, Norma. *How Does It Feel to Be Old?* New York: Dutton, 1979. (Ages 6–9)

Goldman, Susan. *Grandma Is Somebody Special.* Chicago, Ill.: Albert Whitman & Co., 1976. (Ages 4–7)

Guthrie, Donna. *Grandpa Doesn't Know It's Me*. New York: Human Sciences Press, 1986. (Ages 3–10)

Hamm, Diane Johnston. *Grandma Drives a Motor Bed*. Niles, Ill.; Albert Whitman & Co., 1987. (Ages 4–7)

Johnson, Angela. *When I Am Old With You*. New York: Orchard Books, 1990. (Ages 4–8)

Kimmelman, Leslie. *Me and Nana*. New York: HarperCollins, 1990. (Ages 4–8)

Klein, Lenore. *Old, Older, Oldest*. Mamaroneck, New York: Hastings House, 1983. (Ages 4–9)

Knox-Wagner, Elaine. *My Grandpa Retired Today*. Niles, Ill.: Albert Whitman & Co., 1982. (Ages 5–8)

LeRoy, Gen. *Emma's Dilemma*. New York: Harper & Row, 1975. (Ages 8–10)

Leiner, Katherine. *Between Old Friends*. New York: Franklin Watts, 1987. (Ages 9–12)

Miles, Miska. *Annie and the Old One*. Boston: Little, Brown, 1971. (Ages 6–10)

Oppenheim, Shulamith Levey. *Waiting for Noah*. New York: Harper & Row, 1990. (Ages 4–7)

Scott, Ann Herbert. *Grandmother's Chair*. New York: Clarion Books, 1990. (Ages 3–6)

Shane, Anne Zane. *Old Is What You Get: Dialogues on Aging by the Old and the Young*. New York: Viking, 1976. (Ages 10 and up)

Stoltz, Mary. *Storm in the Night*. New York: HarperCollins, 1988. (Ages 5–8)

Thomas, J. R. *Saying Goodbye to Grandma*. New York: Clarion, 1988. (Ages 4–8)

Waddell, Martin. *Grandma's Bill*. New York: Orchard Books, 1990. (Ages 4–7)

Wilson, Christopher. *A Treasure Hunt.* Washington, D.C.: U.S. Dept. of Health and Human Services, 1980. (Ages 6–10)

Zolotow, Charlotte. *I Know a Lady.* New York: Greenwillow, 1984. (Ages 4–9)

Special thanks to the following experts for their input into this chapter: Charles Enzer, M.D., associate clinical professor, University of Cincinnati Medical Center; Paul Fine, M.D., professor of psychiatry, Creighton University; David Keith, M.D., director of family therapy at State University of New York Health Science Center; Clarice Kestenbaum, M.D., director of training, Division of Child and Adolescent Psychiatry, Columbia University College of Physicians and Surgeons; Melvin Lewis, MBBS, DCH, FRCPsych, professor of pediatrics and psychiatry and director of medical studies, Yale Child Studies Center; David Pelcovitz, Ph.D., chief child and adolescent psychologist, North Shore/Cornell University Hospital; Matthew Schiff, M.D., clinical associate professor of child and adolescent psychiatry, Hahnemann Medical School and Philadelphia Psychiatric; Carol Seefeldt, Ph.D., professor of human development, The Institute for Child Study, University of Maryland.

Chapter Nine

"DADDY GOT FIRED ... ARE WE GOING TO BE POOR?"

Talking with Your Child About Job Loss

Eight-year-old Amanda sensed something was awry as soon as her father came home from work. Somehow, her dad looked different—very sad, she thought—and when he didn't reach down to give her a big hug, she grew anxious. Later on, she overheard him tell her mother that he'd been fired—and then her mother started to cry. Worried and confused, Amanda came into the kitchen and asked what was going on; her parents told her that Daddy had lost his job. The youngster wasn't sure why losing a job was so bad, but it scared her to see her mom and dad so upset. Lying in bed that night, she remembered something her mother had told her—that many poor people had to sleep on the sidewalks because they had lost *their* jobs. "Daddy got fired," Amanda repeated tearfully to her mom when she came to tuck her in. "Are we going to have to sleep outside in the cold?"

The economic and emotional turmoil of job loss is not easy to explain to a young child. Some children may not yet fully understand what having a job means; to a child of two, three, or even four, "Mommy goes to work" simply means that mother goes away for many hours and someone else takes care of him during that time. Thus, the significance of job loss cannot possibly make any sense. In fact, when a parent loses her job, a very young child may be quite happy. "If Mommy doesn't have to go to work anymore," the child may think, "she'll have more time to spend with *me.*"

Older children who understand that parents go to work to earn money to support the family may begin to grasp some of the negative repercussions of job loss, even though their thoughts may not be completely rational. Amanda, for example, took the news of her father's job loss and jumped ten steps to worry if she would become homeless. Another child might worry that his parents will no longer be able to afford to send him to summer camp. Still another might insist on getting a job to help his parents recoup some income.

But what usually disturbs kids most about parental job loss is sensing—or witnessing—their parents' emotional devastation. Children rely on their parents for stability and security; when a parent becomes very upset, it can—and often does—threaten the safety of the child's world. Thus, when a parent gets fired or laid off, the emotional shock waves ripple through the entire family.

Why is job loss so stressful? This is a complex question that can't be answered in a sentence or two. In fact, I recently co-authored an entire book (called *Congratulations! You've Been Fired;* see Readings for Parents at the chapter's end) that not only examines the stress of job loss but offers advice on how to get yourself back on track again. Nonetheless, before attempting to talk with your kids about your job loss, it's important to grapple, at least briefly, with why losing your job packs such an emotional wallop.

The Issue in Focus

When mental health researchers T. H. Holmes and R. H. Rahe developed their "social adjustment scale" back in the sixties, they ranked getting fired as one of the top ten most stressful life events, right up there with the death of a spouse and divorce. No matter what you call it—fired, laid off, downsized, terminated, sacked, pink-slipped, axed, or given your walking papers—losing your job hurts. Here's why.

The first reason is the most obvious—loss of income. In *Congratulations! You've Been Fired,* we advise stashing away enough money to pay at least six months worth of expenses to cushion the financial blow of a sudden job loss. But let's face it: how many of us, particularly in today's economy, can afford to leave that much cash untouched? Most of us live from paycheck to paycheck; if the checks stop coming, we feel more than a financial pinch—we feel a stranglehold.

If you have children to support, losing that steady income can be especially terrifying. Even if you're among the

nearly 16 million two-wage-earning families in our country*
—and your spouse has managed to hold on to his/her
job—the loss of one income can be devastating. And if
you're one of the approximately 6 million single parents in
the labor force today, the financial jab of job loss can seem
crippling.

The second but nonetheless cogent reason that job loss
is so painful is that it can damage your self-esteem. Just
think back to the last social gathering you attended: how
many times did someone you just met ask you, "So, what do
you *do?*" In Western society and especially in America, our
work defines us. It makes perfect sense, therefore, that
when we lose what we do, we lose our sense of who we are.

Significantly, people who lose their jobs go through
certain emotional phases similar to the stages of grief Elisabeth Kübler-Ross talks about in her classic book *On Death
and Dying.* Though individuals may not go through them in
the same order, at some point after losing a job, they experience the following:

• Shock—Even if you saw it coming, learning that
you've lost your job shakes you up, often making you feel
numb, dazed, and disoriented. A part of you thinks, "This
can't be happening," as your psyche struggles to absorb the
blow.

• Fear—You worry, "How will I pay the bills? How
will I make the rent or mortgage payments? Who will ever
hire me again? Will I ever find another job? What will
happen to me?"

• Anger—Directed at your boss, the company, or a

*Statistics on the labor force come from the Bureau of Labor Statistics,
Washington, D.C.

colleague, feelings of anger can seem overwhelming. And if you get angry at yourself—"if only I'd been smarter" (or more talented, quicker, more aggressive, more flexible, harder working, etc.)—it can chip away at your self-esteem, lack of which is one of the most common problems in individuals who've lost their jobs.

• Shame—Anger can often lay the groundwork for shame. When you blame yourself for your job loss and see it as a personal failure, and if you feel that others see you as having failed, you are likely to feel a sense of shame and embarrassment.

• Sadness and Despair—It's natural to feel a bit depressed after you experience any kind of loss, and job loss is no exception. You may feel that you've let yourself and your family down and that your future appears bleak. It's not true, though—you can and will get back on your feet again, for most people do return to the work force revitalized. But sometimes you just need to let despair, as well as the other emotional stages I've listed, run their course.

A few ideas to keep in mind that can go far in buoying your deflated spirits: remember that often you have more control over your employment status than you think. You can do lots of things to find yourself another job—write an effective résumé, hone your interviewing skills, network. Sometimes, and particularly if you're in an industry that has become obsolete, you can seek training or additional education to make yourself more marketable. At worst, you may have to rely on unemployment benefits to tide you over until your company, plant, or industry starts rehiring. (The rule of thumb on how long you can expect to be unemployed is one month for every $10,000 of income. For example, if you're replacing a $35,000 job, you may be out of work for three and a half months.)

It's also comforting to know that you're not alone. As of January 1991, the Bureau of Labor Statistics reported that nearly 4.7 million workers had lost their jobs. And if you add in the number of people who lost their jobs and dropped out of the work force or immediately found some kind of new work (even if temporary), that number jumps even higher.

The simple fact is that the marketplace isn't what it used to be. Gone are the days where employer/employee loyalty fostered the kind of security that allowed individuals to work twenty-five years for the same firm. The Department of Labor reports that people entering the work force today will hold between ten and fifteen jobs in their lifetimes; they will change careers at least four times.

And here's another "positive" you may not have considered: Often, losing your job gives you a chance to take inventory of yourself. It gives you the opportunity to assess your likes and dislikes, strengths and weaknesses, and to find a new position that's often more satisfying than the one you had before. Job loss can also spark you to get your priorities in order. I know of a mother of two who had rarely taken any time off, even during her two pregnancies. When she was fired from her job as a human resources manager at a cosmetics firm, she started spending more time at home with her children, and realized she was happier. So she set about finding a new position that offered her more flexibility and would allow her to spend more time with her kids—and she found it!

Still, the upside of job loss doesn't preclude people's

difficulties in dealing with job loss, particularly if they're a parent. One Michigan State University study suggests that parents who have a clear "occupational identity," that is, who hold jobs and feel good about them, are better, more effective, and more confident parents than those whose occupational identities are muddied by such things as job loss. The reason is that the former group is able to focus on their children's wants and needs. They are not distracted by their own woes or sapped of the time and energy it takes to concentrate on finding a new job.

Job loss might dampen not only parental self-esteem, but their children's as well. As Harvard Medical School psychologist Dr. Steven Berglas explains, "Kids may not understand why Mom (or Dad) got fired, but they do know that she is more distracted and less cheerful and demonstrative than before she lost her job. And because the children start getting less nurturance and attention from Mom then, they may feel less worthy."

Still another problem is that parental job loss can effect a change in a child's everyday routine. Even something as simple as Dad's not going to the office can throw off the family's rhythm, undermine life's predictability, and therefore sabotage a child's sense of security. In a panic over getting fired, five-year-old Jackson's mother immediately dismissed the child's long-time baby-sitter and enrolled Jackson in a full-day kindergarten. The radical change in his routine rattled her son to such an extent that he not only became uncharacteristically withdrawn but started to wet the bed, something he hadn't done since he was two. The regressive behaviors vanished once his mom got a new job and Jackson grew familiar with his new routine. But the incident speaks clearly to the problems parental job loss can visit on young children.

As with all crises, job loss can be handled with a minimum of stress on you and your child. And the experience can serve to teach your child a wonderful lesson: while life's path doesn't always run smoothly, your family is loving and strong enough to negotiate the bumpiest of roads.

How to Talk with Your Child About Parental Job Loss

1. Level with Your Child.

You're making a big mistake if you try to hide your job loss from your child. Kids count on their parents for the truth, and if you don't level with them, you're not being honest. Children sense when something's bothering their parents and may conjure up some far worse scenario than job loss if you're not straight with them from the start.

But being truthful doesn't mean going into all the gory details, particularly if your child is very young. A four- or five-year-old need only be told something like "Daddy lost his job today, so he's not going to be working at his office (or factory or hospital, etc.) for a while. But he's going to be looking for a new job and then he'll have a new place to go to work."

A seven- or eight-year-old who understands a bit more about what having a job means may be told, "Daddy lost his job yesterday. He's a little sad because he liked his work and he liked earning money. But he's going to be looking for a new job and maybe he'll find something even better. In the meantime, things will go on pretty much the same. You'll go to school and play with your friends and do all the things you usually do."

You might explain to a ten- or eleven-year-old that "Daddy lost his job yesterday. He's a little disappointed because he liked his work and he liked earning money so that he could buy us lots of nice things. Dad will find a new job, but in the meantime, things will go on pretty much as usual. We are going to have to be a little more careful about how we spend our money for a while—maybe instead of going to the movies this weekend, we'll rent a special video instead—but otherwise, things will stay pretty much the same."

(By the way, you'll want to decide what you're going to say in advance. Chances are you're in a shaky emotional state and perhaps not thinking as clearly as usual, so it's best not to speak entirely off the cuff.)

2. Don't Create a False Sense of Reality.

In an effort to shield children from the emotional and economic stress of job loss, some parents shower their kids with new toys and treats during this time. But that only creates a false sense of reality that confuses young kids. The children can see that Mom and Dad are upset about money—so, they wonder, "why are they still buying us gifts?" They begin questioning their own ability to understand reality and/or their parents' truthfulness. Creating such a contradictory situation also sends the message that it's fine to pretend things are okay when they're not. To avoid falling into this trap, parents need to remember that kids are better served when they are allowed to see a family crisis and to participate, in an age-appropriate way, in dealing with it.

3. Let the Kids Help Out.

Kids are part of the family; when the family is going through a difficult time, they want to help resolve the problem. So let them. Dr. Antoinette Saunders, founder of the Chicago-based The Capable Child counseling centers, suggests creating a chart on which each child lists the way he helped out in a given week. Next to the four- or five-year-old's name might be "Played quietly while Mommy was on the phone," or "Brushed my teeth by myself while Mommy was writing letters." A seven-year-old's contribution might be "Helped clear the table after dinner every night," while an eleven-year-old "helped get the baby ready for bed so Dad could have more time to send out resumés."

Another tactic that will allow you to involve your kids without overburdening them is to make a game of problem-solving. You can say, "You know, since I lost my job, we have to make our money last longer. So let's see if we can make up a list of ways we can have lots of fun without spending lots of money." That list might include things like riding bikes, playing games at home, visiting a favorite relative or friend, or preparing a special family meal. Another suggestion: Take your youngster grocery shopping, and let him help you figure out ways to stretch the budget. Discovering that buying chicken is less expensive than purchasing steak is a great way to introduce your child to budgeting and to help him feel that he's doing his part.

4. Maintain a Normal Routine.

Children depend on routine and predictability to assure them that their world is safe. Thus it is critically important to try and maintain their daily routines as much as possible. If the economic realities of job loss demand that you cut down on expenses, make it the housecleaner and not the child's regular baby-sitter (or nanny) who goes. In that same vein, it's better to have to forgo your planned vacation to Disneyworld than to curtail your child's weekly karate classes.

Make an effort to keep meal-, bed-, bath- and playtimes on the same schedule. If you always read a story to your child at bedtime, continue to do so now, even if you don't feel up to it. Your child will suffer more from a disrupted routine than from your temporary inability to buy her any special toys or goodies she may desire.

5. Don't Overburden Your Child.

Often a parent in crisis, and particularly a single parent who doesn't have a supportive mate to count on, will lean too heavily on his/her children for emotional support. I talked with one single mother of a five-year-old girl who, after she went through a traumatic firing, began asking the daughter to sleep in Mom's bed at night "so Mommy won't feel so alone."

I know you need the support and comfort of your family right now, but try not go overboard. While kids need to be kept informed of a family crisis, they should not be made to feel responsible for fixing it.

Many kids naturally will want to help out. I know of one seven-year-old boy who began break-dancing on the streets for money; he thought this new "income" would help cheer up his out-of-work father. As touching as such an act may be, it's a parent's responsibility to be his child's caretaker, not the other way around. If your child is clearly feeling responsible for making things better, you can simply say, "I know I've been feeling bad and that you want to help. And I want you to know that I really appreciate it and love you for it. But sometimes people have to feel sad for a while. I'll feel fine again soon. The most important thing for you to know is that I'll always be able to take care of you. You don't ever have to worry about that. I love you very much and it makes me feel good just to know you love me, too."

6. Ease Any Necessary Transitions.

If you're out of work for a long time, you may have to make some adjustments in your child's routine. In that case, though, help prepare your child for the change.

Suppose that an extended period of unemployment forces you to pull your six-year-old out of private school and put her into public kindergarten. First of all, try to do it at the beginning of the new term, when the transition will be more natural. Then explain to your child what is going to happen. You can say, "I found a wonderful new school that I would like you to try. I met the teacher and she is very nice and the children seem like lots of fun, too. Tomorrow we'll go over and see the new school and you can meet the teacher." Take the child over to the school, introduce her to the teacher, and, if possible, let her spend an hour or so there. Also, explain anything about her routine that will be different—who will take her to school, how she'll get home, where she'll eat her lunch, and so on. And be sure to answer any and all questions as honestly and simply as you can.

Another possible scenario: You cannot afford to send your child to camp this summer. In that case, simply explain, "You know that daddy lost his job and hasn't found a new one yet. We have to be careful about how we spend money, so we can't afford to send you back to camp this year. But we're still going to take a vacation. We're going to visit Grandma and Grandpa upstate. And we'll go swimming, and play ball, and take the boat on the lake. I can't wait. It will be lots of fun to spend our vacation all together as a family."

7. Seek Outside Help, If Necessary.

Sometimes children act in ways that signal their distress. Regressive behavior, such as a return to bed-wetting, as well as clinginess, withdrawing from friends, loss of appetite, disturbed sleep, a sudden drop in grades or an increase in behavior problems at school may be signs that your child is having trouble coping. If your child is mature enough, try talking with her about how she's feeling. Spending a little extra quality time with your youngster may also help. But if the uncharacteristic behavior persists more than a few weeks, seek outside help. Your child's pediatrician can help you find a qualified mental-health-care professional.

8. Hold Your Emotions in Check.

Nothing disturbs a child more than seeing a parent who is emotionally out of control. A certain amount of sadness is appropriate when you've just lost your job, and there's nothing wrong with showing your child that sometimes Mom or Dad feels sad. But crying and breast-beating should be reserved for times when your children are safely out of earshot. Otherwise, you'll threaten your children's confidence in your ability to take care of them no matter what.

The same holds true for the spouse of the out-of-work

person. You need to avoid mirroring his or her stress, because your kids will be looking to you for reassurance that their world is still safe. If you're nervous or distraught and convey that to your kids, they think, "Well, I guess we really are in trouble if both Mom *and* Dad are this worried."

Try also to be aware of how angry you are. As I discussed earlier, anger is a normal reaction to losing your job. But don't take it out on the kids. Find another way to ventilate your pain—talk to your spouse or friends; get yourself in a support group; seek therapy, if necessary; throw your energy into an exhaustive and exhausting job hunt. But don't let your kids bear the brunt of your rage.

9. Hold Family Meetings.

The importance of pulling together during trying times is one of the most noteworthy lessons parental job loss can teach children. To underscore that message and to help each member of the family deal with this crisis, try to hold weekly family meetings where everyone has an equal opportunity to speak and share. The unemployed parent may offer an update on how his or her job hunt is going. (Don't give too many details if the search isn't going well, though. You don't want to add to the children's anxiety.) Then each family member can express what's been hard about this time and what's been fun about it. Having to postpone buying that great new pair of sneakers was hard, but having Dad at home to play basketball after school has been great. Family conclaves also give parents the opportunity to remind a child of the contributions he's made. For instance: "You know, David, your dusting the living room this week saved me a lot of time that I was able to put into my job hunt. You were really a big help to me."

Dr. Saunders, who strongly recommends these meetings, suggests holding them on Sunday nights. As she explains, "Sundays are family days. They're slower times when you have the chance to regroup, and to prepare for the week ahead. And it's a time when the kids can have Mom and Dad's undivided attention, which is really important during this stressful period."

10. Boost Your Own Spirits.

Children sense when a parent is feeling bad about herself; they notice that the parent is more irritable, sad, and distracted. And often, kids' egocentricity leads them to feel they are to blame for their parents' distress. To counteract these feelings and, of course, to help get you moving again, put some time and effort into buoying your own deflated spirits.

Redoubling your efforts to be a good parent—spending more time with your kids, for instance—is mutually beneficial. Your kids feel happier, and their happiness cannot help but cheer you up. Maintaining some kind of daily routine, exercising regularly, eating a low-fat, high-carbohydrate diet, and spending time with supportive friends will also help you feel better about yourself. Of course, the best antidote to these pink-slip blues is to get another job. But that will come with persistence, effort, time, and a little luck. In the meantime, though, keeping yourself together—for the sake of yourself and your kids—has never been more important.

Sample Questions & Answers

Q: When you got fired, did you get burned?

A: No, getting fired is just a way of saying that Daddy lost his job. But there was no fire and Daddy didn't get burned.

Q: Why is Daddy home so much now?

A: Daddy's home because he lost his job, so for a while he won't be going to work. But he's looking for a new job, and when he finds one, he'll go to work every day again.

Q: Why is Mommy feeling so sad?

A: Mommy's feeling sad because she lost her job. Mommy likes to work and she likes to make money to buy us things, so she feels bad that she isn't working now. Sometimes things happen in life that make us sad. But it doesn't last forever. Mommy will find a new job and then she won't feel sad anymore.

Q: If you lost your job, does that mean we'll be homeless?

A: No, we will not be homeless. Mom and Dad have put aside money to use in a difficult time. That's what savings are for. And so we will live on our savings. But don't worry. Dad (or Mom) will find another job, and in the meantime, things will be pretty much like always. You'll go to school, play with your friends, watch TV, sleep in your own room, just like always. And you don't ever have to worry about being homeless. We will have a place to live and we will stay together as a family.

Helpful Resources

ORGANIZATIONS*

Employment & Training Administration
Office of Public Affairs, room S2322
200 Constitution Avenue, NW
Washington, DC 20210
(202) 523-6871
(Employee legal rights)

National Association for Female Executives (NAFE)
127 West 24th Street
New York, NY 10011
(Networking groups)

Pension & Welfare Benefits Administration
Office of Assistance & Technical Inquiries
Room N5658
U.S. Dept. of Labor
200 Constitution Avenue, NW
Washington, DC 20210
(202) 523-8776
(Employee pension and health benefits)

*The laws governing unemployment rights and benefits vary from state to state, so be sure to check with your local employment service or job service office and ask for someone who can provide you with specific information for your state. Also request information on the Dislocated Worker Program in your town. These programs—the titles of which often vary; I've heard them called Title III or Worker Retraining and Adjustment—are federally funded and provide support services and training for workers who've lost their jobs.

Unfortunately, no national organization yet exists that offers counseling and emotional/psychological support for the involuntarily unemployed. Often, however, local Y's or churches offer such services, so check your local phone book for an appropriate listing.

Women's Legal Defense Fund
1875 Connecticut Avenue, NW, suite 710
Washington, DC 20009
(Sex discrimination issues, for women and men)

READINGS FOR PARENTS

Bird, Caroline. *The Two-Paycheck Marriage.* New York: Pocket Books, 1979.

Bolles, Richard Nelson. *What Color Is Your Parachute?* Berkeley, Calif.: Ten Speed Press, 1989. (Updated annually).

Ciabattari, Jane. *Winning Moves: How to Come Out Ahead in a Corporate Shakeup.* New York: Rawson Associates, 1988.

Hall, Francine, and Douglas T. Hall. *The Two-Career Couple.* Reading, Mass.: Addison-Wesley, 1979.

Hyatt, Carole, and Linda Gottlieb. *When Smart People Fail.* New York: Viking/Penguin, 1987.

Koltnow, Emily, and Lynne S. Dumas. *Congratulations! You've Been Fired: Sound Advice for Women Who've Been Terminated, Pink-Slipped, Downsized, or Otherwise Unemployed.* New York: Ballantine Books, 1990.

READINGS FOR CHILDREN

Ancona, George. *And What Do You Do? A Book About People and Their Work.* New York: Dutton, 1975. (Ages 7–10)

Delton, Judy. *My Mother Lost Her Job Today.* Niles, Ill.: Albert Whitman, 1980. (Ages 4–8)

Florian, Douglas. *People Working.* New York: Harper & Row, 1983. (Ages 3–7)

Hazen, Barbara Shook. *Tight Times.* New York: Viking Press, 1979. (Ages 7–9).

Leiner, Katherine. *Both My Parents Work*. New York: Frank-
   lin Watts, 1986. (Ages 5–10)
Mitchell, Joyce Slayton. *My Mommy Makes Money*. Boston:
   Little, Brown, 1984. (Ages 3–7)

Special thanks to the following experts for their input into
this chapter: Steven Berglas, Ph.D., attending psychologist,
McLean Hospital/Harvard Medical School; Antoinette
Saunders, Ph.D., founder, The Capable Child Counseling
Centers; Matthew Schiff, M.D., clinical associate professor
of psychiatry, Hahnemann Medical School; William Sonis,
M.D., associate professor of psychiatry, The Philadelphia
Child Guidance Clinic, University of Pennsylvania School
of Medicine.

Chapter Ten

"WILL WE BE OKAY IF AN EARTHQUAKE HAPPENS?"

Talking with Your Child About Disasters

Patrick awoke to feel his bed shaking violently. As the six-year-old clutched the covers in the dark, he peeked out just in time to see his toy trucks and games falling helter-skelter off their shelves and his Batman mirror come crashing to the floor; it barely missed Max, the cocker spaniel puppy who, sensing the impending rumble, had just sneaked into the youngster's room. Thirty seconds later, all was quiet; Patrick and his family had survived the earthquake. But two weeks later, as the little boy snuggled in his mother's arms for a bedtime story, he spotted an unrecovered piece of broken mirror on the floor and the whole scary scene flashed through his mind. "Mom," asked little

Patrick anxiously, "will we be okay if the earthquake happens again?"

Living through an earthquake, tornado, hurricane, flood, plane crash, or any such catastrophic event can leave an indelible mark on the psyches of adults and children alike. Even if you are not physically injured in a disaster—as was the case, thankfully, with Patrick and his family—the experience can trigger enormous emotional distress. It rips apart, at least for a time, your sense that the world is a safe, predictable, controllable, and secure place.

Furthermore, disasters, whether natural, like an earthquake, or man-made, like a hostage situation, affect not only those immediately involved, but also those who see or hear about them. The explosion of the space shuttle *Challenger*, for example, echoed disturbingly in nearly every American's mind and heart, even though most of us only experienced its devastation from a distance.

When I spoke with Dr. Jim Wells, a psychologist from Concord, New Hampshire, Christa McAuliffe's hometown, he told me that merely watching the explosion on TV made many of the children, even those who did not know Mrs. McAuliffe at all, feel angry (some smashed the space shuttle models they had made so painstakingly), anxious (many had frequent nightmares in which their parents blew up in the shuttle), fearful, and clingy. Children countrywide remember exactly where they were when the *Challenger* exploded, just as people of my generation remember where we were when we heard President Kennedy was shot. As childhood psychic trauma expert Dr. Lenore Terr recently commented to me, "TV brings us so close to disasters. It may be that our TV screen doesn't really screen at all."

Clearly, though, the closer your contact and involvement with a disaster, the greater your risk for emotional problems in its aftermath. Still, children who depend on their world to be safe and secure are particularly vulnerable to the chaos a disaster can cause, whether they experience that calamity firsthand or from a more remote vantage point. But before we can help our children cope with the short- and long-term psychological consequences of *any* contact with disasters, we need to gain better insight into the emotional impact of these frightening events.

The Issue in Focus

Disasters, according to studies by the National Institute of Mental Health,* consist of four phases:

• the "heroic phase," which occurs as the disaster hits and includes its immediate aftermath. During this time, people rise to the occasion and often behave heroically in the rescue of both people and property.

• the "honeymoon phase," during which survivors count their blessings and begin the process of cleaning up; individuals and community-outreach organizations promise help. This optimistic period usually begins about one week after the disaster and lasts for up to two months, though it can go on for longer.

• the "disillusionment phase," which follows the hon-

*The information on disaster stages comes from the National Institute of Mental Health *Training Manual for Human Service Workers in Major Disasters.*

eymoon period and lasts anywhere from a couple of months to a couple of years. It occurs when and if the promises of help and dreams of rebuilding go unfulfilled. Victims stuck in this phase often feel disappointed, angry, bitter, and resentful.

• the "reconstruction phase," which can last for several years. This period is characterized by the survivors' acceptance of the situation at hand and their ability to approach the difficult business of reconstructing their lives. New buildings go up, community programs are set in place, and routines begin to normalize, all of which helps the victims reaffirm their belief in a positive outcome.

Very young children do not necessarily experience each of these phases. They are influenced by them, however, because children are affected by their parents' reactions. That is, a bitter, angry parent caught in the disillusionment stage may be less accessible to his child than one who has moved into the more positive reconstructive phase.

But disasters can affect more directly the children themselves. Studies show that kids who have experienced some sort of devastating event share certain characteristics. Contrary to popular belief, for instance, children don't usually become hysterical while the stressful event is going on; instead, they continue with their normal behavior. Child psychiatrist Lenore Terr observed this when she studied the youngsters who endured the Chowchilla kidnapping: in 1976, a bus load of elementary school kids was kidnapped, held at gunpoint and terrorized in Chowchilla, California. She recounts in her book *Too Scared to Cry* that even as the children's captor drove them away, the kids sang songs. Why? Posits Terr, it's not that the children weren't aware of the danger, but that at the "moment of terror" when children's "psychological underpinnings were being torn asunder," the youngsters were "too scared to cry."

Jane Myer observed the same phenomenon at New York's East Coldenham Elementary School after a building there was hit by a freak tornado in 1989, causing a wall to blow off the cafeteria. Nine children were killed and seventeen were injured. Myer, a social worker, told me, "In the short term, many of the kids said they did not feel frightened, worried, or anxious. In fact, they explained what had happened in a somewhat cold, narrative, factual style."

But while children may *seem* normal and even claim to feel "okay" during and immediately after a disaster, studies show that their inner turmoil is often great, filling them with anxiety and fear. Many children worry that the disaster will strike again; they fret that they or their families will be injured, or even worse, die and leave them unprotected. Such fear of abandonment is common in disaster victims and leads to intense separation anxiety.

Child psychiatrist Dr. Elizabeth Weller, who was called to Armenia after a devastating earthquake hit that country in 1988, told me she saw rampant evidence of separation anxiety in the Armenian children. "They didn't want to go to school, not only because many of them had been in school when the earthquake hit and didn't want to be reminded of what had happened, but also because they didn't want to be separated from their families. I remember one little boy who told me he would only go to school if his mommy and daddy would go with him. It was really very heartbreaking."

Separation anxiety also can cause sleep problems, another common difficulty for disaster's youngest victims. Typically, the children refuse to go to bed or to sleep alone;

they may wake frequently during the night, rise unusually early in the morning, or suffer nightmares.

Young children also tend to regress. They may start sucking their thumbs again or wetting the bed, even though they may have outgrown such behavior months or even years before. Some kids may exhibit a sudden change in their normal behavioral style; that is, an outgoing child may become withdrawn, or a normally gentle child may become aggressive. Too, experiencing an uncontrollable, devastating event makes some children lose the sense of invincibility so common in young kids. If that occurs, the children can become very pessimistic and gloomy, an attitude that can last well into adulthood.

Young victims of disasters also may be plagued by shame and guilt. Some of the children who survived the East Coldenham school disaster, for example, felt ashamed that they hadn't been able to stop the cafeteria wall from collapsing on their friends. Later, they worried about what they could have done to help, and felt guilty about what they perceived they *should* have done to assist their schoolmates.

Fear, anxiety, regression, shame, and guilt are fairly common to childhood disaster victims, no matter how old the youngsters are. Still, age does influence how a child responds to a terrible event. Let's take a moment to examine more specifically how children react at key stages:*

• Preschool to age five—The degree to which a disaster affects a very young child largely depends on how it affects that child's immediate family. The preschooler who

*The following information comes from the National Institute of Mental Health's *Manual for Child Health Workers in Major Disasters.*

loses his mother, father, or sibling in a flood will suffer much more intensely than the child whose entire family survives in good health. Children who watch news footage of an earthquake on television will be less disturbed by the images they see if their parents react to those images in a relaxed, though concerned, manner.

Preschoolers may not be able to express their anxieties and fears verbally; instead, such feelings often reveal themselves in drawings or play. Children's upset may also manifest itself in such regressive behavior as bed-wetting, thumb-sucking, or using baby talk. Additionally, kids may develop eating or sleeping problems, as well as a sudden fear of animals, strangers, or the dark. Preschoolers may become sad, irritable, or confused. Happily, though, most of these symptoms disappear, or at least fade somewhat, within a few weeks of the event.

• Ages six to eleven—Slightly older children are able to express their fears and anxieties a little more directly; some may even verbalize their worries or write about them in simple stories or poems. Communicating their feelings through drawings is also common in children of this age.

Like their preschool counterparts, school-age children may slip into such regressive behavior as bed-wetting or clinginess; they may also experience nightmares and such sleep difficulties as wakefulness or fear of sleeping alone.

Children in this age range may become irritable, sad, withdrawn, or more disobedient at home and in school; their grades may drop and concentration may slide. Physically, they may also suffer from headaches or nausea. Again, most of these reactions usually subside within a few days or weeks.

Since very little research has been done on children's

reactions to disasters, no real studies exist, at least to my knowledge, that show any gender difference. However, several experts I spoke with did observe certain differences in how boys and girls reacted to specific disasters. Myer noted that boys' play at the East Coldenham school became more aggressive after the tornado; games in which the Ninja Turtles or other superheroes battled the evil tornado were popular. Girls became more angry and directed that anger inward. "The feeling they had was 'What did I do to deserve this?' They found it more difficult than the boys to direct their anger at the tornado itself or, say, the people who put up the building in the first place," Myer said.

Lydia Walker, the national director of Cooperative Disaster Child Care, an organization that provides trained volunteers to help in disaster sites, told me that she often sees little boys reenact whatever disaster hit; they play hurricane, for instance, and knock down all the buildings. Girls, on the other hand, are more apt to play with puppets, to cuddle their toys or read a book.

Amid all this rather disheartening information lies an upbeat note: experiencing a disaster, either first- or second-hand, can actually have some positive effects. It is not by accident that the Chinese character for crisis has elements of both danger and opportunity. Kids who survive can grow emotionally stronger from the experience. Just as losing a cherished pet helps prepare a child for the death of a grandparent later on, living through a disaster can serve as a kind of psychological inoculation against other crises that may come along and may help a child deal more effectively with them. Family and friends who weathered a calamity together can also draw closer together and children can benefit from these more secure social ties.

A few more pluses: children can and sometimes do become more self-assured and outgoing after a disaster, possibly from all the increased attention and support from family, friends, and community groups. With the proper guidance, children can also learn an important lesson in compassion: they may become more sympathetic and sensitive toward others in need after having experienced, at least on some level, a crisis of their own.

Finally, the crisis that occurred in childhood may positively shape the course of an individual's entire life. We've all heard stories about the youngster who eventually went into medicine because she was inspired by a doctor who treated her after her plane crashed; or the child who became a fireman because of the firefighter who pulled his mother out of their burning home.

The advice that follows is intended to help you, as parents, maximize the positive and minimize the negative aspects of your child's disaster experience. As you begin, you'll see that some pointers pertain more to direct victims of disasters, while others are more applicable to secondhand observers. But read through them all. Each tip will give you just a little more insight into helping your children deal with the emotional upheaval any disaster can provoke.

How to Talk with Your Child About Disasters

1. Tune Into Your Kids.

Parents whose children have actually been through a disaster may be more apt to tune into their youngsters' behavior than parents whose kids may have simply watched a catastrophic event on TV. In both cases, though, children can be affected by the calamity; you need to pay close attention to understand to what degree.

A child who has just mastered the intricacies of a two-wheeler—but who, after a disaster, suddenly develops a fear of the bike—is communicating a new sense of anxiety and vulnerability. Some children who saw the *Challenger* explode suddenly started worrying that their family cars or space heaters would blow up. A day-care-center worker told me that for weeks after Hurricane Hugo struck, many four-year-olds who lived through the disaster would color all their drawings over with brown crayon to show "how the hurricane covered everything up." Pay close attention to your children's behavior or verbalizations; it will give you a better understanding of how upset or discomfited they may be.

2. Build a Protective Shield.

We've already discussed the possibility that your child may regress following a disaster, that he may become more clingy and "babyish" in the event's wake. My advice: go along with it, at least for a while. You won't be damaging your child if you offer a little extra cuddling and comfort during this stressful time. In fact, kids who know that their parents will build a protective shield around them during periods of stress will weather those times more easily and be less at risk for chronic fearfulness as they grow into adulthood.

3. Keep the Family Together.

During World War II, many English families sent their children out of London to protect them from the frequent bombings. But subsequent studies revealed that those children who remained with their families during this stressful period actually fared better, at least emotionally, than did those youngsters who were sent from their homes. The same seems to be proving true with the children of Chernobyl; those who were sent away were physically safer but had more emotional problems than children who remained with their families.

These experiences strongly suggest that if at all possible, parents should try to stay with their children during a disaster and its aftermath. Children feel more comfortable and secure when they are in the company of their parents and family.

4. Accept Your Children's Feelings.

Sometimes children's feelings can seem foolish to adults: the six-year old who burst into tears after seeing the *Challenger* explode because he feared that his grandmother, who lived in Florida, must have exploded, too, can seem silly to a grown-up mind. But whether or not your child's fears seem warranted to you, they are very real to the youngster and need to be taken seriously. Avoid saying things like "You shouldn't feel that way" or "Just don't think such a silly thought." Instead, try something like "I understand that you are afraid, but Grandma is fine. Where this happened is very far from where she lives. Why don't we call her up so you can talk to her?" Such a response validates a child's feelings, acknowledges his emotions, and helps alleviate his concerns.

The same holds true for anger. Children can become very angry after a disaster. Often, they direct that rage at Mom or Dad who was not there to protect them. But instead of returning their ire, you can explain to a five- or six-year-old that "I know you're angry at me, but there was nothing Mommy could do; you were in school when the storm came. I came and got you as soon as possible and I'm here now to protect you." To a ten- or eleven-year-old you might add something like "You know, Mom can't always be there to protect you; that's just the way things go. But I will always be there whenever it is possible."

Feelings of loss are also common in children who have witnessed a disaster. They may lose a cherished teddy bear, a special blanket, or a pet they truly loved. Don't belittle their loss or patronize them in any way. Instead, let them know that you understand their upset, then give them time to grieve and mourn. Children's various feelings of loss tend to diminish when their family, and especially their parents, let them know they understand.

5. Share Your Own Feelings with Your Child.

One of the best ways to bridge the gap between children and adults—and to reassure young children that their fears and anxieties are normal and natural—is to show them that grown-ups have those feelings, too. Terr told me that the kids who saw their teachers cry after the *Challenger* exploded "were really up on those teachers for a long while afterwards because before that, they didn't realize that teachers were real people who had feelings, too." So don't be afraid to share your emotions with your child. You can say, "I know that you're frightened; I am, too. But we'll get through this together and feel better again soon."

6. Stay Calm and Remain in Control.

While it's perfectly acceptable, even preferable, to share your feelings with your children, it is not a good idea to let your child see you panicked or engaged in uncontrolled hysteria. Because children take their cues about how dangerous (or safe) a situation is from watching their parents, it's important to try to remain calm and in control in their presence. Keeping your cool also teaches your child an important lesson: that people can behave with courage and dignity even when they are afraid.

7. Demystify the Event.

Children, like adults, are more fearful when they don't understand what's happening around them. Try, then, to keep your kids informed about what is going on. After the cafeteria wall collapsed at the East Coldenham Elementary School, for example, teachers and counselors regularly let students know how the rebuilding was progressing; they gave them tours throughout the reconstruction period and let them touch the strong steel beams.

In the absence of, or in addition to, such a hands-on educational opportunity, books can also serve as a rich source of information for children. Spend some time reading with your child about a particular disaster. (The Readings for Children list at the end of this chapter will give you some good titles with which to begin.) Just make sure that all information presented is appropriate for your child's age.

8. Remove the Blame.

Keep in mind when talking to your kids about any catastrophic event that you need to reassure them that the occurrence was not anyone's fault. When five-year-old

Tommy died in a tornado, a teacher-led discussion revealed that the child's classmates thought he'd died "because he did something bad." If you discover such a misconception, correct it immediately by saying something like "Tommy didn't do anything bad. None of you did anything bad. Tornados just happen in nature; they are nobody's fault. Let's get a book about tornados and read why they happen, okay?"

9. Prepare for Bedtime.

As we discussed in the Issue in Focus section, disaster experiences often trigger sleep disturbances in children. With a little patience and understanding, however, these problems should dissipate, if not totally disappear, within a few weeks. Children who begin refusing to go to bed may be helped by a soothing bedtime story or a quiet game, or by Mom or Dad lying down with them for five or ten minutes.

Kids who suddenly become fearful of the dark will appreciate a night light, or being allowed to go to sleep with their bedroom door slightly ajar and a comforting hall light glowing. If your child seems frightened of sleeping alone, be flexible with a new bedtime arrangement. You can move the child in with another sibling for a short time, or put the child's mattress or sleeping bag on the floor in your room for three or four nights. Do make sure that you and your child understand that these new arrangements are temporary and that you both know when they will end. But don't yell or punish your child for his sleep difficulties. It will only exacerbate your child's anxiety and prolong the problem.

10. Normalize Your Child's Routine as Soon as Possible.

Kids feel most secure when their everyday routines remain intact, but the turmoil surrounding a disaster often sets these routines spinning. Try to normalize your children's lives as soon as possible: get them back in school, reinstate regular bedtimes and mealtimes, and remind them that they need to start doing their chores again. While you may want to ease up on discipline—at least immediately after the catastrophic event occurs—don't adopt an anything-goes attitude. If your eight-year-old takes a swipe at his little brother, remind him, "You cannot do that; we don't hit each other in this house. I know you are feeling angry right now, but that's not how we deal with it. Maybe you and I can think of something else you can do when you're angry."

11. Anticipate Problems with Separation.

As we discussed earlier, the trauma of a disaster can make children extremely fearful of being abandoned, and thus anxious over any separation from Mom or Dad. Expect your kids to kick up a fuss when they have to go to bed, get dropped off at day care or school, or are left with a caretaker while you go to work. Although having to deal with an upset youngster is the last thing you need during this time, be patient. Spending a little time before you have to say good-bye may be helpful, as will offering some extra reassurance that you and your youngster will be reunited very soon.

12. Encourage, but Don't Force, Communication.

It's always helpful if your child can get his feelings out in the open, and you will want to do all you can to encourage such communication. Give your child every opportunity to speak with you when you're both calm and relaxed. Offer her lots of chances to draw, paint, play with clay, or, if she is old enough, write, or encourage your child to express herself through puppet play or other kinds of pretend games.

But don't allow your good intentions to push you or your child overboard. Children are entitled to keep some of their feelings private, or at least separate from the scene of the disaster. Here's what I mean.

The five-year-old daughter of a friend of mine witnessed a tragedy at her school: during a major storm, a tree limb fell on the school principal, crushing him to death. Concerned that her daughter would be traumatized by the event, my friend tried to discuss the incident with her daughter at home. But the youngster only responded with "Oh, Mommy, we already talked about that in school. I don't want to talk about it anymore." Her mom wisely backed off.

It's good to respect your child's wishes at times like these. It may well be that to this youngster, talking about the disaster with Mom in some way would link the event with home—and she would prefer, understandably so, to keep it very separate.

Child psychiatrist Dr. David Fassler agrees. "I see a lot of that in my practice. Kids who witnessed some terrible incident, like a parent's heart attack, don't want to talk about it when they come to my office. And that's okay. But it doesn't mean they are not distressed. Usually, their upset comes out in other ways—through games or the objects they make with clay—and then I can use those times to begin to talk about what they are expressing in nonverbal ways."

13. Allow Kids to Participate in Clean-up Activities.

Letting your child take part in cleaning up after a disaster—whether it's sweeping out his room, putting fallen items back on shelves, giving the dog a bath—can help him reestablish a sense of control over his environment and speed the healing process.

Another important tactic: Let your child have a say in any reconstruction or redecorating. If his room has to be repainted after a flood, let him pick out the paint color or choose the new wallpaper. Such participation will help your child feel more in control and ameliorate feelings of helplessness.

14. Encourage Schools to Hold Group Discussions.

Today educators and school administrators are much more sensitive to the emotional and psychological ramifications of disasters than they were even as little as fifteen years ago. Following any such event, most schools now hold assemblies, offer counseling, and encourage student participation in a variety of programs geared to minimize a disaster's negative effects.

But if your school is not doing anything to help the children work through their feelings, urge both teachers and administrators to do so. One of the most beneficial activities they can offer is to hold group discussions following a catastrophe. When I was teaching, I found that children felt reassured when they learned that other kids had the same feelings that they did, particularly when it came to being afraid. Such group talks also can help even the most reticent child to open up.

15. Be Realistically Reassuring.

If you live in an area of the country where a certain kind of disaster does not occur—a child living in New York City is not likely to experience a devastating flood—offer reassurance that there is almost no chance that such an event will happen where you live.

If you live in an area where a similar disaster could strike, let your children know the facts but stress your family's preparedness for any emergency. And make sure your child knows some simple survival skills, too. Your local chapter of the American Red Cross has some helpful pamphlets that detail specific safety measures you can take to help your family cope with different kinds of disasters; just call or write to get them. (See sample questions and answers for specific language you can use in responding to your child.)

After a disaster hits, it's also reassuring for a child to hear what is still the same about his world. For instance, once things calm down a bit, you might take your child for a walk and note "Look, our church is still standing and the playground looks just fine. We're really pretty lucky. Our house wasn't hit and neither was your school. So we'll get up on Monday and I'll make you some breakfast, then drive you to school, just like always. Okay?"

16. Put the Event in Context.

Young children often perceive that the world they see on television or the world in which they live is the *entire* world. In the aftermath of the San Francisco earthquake a few years ago, TV news showed repeated footage of the same block of devastated buildings. But many young children did not realize that they were seeing the same image over and over again; they got the impression that the entire city was torn apart. It's up to parents to help put the event in context for their children. Simply say, "Did you notice that that's the same grocery story that was in the news last night? They keep showing the same block. But you know, not all the buildings in San Francisco were hurt. Lots of places are just fine. Let's take out a map and find San Francisco and I'll show you what I mean." If your child experienced the disaster firsthand, it's also important to offer some perspective. Driving out to the places that were totally unaffected, for instance, can help the child see the bigger picture and assure him that the larger world is still intact.

17. Provide Safe Opportunities to Release Tension.

Living through or watching a disaster can make any of us, including children, anxious and tense. That's why it's a good idea to provide your child with safe outlets to release any pressure. A few ideas: Give your four- or five-year-old a ball to kick; introduce your seven-year-old to the joys of a pillow fight; encourage your nine-year-old to get up a game of soccer. And remember: the more rigorous the play, the better.

18. Limit TV Viewing of the Tragedy.

Seeing an image of devastation again and again can stir up feelings of anxiety, fearfulness, and insecurity. Take care to limit your child's viewing of the disaster on television and to provide your child with an opportunity to express his fears or concerns about what he sees and hears. It takes a good deal of vigilance—news programs are relentless once they get compelling footage of any devastation—but making sure your children do not overdose on disaster is important for their emotional well-being. (Because what children see generally has a more powerful effect than what they hear, radiocasts can be a little less threatening. Again, though, it's wise not to keep the radio news on all day. News coverage, whether on radio or television, can overwhelm and disturb children, even in measured dosages.

19. Involve Kids in Preparedness.

If you live in an area vulnerable to certain kinds of disasters—earthquakes, floods, tornadoes—it's important to involve your children in learning how to protect themselves. Make sure your child knows where the "safe" place in the house is; how to dial 911 and ask for help; who to call if Mom or Dad isn't home. Rather than scaring children, familiarizing them with disaster-preparedness tactics makes them feel more in control and therefore safer and more secure.

20. Find Your Own Support Network.

It's hard to parent a child traumatized by anything, and that includes disasters. Because the child may become extremely needy, anxious, frightened, and angry, the demands placed on the parent intensify; you may begin to doubt your own ability to rise to this parenting challenge.

For precisely these reasons, you may want to take advantage of any adult support groups that will undoubtedly pop up at churches, synagogues, Y's, or your local Red Cross chapter immediately after a disaster. Such groups can go far in soothing jagged nerves and giving you the confidence and courage it takes to continue parenting well.

21. Encourage Empathy.

As awful as they are, disasters can offer us a chance to teach children that while the world can be troubling, it is also a place where people care about one another and, in times of distress, help each other out. Keep in mind, though, that this lesson can't be taught with words alone; actions do speak louder here. So if you and your child are watching a newscast about an earthquake in Mexico, you might say, "Isn't this terrible? I bet those people will need lots of food and clothing and toys. Why don't we call the Red Cross and see what we can send? Then, maybe you can pick out one or two of your toys or sweaters and we can send them to the children in Mexico." Not only does such action encourage empathy by helping children to think of the less fortunate, but it gives them a sense of power. They learn that they have the ability to make a difference in someone else's life.

22. Stress the Positives.

So many negatives surround disasters that it's important to offer children a little balance by pointing out the positives. Of course, survivors will always say, "Aren't we lucky that we survived," and that's important to note. But you can go a step further; you can stress that not only do people weather a disaster but they rebuild after one. Even a four-year-old can appreciate this: "It's very sad that the ice cream store collapsed in the tornado, but I read that they are already starting to rebuild it and that the new store will be even better. Won't that be nice?"

A slightly older child can also appreciate other pluses, like how well people reacted in the disaster. You can point out to your nine-year-old, "You know, this flood was pretty awful. But look at how we learned to help each other, and to help our neighbors since it happened. Not only that, but we've made lots of new friends [give examples]. Also, we've learned how to share our feelings a little more. We know that we can cry in front of each other and that no one will make fun of us. Sometimes even bad events can make good things happen. And that's nice to know."

Sample Questions and Answers

Q: What makes a hurricane (tornado, earthquake, flood, etc.) happen?

A: A hurricane is something that happens in nature; it's like a thunderstorm, only bigger. It is nobody's fault; it doesn't happen because anyone was bad. Let's go to the library and find a book that will explain exactly what makes a hurricane happen.

Q: Why did our house fall down and not Timmy's?

A: Well, our house happened to be in the path of the tornado, so it got hit harder than Timmy's house did. It didn't hit our house because you were bad or because anyone in our family was bad. A tornado is nobody's fault. It just happens sometimes in this part of the country.

Q: What if it happens again?

A: We know what to do if it happens again. We will get

to a safe place [name the place] where we have food and water and lights. Our town has also made its new buildings very strong—much stronger than before. So we are well prepared in case another tornado comes along.

Q: I saw the earthquake on TV. Could we have an earthquake here?

A: No, it's not likely. We're very lucky because we don't get earthquakes in this part of the country. But what happened in San Francisco was terrible. Maybe we could send some money to the Red Cross to help the people in San Francisco rebuild their homes.

or

A: It's possible. We have had some earthquakes in our part of the country. But we are prepared. We know where to go to stay safe and we have extra food and water and emergency lights just in case. Our whole community is prepared for an earthquake and that makes me feel nice and safe.

Helpful Resources

ORGANIZATIONS

American Red Cross
(Contact local chapter listed in telephone book)

The Violence and Traumatic Stress Research Branch
National Institute of Mental Health
Park Lawn Building, room 18105
5600 Fishers Lane
Rockville, MD 20857
(301) 443-3728

Federal Emergency Management Agency (FEMA)
500 C Street, SW
Washington, DC 20472
(202) 646-4026

Cooperative Disaster Child Care
P.O. Box 188
500 Main Street
New Windsor, MD 21776

Readings for Parents

Johnson, Kendall. *Trauma in the Lives of Children*. Claremont, Calif.: Hunter House, 1989.

San Fernando Valley Child Guidance Clinic. "Coping With Children's Reactions to Earthquakes and Other Disasters." Northridge, Calif.: San Fernando Valley Child Guidance Clinic, 1986. (Also available through FEMA)

Terr, Lenore. *Too Scared to Cry: Psychic Trauma in Childhood*. New York: Harper & Row, 1990.

Wolfenstein, Martha, and Gilbert Kilman, eds. *Children and the Death of a President*. Garden City: Doubleday, 1965.

READINGS FOR CHILDREN

Arnold, Caroline. *Coping with Natural Disasters*. New York: Walker & Co., 1988. (Ages 10 and up)

Branley, Franklyn M. *Earthquakes*. New York: Harper Junior Books, 1990. (Ages 5–10)

————. *Flash, Crash, Rumble and Roll*. New York: Thomas Y. Crowell, 1964. (Ages 4–8)

Rutland, Jonathan. *The Violent Earth.* New York: Random House, 1987. (Ages 7–11)

Zolotow, Charlotte. *The Storm Book.* New York: Harper & Row, 1952. (Ages 5–8)

Special thanks to the following experts for their input into this chapter: Victor Fornari, M.D., director of clinical services, Division of Child and Adolescent Psychiatry, North Shore University Hospital, Cornell University Medical College; Sandra Frick, Ph.D., associate professor, University of South Carolina College of Nursing; Jane Myer, C.S.W., clinical director, Orange County Dept. of Mental Health; Diane Myers, RN, trainer-consultant in disaster mental health; Lynn Ponton, M.D., associate professor of psychiatry, University of California at San Francisco; Sherry Thaggard, M.D., child psychiatrist, Madison County Mental Health Center; Lenore Terr, M.D., clinical professor of psychiatry, University of California; Lydia Walker, national director, Cooperative Disaster Child Care; Elizabeth Weller, M.D., professor of pediatrics and psychiatry, Ohio State University, and Children's Hospital; Jim Wells, Ph.D., senior vice president, Central New Hampshire Community Mental Health Services.

Chapter Eleven

"MY MOM'S IN THE HOSPITAL....

WILL SHE DIE?"

Talking with Your Child About Cancer

"Ever since Mom went to her doctor for some sort of test, things at home have been just awful," thought nine-year-old Susannah. Her mother was tired all the time; Dad was nervous and jumpy. So when Susannah came home from school to find her aunt Kathy sitting in the living room, eyes red and swollen as if she'd been crying, the youngster became frightened. "Your mother is upstairs lying down, sweetheart," Aunt Kathy explained after kissing Susannah hello. "She got the tests results from the doctor and she is very sick. She has to go into the hospital for an operation." Susannah felt her heart race. "What's wrong with her?" she asked, a sick feeling knotting her stomach. "Is my mom going to die?"

Susannah's aunt faced a difficult dilemma: should she tell her niece that her mother had cancer or try to shield her from the pain that such information could inflict? And should Susannah's aunt offer reassurance to her niece or admit that the child's mom might die?

Cancer, as Susannah's aunt was fast learning, is not just an individual's disease, but a family problem. Such a serious illness, particularly when it strikes the parent or sibling of a healthy child, raises numerous questions and concerns. How much do you tell a young child? Can he understand the diagnosis and absorb the news without being traumatized by it?

And here's another issue: What if the youngster himself has cancer? Does the very young patient have a right—or a need—to know?

This chapter will tackle all these questions and more. But first, let's take a closer look at the issue of cancer and children's reactions to serious disease.

The Issue in Focus

What is cancer? At the risk of oversimplification, cancer is an illness characterized by the presence of certain abnormal body cells that grow and divide rapidly, crowding out and destroying healthy, normal cells. We know of over one hundred different types of cancer today, but there are only three main forms of treatment: surgery, chemotherapy, and radiation, or some combination thereof. In many cases, the treatment causes a number of unpleasant side effects, including nausea, vomiting, mouth sores, hair loss, and fatigue.

Cancer can be deadly. In fact, it is the second leading cause of death in the U.S. today, second only to heart disease.* In the last decade alone, some 9 million new cancer cases appeared, and there were over 4.5 million cancer deaths.

But thanks to better diagnostic procedures and treatments, cancer is no longer a death sentence. Today, approximately 40 percent of all patients who learn they have cancer will be alive five years or longer after diagnosis. Some forms of cancer, like cervical cancer and skin cancer, are curable if diagnosed early.

The news for children with cancer is even brighter. While the disease remains the leading cause of death in all ages of children (except for infancy), some forms of cancer—such as leukemia—are 60 to 90 percent curable in kids up to age eighteen. By the year 2000, one in every one thousand adults age twenty to twenty-nine will be a person *cured* of cancer.

Despite the fact that millions of Americans once diagnosed with cancer are living active, healthy, productive, and long lives, the "C" word still carries a legacy of fear and uncertainty. It triggers such a profusion of emotions that it remains a difficult topic for parents and caregivers to broach with young children.

And understandably so. Often healthy children whose

---

*All statistical information comes from the American Cancer Society.

families are touched by cancer become sad, depressed, angry, irritable, and resentful. They may become clingy and withdrawn, or act out their anxieties in uncharacteristic and unruly behavior. They also may experience such physical problems as headaches, loss of appetite, stomach upset, or sleep disturbance.

If a parent becomes ill, children fear being abandoned. They worry, "Who will take care of me?" and may become particularly clingy or upset when separated from either parent.

If a sibling has cancer, the healthy child may feel anxious and guilty. An angry thought like "I wish you were dead" can stir up great self-blame in a child who learns that his sibling (or parent, for that matter) has cancer and may, in fact, be dying. Siblings of cancer patients may also feel jealous and resentful of all the attention being showered upon the sick child; they may feel sorry for themselves because they feel they are being neglected. On the other hand, the healthy child can become very protective of his sick sibling, even if that sibling is older.

A youngster's reaction to a loved one's cancer also depends upon the age and developmental level of the healthy child. Children age six and under may not be verbal enough to express their feelings in words, but may communicate more obliquely. Lisa Bard, the clinical coordinator of children's services for Cancer Care, Inc., told me of a six-year-old she worked with whose father had cancer. The youngster's anxiety came out in play: he started hammering the heads of all the dolls in the playroom, and creating war games in which someone always got eaten up.

Very young children may also engage in egocentric magical thinking. For instance, one five-year-old knew that his brother Billy had lots of bruises on his body and that Billy had leukemia. The youngster believed that his getting angry at Billy and hitting him, causing his arm to bruise, made him responsible for his brother's illness.

Older children are better able to separate reality from fantasy; that is, their worries and fears are more grounded in the real world. They are less likely to believe that punching their brother and giving him a bruise gave him cancer, particularly if their parents take the time to explain what cancer is. They also may be able to express their anxieties and concerns more directly. That is, a four-year-old whose Mom has cancer and who asks "Is Mommy going to die?" is worried primarily about Mom leaving him; he'd probably ask the same question if Mom went to the hospital for a broken leg. But the ten-year-old who asks that same question most likely understands the seriousness of his mother's illness and the real possibility that his mom might die and leave him forever.

Children dealing with a family member's cancer may also become developmentally accelerated; that is, they may *seem* more emotionally mature than kids whose lives have been more carefree. (Remember, though, that even the most "mature" youngster is still a child inside.)

Such precociousness is also true of kids who are suffering with their own cancer. One eight-year-old with leukemia, for example, listened to her mom say, "I wish I could take this pain away from you," and then responded with "Mommy, you couldn't go through this; you're not strong enough. I'm glad it's me and not you who is sick."

On the other hand, Cancer Care's Lisa Bard has observed that these same kids may in some ways be less mature than their healthy peers. She explains, "Because they've been in the hospital so much and maybe out of school for long periods of time—really living in an adult world—they may not know how to relate to other kids. So what you wind up with is a child who is a strange mixture of developmental acceleration and immaturity."

When a young child's life is touched by cancer—whether his parent's illness, a sibling's, or his own—it can precipitate a great deal of emotional and psychological stress. However, it also can present some opportunities for growth. The family dealing with cancer is sharing a deeply emotional time which may forge closer bonds among parents, children, and siblings. Children learn an important lesson: Our family is strong and can weather any crisis together. Kids can become more independent, resourceful, and self-confident as they learn that they can survive such a trauma successfully.

Fortunately, parents have a good deal of influence over how well their young children deal with cancer. The advice offered in the following section can help you ease the potential trauma. (Please note: The following suggestions focus primarily on how to talk to a healthy child when his parent or sibling has cancer. Later on, I offer some tips on how to talk to your child about his own cancer. Since space constraints permit me to deal with the latter subject only very briefly, I urge you to contact the organizations listed at the end of this chapter to get the kind of in-depth support and information you and your ill child need.)

How to Talk with Your Child About the Cancer of a Parent or Sibling

1. Tell Them About the Illness.

Children are amazingly sensitive to what's going on around them. They pick up their parents' distress through facial expressions, body language, and overheard snippets of conversation. If unguided, their active imaginations will piece together these bits of information to create a false scenario that's often far scarier than the reality. To help prevent this, tell your child about the illness. Once you have a clear diagnosis and some idea of the treatment, explain what's going on as simply and objectively as possible, and, of course, in an age-appropriate manner.

Here's how. Suppose Mom is diagnosed with breast cancer. You can tell your four- or five-year-old that "Mommy is sick and has to go to the hospital to have an operation. Later, she will have to take some very strong medicine to help her get better again. But then she will come home and we'll all be together." To an eight- or nine-year-old you might explain, "Mom has something called cancer in her breast. The doctor has to take her breast off to get rid of it. She has to go to the hospital for the operation, and then she has to take some strong medicine. But after that, we think she'll be just fine." A ten- or eleven-year-old can understand a more detailed explanation, such as "Mom's doctor found a lump in her breast and she's going into the hospital next week to have her breast removed by a surgeon. It's really good that it was found because it was cancerous. Mom may be uncomfortable during her treatment, but we think that after the surgery, and after taking some very strong medicine for a while, she will be just fine."

2. Practice Your Explanation Beforehand.

It's hard to tell a child that Mom, Dad, brother, or sister has cancer. Because you may be overwhelmed by your own fears, anxieties, and concerns and may not be at your "parental best," try practicing what you will say before sitting down and talk to your youngster. You can use the sample "scripts" offered in tip #1 as a springboard. But don't try to broach the subject without at least one brief run-through; it's an important conversation that requires you to be as calm, objective, and concise as possible.

3. Remove Any Blame.

Because young children feel that everything that happens in their world centers on them, they often feel responsible for their parent's or sibling's cancer. You need to set them straight by explaining, "Your sister Amy has a disease called leukemia. No one knows what caused it, but we do know that people can't make it happen. You didn't do anything bad to make her sick and Amy didn't do anything bad to get sick either. Anyway, now the doctors are doing whatever they can to make Amy well again."

4. Reassure Your Child That Cancer Is Not Contagious.

Young children (and some not-so-young adults) may worry that they can "catch" cancer from someone else. This simply is not true. So reassure your child that even if Mom or Dad has cancer, or if big brother or little sister has cancer, that does not mean he will get it, too.

5. Strike a Balance Between Optimism and Pessimism.

Telling your child that Dad or sister will be "just like new"—at least until you're certain that that's true—is neither honest nor helpful. On the other hand, conveying a "woe is me, I'm helpless" attitude won't do any good, either. Instead, it's better to offer a realistic but hopeful assessment of the situation. You might say that "cancer is a serious illness and Dad is very sick. But he has an excellent doctor who is doing everything she can to make him well again. That's why I think Daddy will feel better again soon." Such an explanation assures that you won't be making any false promises and thus risk your child's trust.

6. Stay in Contact with the Healthy Child.

Frequently, cancer treatment is only available at a hospital or cancer center far from home, which means that the patient and the accompanying parent (or spouse) may be away for long periods of time. Since such separations can make the healthy child who remains at home feel anxious and left out, you need to try to make an effort to stay in close touch. Call, write, or send a tape recording back home as often as possible. The goal is to minimize your well child's anxiety and insecurities by keeping the familial ties tight.

7. Validate *All* Your Child's Feelings.

Healthy children often experience lots of different emotions when dealing with the cancer of a loved one—anger, sadness, guilt, fear, and more. That's why it's important to let your child know that all feelings are okay. And that includes anxieties about his own health. As Dr. Gerry

Koocher, chief of psychology at Boston Children's Hospital, explains, "If your child knows Tommy had lots of bruises and he got leukemia, he may become worried about all the bruises he himself has (even though you're certain he got them in last Saturday's soccer match). Don't treat his health concerns lightly. Enlist the aid of your pediatrician or other credible source who can assure your child that he is well." Acknowledging your children's emotions will let them know that they are important people whose feelings are taken seriously.

8. Answer All Questions Honestly.

In researching this chapter, I met with Dr. Lynna Lesko, the assistant attending psychiatrist at the world renowned Memorial Sloan-Kettering Cancer Center in New York. Lesko spoke of an interesting pilot study of one hundred kids and their parents that was conducted at the hospital. The study revealed "that the better the communication between parents and children, and the better the communication within the family, the less distress the child has. It just showed us how important honest communication with your child is."

One key aspect of such communication is answering your children's questions about cancer accurately, honestly, and according to their cognitive abilities. If, for example, your six-year-old asks, "Can I catch cancer?" you might respond with, "No, you can't. You cannot catch cancer like you caught a cold from your brother last month." If your ten-year-old asks the same thing, you might say, "No, cancer is not contagious. We don't know how people get cancer, but doctors do know that we can't catch it from someone else."

What if your child poses a question that stumps you? Say so! I know that many parents are uncomfortable admitting they don't know something for fear that their child will think less of them, but it's simply not the case. Children react just fine when a question is answered with "That's a good question, but I don't know. The next time I speak with Mom's doctor, I'm going to ask him."

Sometimes, however, kids don't verbalize their questions and concerns. Still, paying close attention to their behaviors and play—e.g. drawings or games—might help you figure out what's on their minds. Jesse, six years old, first expressed her anger and anxiety over losing her father to cancer when she began smacking her dolls. Noting that behavior allowed her mother to ask why she was hitting the dolls and presented an opportunity to talk about angry feelings. Psychologist Koocher often uses another approach. When he senses that a young patient dealing with his mother's cancer is blaming himself for her illness, for example, he might try to explain what "other children" think as a way to reassure his young patient. For instance, he might say something like "You know, lots of kids think that they made their mom sick. But they didn't. Nothing a person does can make another person get cancer."

9. Visit the Treatment Setting.

When a well child's parent or sibling goes off to a hospital or cancer center for treatment, the healthy youngster may fantasize either that the patient is being tortured in a horrible place, or is having a great time without him. To give your child a clearer picture of the situation, try to take him to visit the treatment setting. If possible, show your youngster where the patient goes for chemotherapy or other treatment; introduce her to the doctor and the nurses. Such a visit also will make the child feel less isolated and more a part of all that's happening.

10. Try to Maintain Everyday Routines.

When cancer strikes, the family's world is turned upside down. Routines are completely disrupted as everyone struggles to deal with the disease and its enormous new demands. But since young children need stability and predictability to make them feel secure, it's important to reinstate your healthy child's routine as soon as possible. Enforcing regular bedtimes, mealtimes, and playtimes and allowing your child to continue attending after-school activities can help create a sense of certainty amid the turmoil.

If your child's routine must be disturbed, however, make sure you explain any changes fully. For instance, you can say, "Mommy has to stay at the hospital with Maria while she has her chemotherapy. So Uncle Jeff will pick you up from school, bring you home, and make dinner. Then he'll stay with you until I get home at about seven o'clock. Okay?"

11. Prepare the Child for the Patient's Homecoming.

Cancer and its treatment are so powerful that they can change a person's appearance: patients can lose a great deal of weight or experience temporary hair loss; sometimes amputation is necessary or other significant bodily changes occur. Young children need to be prepared for such physical transformations so they won't be frightened by them. A day or two before the ill family member returns, you can explain, "When Daddy was sick in the hospital he got very thin and his hair fell out. He'll gain weight back and later on his hair will grow. For now, though, he looks different from the way you remember him. But remember: No matter how he looks on the outside, he is the same Daddy on the inside. He loves you very much and he is going to be very happy to see you again."

Even the most prepared child, however, may still experience fear and concern over these physical changes. After all, these visible signs are the only concrete proof a young child may have that the patient is indeed ill. Try, then, to give your child permission to express his anxieties openly, and do your best to comfort and reassure him. Simply explain that, as I mentioned before, the patient is still the same person inside even though his outside may be very different.

12. Let Children Participate in Home Care.

Many healthy children adjust more easily to the patient's homecoming if they are allowed to lend a hand in their care. A four-year-old can bring Mommy a glass of water each morning so she can take her medicine; an eight-year-old can run down to the corner store and buy the newspaper so Dad has something to read while he rests in bed. Be careful, however, not to overburden your youngster with added responsibilities. He may already resent being out of the spotlight; having to do too many extra chores may only exacerbate that resentment. Further, with all the tension and anxiety that surrounds cancer, more than ever your youngster needs plenty of responsibility-free time to relax and play.

13. Try to Make Special Time for the Well Child.

Yvonne Soghomonian, an associate director of Candle-lighters Childhood Cancer Foundation and a parent who lost her own child to leukemia, spends a great deal of time working with the families of children with cancer. Over and over again she finds that "the healthy sibling feels rejected. He has a hard time understanding why his parents have to give so much attention to the sick child. And since treatment for leukemia can go on for two or three years, the healthy child's sense of rejection can go on for a long time."

It's helpful, says Soghomonian, to "explain to the healthy child that this illness is a fact of life and that there's really not much he or you can do about it. But what helps even more is for parents to forget about the messy house or catching up on other chores and devote some time when they're home to their well child." Such quality time goes a long way in helping the healthy youngster remember that he, too, is much loved.

14. Keep Caretakers, Teachers, and the Members of Your Community Informed.

Some families have a tendency to retreat into a protective shell when illness or other tragedy strikes. They don't tell anyone for fear of seeming helpless or vulnerable. For your healthy child's sake, though, don't keep cancer a secret. Inform teachers, coaches, baby-sitters and other key members of the child's life so that they will be better prepared to give your youngster the emotional support he needs during this stressful time.

Another suggestion: If you know of a child whose family is suffering with cancer, why not invite that youngster to join your brood in a family outing? Or offer to take the child to his Cub Scout meeting or to bring him home from Little League practice. His family will appreciate your support—and your child will learn something about helping others.

15. Be Prepared to Discuss Death.

Don't be surprised if your discussions about cancer prompt your child to ask questions about death. Despite the facts, our society still links cancer with dying, and children often pick up on that.

Keep in mind that kids understand death according to their age and cognitive capacities. Preschoolers, for instance, rarely grasp death's finality. The four-year-old who helped his pal bury a pet gerbil, then peered into the cage at the remaining animals and asked, "Which was the one that died?" is typical of a preschooler's level of understanding. School-age children tend to comprehend a bit more. They know that dead things don't eat or breathe or sleep; however, they often believe that only old things die. Children age ten and older can grasp the concept of death more clearly, and are able to understand that it is the end of life. It's essential to take your child's developmental level into account when answering any questions about death.

As for specific suggestions on how best to talk with your children about death, it would be impossible for me to cover that satisfactorily in this one chapter. Entire books have been written on the subject; in fact, I recommend some of them in the Readings for Parents section at the end of this chapter. But I do want to emphasize three key points about talking with your children about death:

First, remember to use very concrete terms. The dead bird your child spotted in the street won't ever eat, sleep, fly, or breathe anymore. Daddy died of cancer; he won't be able to eat dinner with us or take you to school or kiss you goodnight.

Second, take care not to use terms like "put to sleep" or "sleeping with the angels" when describing death. If you say, "Johnny went to sleep for a very long time," your child might worry that whenever he goes to sleep he might die.

And lastly, be patient. It will take many, many brief discussions of death over a long period of time—even years—before your child comes to grips with the concept. Just be tolerant and receptive; eventually your child will understand.

16. Tell Your Children When a Loved One Is Dying and Allow Them to Mourn.

One of the most difficult things you may ever have to tell your child is that his mommy, daddy, brother, or sister is dying. But it is important that you do so; anything else is but a stopgap measure that may, in the long run, damage your child's trust. The following advice will help you break the news as honestly and sensitively as possible:

• Give him fair notice. It's best to warn your child that a loved one is dying. You can say, "Remember when I told you that Daddy was very, very sick? Well, now he is even sicker and he may die."

• Allow the child to say good-bye. If your child wishes to say good-bye, let him do so in whatever way he can. That may mean speaking to the patient directly, writing him a note or poem, or even drawing a picture. But saying good-bye will help your child get an important sense of closure.

• Tell her when a loved one dies. Hopefully, you've been able to prepare your child for this eventuality, so you can now say, "Remember how I said that Daddy might die? Well, he did die. I feel very sad and I know that you do, too. Daddy didn't want to die and leave you, but he was so sick that he did die. But he always loved you very, very much. And I love you very, very much."

• Allow your child to attend the funeral. The funeral is a ritual that allows mourners, including children, a time to share their grief with others, safely air their emotions, and find a certain sense of relief from the upset of a loved one's death. Protectively excluding your child from attending the service can hinder this grieving process. But forcing an unwilling child to attend can also be harmful. The consensus among childhood grief experts such as pediatrician Dr. Morris Wessel, therefore, is to encourage but not pressure your youngster to go to the funeral. If he does go, be sure to have an adult ready to take the child outside or back home early if she becomes fidgety or uncomfortable.

• Allow your child to grieve. Wessel puts it well: "Give the child the opportunity to mourn. Comfort him in his sadness rather than try to prevent his sadness." It's wonderful advice and I heartily agree. Know, however, that while children often go through the typical stages of mourning—denial, protest and anger, despair, and resolution—because of their developing cognitive and emotional capacities, it may take them years to do so. Be patient, and give your child the time and understanding he needs to come to terms with the death of a loved one.

• Let your child keep some of the loved one's possessions, particularly if he requests a certain item. Over the years, special mementos help keep loving and comforting memories of the deceased close at hand.

• Maintain consistency. Many parents, with the best of

intentions, send their children to stay with a distant relative or friend when a family member dies. In part, they do this to shield the child from all the upset, as well as to relieve themselves of the child-care burden for a short time. But it's not a good idea. Keeping some consistency in your child's life—letting her sleep in her own bed, play with her own toys—offers needed reassurance that life goes on.

• Help children deal with the realities of death. After the death of a parent or sibling, very young children may practice insistent denial. Even though a youngster's mother has died, he may say something like "Mommy called and she is going to pick me up at school tomorrow." Rather than ignoring such comments, as many parents or caretakers tend to do, grief expert Wessel recommends addressing them matter-of-factly with a comment like "I know that you wish Mommy would pick you up from school. We both would like to believe that Mommy's not dead. But she is and that makes us both very sad." Don't argue with the child or insist he acknowledge the loved one's passing. But as often as is necessary—and that may be quite often—try to counter denial with a gentle dose of reality.

• Permit your child's honest emotions to surface. Sometimes the relative who dies may not have had a positive relationship with your child. If, for instance, the child's deceased father was an alcoholic, the youngster might harbor mixed emotions about his dad. It's important to give your child permission to express these feelings openly and honestly. If your child says something like "I don't care that Daddy died. He was mean to me and Mommy," you might say something like "I know that we were mad at Daddy a lot and that he wasn't always very nice to us. You may still feel angry at him and that's okay. But let's try to remember some of the good things he did, too." Then offer an example or two. The point is to allow your child to vent his emotions honestly and to provide a balanced picture of the deceased.

• Offer caretaking reassurance. Little children often worry about who will take care of them when a parent dies. Be sure, then, to offer reassurance. In a quiet moment, you can say, "I feel sad that Daddy died and I know you do, too. But I want you to know that I am fine and I will be here to take care of you for a long, long time." If your child then asks, "But what if something happens to you?" you can simply say, "Then Grandma [or other trusted caretaker] will take care of you. And she loves you very, very much."

• Let the surviving child know he is valued. When I spoke with psychologist Gerry Koocher, he described a phenomenon that sometimes occurs in a family who loses a youngster to cancer. "Occasionally, there will be an idealization of the deceased child which may be confusing to the surviving sibling. Mom and Dad keep saying how courageous and wonderful Billy was, but Johnny remembers him as sometimes being a bully, too. Add to that the surviving child's sense that his parents are very unhappy over the idealized child's death, and you may find that the well child begins trying to become the deceased."

To insure that this doesn't happen in your family, explain why you're sad—that is, because Billy died. But also add something like "But I'm really glad that you are here alive and well. You're such a great kid and Dad and I love you so much. We're so happy that you're with us."

How to Talk to Your Child When He or She Has Cancer

1. Let Him Know What's Wrong.

In an effort to protect your child, you may choose not to tell him that he has cancer. But that's really a mistake. As I've said before, kids sense that something's wrong anyway; they pick up cues from your facial expressions, body language, the changed attitude of siblings, neighbors, and friends, the strange tests they have undergone at the hospital—even the word "cancer" on the hospital menu. So rather than having your child learn of his illness from another source, tell him as soon as you know the diagnosis and have some sense of what the treatment will be.

2. Make Sure Your Explanation Is Age Appropriate.

When informing your child of her illness, try to keep her developmental level in mind. Of course, every child is different: some four-year-olds can understand more than some seven-year-olds. But in general, following a few age-related guidelines can help when telling your child he has cancer:

• Ages three to four—Such young children need only a simple, general explanation along the lines of "You are sick and the doctor is going to give you some strong medicine to make you better again. I'll be with you the whole time because I love you so much."

• Ages five to eight—At this stage, you should name the disease and offer some simple description of what it means. There's a wonderful brochure called "Talking With Your Child About Cancer" (you can get it free from the

National Cancer Institute—see the Helpful Organizations section at the end of this chapter) that suggests you explain cancer in terms of "good- and bad-guy cells." For instance, you might say, "You have a sickness called leukemia. It is serious. And you are going to take some very strong medicine to help you get well. The medicine will help the good-guy cells in your body become strong enough to fight off the bad-guy cells that are trying to hurt your body."

• Ages nine to eleven. At this age you can offer a slightly more detailed explanation of your child's illness by saying, "You have a disease called leukemia. It is a cancer of the blood and it is very serious. You see, some bad cells that have gotten into your blood are crowding out the good, healthy cells. You are going to get some very strong medicine to fight leukemia and to make your healthy blood cells strong enough to destroy the bad cells. I'll be with you when you get your medicine and I'll always be here to take care of you. The doctors and Mommy and I all think you are going to be just fine."

3. Keep the Child Informed About What Will Happen Next.

Let your child know the next procedure he will have to undergo. It will help give him a sense that he's in control of what's happening to him. Just a day or two in advance—much farther ahead may give your child too much time to worry about it—you might say, "On Thursday we are going to go to the hospital so Dr. Jones can see how you're doing. He's probably going to take some blood from your arm. We'll be there for a few hours and then we'll come home. Okay?"

4. Don't Hover.

Several of the nurses I met with at Memorial Sloan-Kettering Cancer Center told me that over and over again, they see parents overprotecting their ill children. But refusing to normalize your youngster's life may make your child overly and unnecessarily anxious about her illness. Instead, let your child ride her bike or play fetch with the dog—assuming, of course, that the doctor says it's okay. Remember: Even though she is sick, she is still a child and needs to be allowed to feel like one.

5. Acknowledge Your Child's Feelings.

Let your child know that it's okay to feel scared, sad, or even angry. If and when you notice his long face as he watches his brothers and sisters go out to play, let him know you understand. You might say, "It must be terrible to have to go to the hospital every week and get your treatments. And I know you don't like staying in the house. But you are sick and we must do everything we can to make you all better. Hopefully, you'll soon be able to go out and play just like your brothers and sisters."

6. Tell Your Child When You Are Coming and Going.

Children dealing with cancer, and particularly those staying at a cancer center for treatment, may be especially sensitive to any separations. It's a good idea, therefore, to let them know when you are coming and when you will be leaving. Keeping them informed helps them gain a sense of control and security at a very insecure time.

7. Overcome Your Own Taboos.

Children with cancer may have lots of questions about their illness. But if they sense that asking them gets you too upset, they might well keep their concerns to themselves, which can deny them the emotional support and information they need.

Try to get over your own taboos. Cancer is a subject that can and should be discussed openly with your ill child. No matter what the youngster's questions, he needs to hear clear, factual answers. And these may include questions about his own death.

If your child does raise questions about dying, don't answer too fast. First, try to find out what the child is really asking by saying, "Why are you asking me that today? Are you feeling worse?" or "It sounds like you are feeling upset today." Then, see what your child says. It may be that he is just looking for emotional support and encouragement and not a factual acknowledgment of whether or not he is going to die.

Interestingly, health-care professionals who regularly work with dying children say that children who are truly dying rarely pose the question "Am I going to die?" Instead, they seem to sense it, like the five-year-old who told his grandfather, "You know, Grandpa, I'm a lot sicker than I seem." He died twenty-four hours later. Or the six-year-old who, gently cradling her favorite teddy bear, confided to her mother, "Teddy told me he is going to die." She, too, passed away shortly.

But should your child actually raise the question, answer it sensitively and honestly. The most important messge to convey to your child is that he is safe, comfortable, and not alone. You can bring in your religious beliefs here and say something like "You are going to join Grandma and Grandpa in heaven. And that will be very nice. But until then, I will be with you all the time and we will all do whatever we can to make you comfortable. I love you very, very much." As one pediatric nurse at Sloan-Kettering told me, "When death is able to be discussed, when the subject is out in the open, children who are dying seem quite peaceful and serene."

Sample Questions and Answers

(If parent or sibling has cancer)

Q: How do you get cancer?

A: No one knows exactly how people get cancer. But we do know it's not anyone's fault. Nothing you did made Dad get cancer.

Q: Can I catch cancer?

A: No, you cannot catch cancer like you can catch a cold or the flu. Just because Dad [or brother Tony] got cancer doesn't mean that you or I will. We are both strong and healthy and we hope to stay that way.

Q: If Mommy has cancer and dies, who will take care of me?

A: First of all, just because Mom has cancer doesn't mean she will die. The doctors are treating her and doing all they can to make her well. But if she should die, then I will be here to take care of you because I intend to live for a very long time and because I love you very much.

Q: Does cancer hurt?

A: Sometimes cancer can hurt. But most of the time it's the treatment of cancer—the medicine that Mom takes to kill the cancer cells—that makes her feel sick. But we think that soon, Mom will feel better again.

(If child has cancer)

Q: Why did I get cancer?

A: No one knows why. But we do know that nothing you did made you get cancer and that you didn't catch it from anybody else. And the doctors are doing everything they can to make you feel well again.

Q: Will it hurt?

A: Well, some things may hurt for a very short time; a needle may hurt for just a few seconds. And some things will hurt for a longer time. But the doctors and the nurses and I will do whatever we can to help.

Q: Will I be able to go to school again?

A: We think so; most kids who get cancer can go back to school as soon as they are feeling a little better.

Q: Why do I have to take medicine even when I feel okay?

A: Well, even though you don't feel sick, inside your body you have these bad cells that are hurting your good cells. So you have to take medicine to kill these bad cells and make your body all well again.

Q: Will I ever get all well again?

A: We hope so. Most kids who get cancer do get well. And remember, all the doctors and nurses at the hospital are doing everything they can to make you better. And Daddy and I and your brothers and sisters are doing our best to help you get well again because we all love you very, very much.

Helpful Resources

ORGANIZATIONS

American Cancer Society
(Contact local chapter)
(800) ACS-2345

Cancer Care, Inc., and The National Cancer Care
Foundation
1180 Avenue of the Americas
New York, NY 10036
(212) 221-3300

Candlelighters Childhood Cancer Foundation
1312 18th Street, NW
Washington, DC 20036
(800) 366-2223

Leukemia Society of America
733 Third Ave.
New York, NY 10017
(800) 955-4LSA

National Cancer Institute
Office of Cancer Communications
Building 31, room 10-A24
Bethesda, MD 20892

National Childhood Grief Institute
300 Edinborough Way, suite 512
Minneapolis, MN 55435
(612) 832-9286

National Coalition for Cancer Survivorship (NCCS)
323 Eighth Street, SW
Albuquerque, NM 87102
(505) 764-9956

READINGS FOR PARENTS

(About cancer)

American Cancer Society. "Helping Children Understand: A Guide for a Parent with Cancer." New York: American Cancer Society, 1986.

Bombeck, Erma. *I Want to Grow Hair, I Want to Grow Up, I Want to Go to Boise.* New York: Harper & Row, 1989.

Bracken, Jeanne Munn. *Children With Cancer: A Comprehensive Reference Guide for Parents.* New York: Oxford University Press, 1986.

Chesler, Mark A. *Childhood Cancer and the Family: Meeting the Challenge of Stress and Support.* New York: Brunner/Mazel, 1987.

Johnson, Joy, and S.M. Johnson et al. *Why Mine? A Book for Parents Whose Child Is Seriously Ill.* Omaha, Nebr.: Centering Corp., 1981.

National Cancer Institute. "Talking With Your Child About Cancer." Bethesda, Md.: National Institutes of Health, 1986.

(About death)

Colgrove, Melba, Harold Bloomfield, Peter McWilliams. *How to Survive the Loss of Love.* New York: Bantam Books, 1977.

Grollman, Earl A. *Talking About Death: A Dialogue Between Parent and Child.* Boston: Beacon Press, 1976.

Kübler-Ross, Elisabeth. *On Death and Dying.* New York: Macmillan Publishing, 1969.

Kushner, Harold S. *When Bad Things Happen to Good People.* New York: Schocken Books, 1981.

La Tour, Kathy. *For Those Who Live: Helping Children Cope With the Death of a Brother or Sister.* Omaha, Nebr.: Centering Corp., 1987.

National Institute of Mental Health. "Caring About Kids: Talking to Children About Death." Rockville, Md.: U.S. Dept. of Health and Human Services, 1979. (Reprinted 1980).

Rogers, Fred. "Talking With Young Children About Death." Pittsburgh: Family Communications, Inc., 1979.

Schiff, Harriet Sarnoff. *The Bereaved Parent.* New York: Penguin Books, 1978.

Stein, S.B. *About Dying: An Open Family Book for Parents and Children Together.* New York: Walker, 1976.

Readings for Children

(About cancer)

Amadeo, Diana M. *There's a Little Bit of Me in Jamey.* Niles, Ill.: Albert Whitman & Co., 1989. (Ages 7–12)

Fine, Judylaine. *Afraid to Ask: A Book About Cancer.* New York: Lothrop, Lee & Shepard, 1986. (Ages 10 and up)

Gaes, Jason. *My Book for Kids With Cancer.* Aberdeen, S.D.: Melius/Peterson Publishing Corp., 1987. (Ages 5–11)

Krementz, Jill. *How It Feels to Fight for Your Life.* Boston: Little, Brown, 1989. (Ages 7–16)

Lancaster, Matthew. *Hang Tough.* New York: Paulist Press, 1983. (Ages 8–12)

Lindberg, Carol. "It Helps to Have Friends When Mom or Dad Has Cancer." Atlanta, Ga.: American Cancer Society, 1989. (Ages 7–12)

Silverstein, Alvin, and Virginia Silverstein. *Cancer.* New York: Harper & Row, 1977. (Ages 8 and up)

Swenson, Judy H., and Roxanne B. Kunz. *Cancer: The Whispered Word.* Minneapolis: Dillon, 1985. (Ages 7–12)

(About death)

Bernstein, Joanne E. *Loss: And How to Cope With It.* New York: Clarion, 1981. (Ages 10 and up)

Brown, Margaret Wise. *The Dead Bird.* New York: Young Scott Books, 1958. (Ages 4–8)

Fassler, Joan. *My Grandpa Died Today.* New York: Human Sciences Press, 1971. (Ages 5–8)

Keller, Holly. *Goodbye, Max.* New York: Greenwillow Books, 1987. (Ages 4–9)

Stiles, Norman. *I'll Miss You, Mr. Hooper.* New York: Random House/Children's Television Workshop, 1984. (Ages 3–6)

Thomas, J. R. *Saying Goodbye to Grandma.* New York: Clarion, 1988. (Ages 4–8)

Varley, Susan. *Badger's Parting Gifts.* New York: Lothrop, Lee & Shepard, 1984. (Ages 5–9)

Viorst, Judith. *The Tenth Good Thing About Barney.* New York: Atheneum, 1971. (Ages 4–8)

Vogel, Ilse-Margaret. *My Twin Sister Erika.* New York: Harper & Row, 1976. (Ages 5–8)

Special thanks to the following experts for their input into this chapter: Lisa Bard, C.S.W., clinical coordinator, children's services, Cancer Care, Inc.; Diane Blum, executive director, Cancer Care, Inc.; Allan Brenman, Ed.D., staff psychologist, Department of Child and Family Psychiatry, Rhode Island Hospital; Toni Cabat, assistant director, Department of Social Work, Memorial Sloan-Kettering Cancer Center; Genevieve V. Foley, RN, MSN, director of pediatric and surgical nursing, Memorial Sloan-Kettering Cancer Center; Gerry Koocher, Ph.D., chief of psychology, Children's Hospital (Boston) and Judge Baker Children's Center; Lynna Lesko, M.D., Ph.D., assistant attending psychiatrist, Memorial Sloan-Kettering Cancer Center; Shelley McKay, RN, nurse manager, pediatric in-patient unit, Memorial Sloan-Kettering Cancer Center; Ide Mills, CSW, pediatric oncology social work supervisor, Memorial Sloan-Kettering Cancer Center; Edy Nathan, psychotherapist; Dana Naughton, national program manager of Family Support Groups, Leukemia Society of America; Marc

Nemiroff, Ph.D., coordinator of children's programs at Woodburn Center for Community Mental Health; Robert Schacter, Ph.D., assistant professor in psychiatry at Columbia University College of Physicians and Surgeons and at Mt. Sinai School of Medicine; Yvonne Soghomonian, associate director for group liaison, Candlelighters Childhood Cancer Foundation; Morris Wessel, M.D., clinical professor of pediatrics, Yale School of Medicine; Marianne Wientzen, RN, nurse manager, pediatric day hospital, Memorial Sloan-Kettering Cancer Center.

Chapter Twelve

"MOMMY, I KNOW A BAD SECRET"

Talking with Your Child About Sexual Abuse

Four-year-old Kim sat on a kitchen stool quietly watching her mom prepare dinner. These days the normally chatty youngster seemed withdrawn, particularly on those afternoons when her fourteen-year-old baby-sitter, Danny, would pick her up at preschool and stay with her until Kim's mother returned from work. Kim's mom chalked up her daughter's uncharacteristic moodiness to "a phase" and didn't pay too much attention. But today, when Kim suddenly said, "Mommy, I know a bad secret. But I'm not supposed to tell," she took note. "You can always tell me," she said to the youngster, turning to look into her eyes. "Daughters can tell mommies anything." "Well," said Kim anxiously, "sometimes Danny shows me his pee-pee. And today I saw snow come out of it. He told me not to tell you. He said it was a secret. He said you would get really angry at me if I told. Are you angry, Mommy?"

Like most other parents who learn that their innocent young child has been sexually abused, Kim's mother was shocked—and deeply angered—by her daughter's revelation. It's hard for *any* caring adult to imagine how someone could take such brutal advantage of a child, but unfortunately, such outrages happen. Thousands of children are sexually abused* each year, many in their own homes. Ignoring that such a horrifying practice can occur—and/or assuming that your child is not vulnerable to it—does your youngster a terrible, and perhaps dangerous, disservice. To help insure your child's safety, and to give him or her the best chance to remain safe, secure, and happy, you need to stay informed about child sexual abuse and the factors that may put your child at risk.

The Issue in Focus

Retrospective studies of adult populations lead experts to believe that anywhere from one in three to one in four girls will be sexually abused by the time she turns eighteen. Male

---

*Child sexual abuse includes both "touching offenses" as fondling, oral, anal, and genital sex, and such "nontouching" offenses as exhibitionism, voyeurism, and child pornography.

victims of abuse number one in eight to one in ten. And here's another appalling statistic: The mean age of the victim is somewhere between six and nine. That means that little Julie is just one of thousands of youngsters under the age of six who are sexually abused each year.

The incidence of reported child sexual abuse has grown dramatically over the past decade. According to the most recent statistics from National Center on Child Abuse Prevention research, reported cases of child abuse climbed 147 percent between 1979 and 1989; sexual abuse accounts for some 15 to 16 percent of these reports.

Several factors have contributed to this increase. One is the rise in substance abuse, which has affected the level of violence in our society overall. Another is the changing structure of the family; more and more children are left in day care or out of the protective eye of their parents for long periods of time, leaving children more vulnerable to abuse. Mass media may also shoulder some of the blame, as sex and violence permeate TV, movies, and the print media. On the other hand, the media must be congratulated for getting the word out about child sexual abuse; it may well be that at least some of the apparent increase in *reports* of sexual abuse is due to heightened awareness of the problem.

Knowledge of these facts and figures is important when trying to understand sexual abuse. But what calls forth an even greater sense of urgency are the emotional repercussions of such actions. When a child is sexually abused, the impact reverberates throughout the entire family. In the short term, the victim often feels confused, fearful, embarrassed, shameful, and guilty that somehow he or she encouraged or at least permitted the abuse to take place. The child may be plagued by nightmares, become clingy or withdrawn, display regressive behavior, or act out her upset in school.

Long-term effects of abuse also vary, and can be particularly severe if the child has suffered repeated abuse over a long period of time. In *Too Scared to Cry,* Dr. Lenore Terr's powerful book on psychic trauma in childhood, she points out that the rage such abuse engenders can turn a child into either a cruel and abusive bully or an extremely passive "victim," perhaps for the rest of her life. Alternatively, says Dr. Terr, such ongoing abuse can render a child unable to tolerate any frustration even in adulthood; when frustrated, the victim may well fly into a "wild rage" or engage in a "self-destructive spree."

Other research suggests that long-term effects of sexual abuse often depend upon gender. While both female and male victims suffer problems with self-esteem and intimacy, sexually abused women tend to suffer from chronic depression and to view the world as an unsafe place in which they remain vulnerable. They may become promiscuous and highly manipulative in an effort to control their relationships with others, particularly men. Men who were abused as children tend to exhibit a more angry kind of acting out; they may be more physically abusive of others, and become dependent upon drugs and alcohol in a misguided effort to manage their rioting feelings.

Parents of an abused child also feel a strong sense of shame. If a father or other family member has been the abuser, the mother may feel intense anger, anguish, and guilt over not protecting her child sufficiently. Even siblings suffer when a child is abused. If the abuser is a parent, brothers and sisters often feel angry at both the abuser and the victim for breaking up the family. Siblings also may feel ashamed, confused, or guilty, particularly if they themselves have been maltreated by the abuser and kept it a secret.

Clearly, a one-time abusive occurrence is a lot less likely to cause long-term psychological damage than repeated sexual abuse, especially when perpetrated by a family member. But too often the sexual abuse goes on for a long period of time, sometimes years. And in some 80 percent of the cases, the abuser *is* either a family member—42 percent of the time, the perpetrator is a parent; 22.8 percent of the time, another relative*—or friend, baby-sitter, neighbor, or someone else the young victim knows well and trusts.

Most often abusers are men, although women can and do abuse children as well. Despite the prevailing myth of the "dirty old man," perpetrators cut across all ages: pre-teenagers and grandparents can and have sexually abused young children. Another myth dispelled: rather than using force on their victims, abusers most often manipulate their subjects into compliance, first by gaining their trust—"Let's play a game of tickle" or "Come sit on my lap and I'll give you a special hug"—and then by gradually progressing toward more sexually aggressive acts. Abusers often warn the child that these "friendly encounters" are secret and that if the youngster tells, there will be dire consequences—"Mommy won't love you anymore if you tell her."

What's more, abusers exist in all walks of life; they know no economic, race, or religious boundaries. In short, no parent can afford the luxury of believing that his or her

*Percentage breakdowns for family members/abusers are from the American Association for Protecting Children, a division of the American Humane Association.

child is totally immune from the outrage of child sexual abuse.

The good news, however, is that prevention programs, which include learning how to talk to your own children about sexual abuse, seem to be working. According to a fifty-state survey by the National Committee for Prevention of Child Abuse, Hawaii has seen a 30 percent decline in reported incidences of sexual abuse, thanks to rigorous public and private prevention programs. In this chapter I'll be focusing primarily on talking to your kids about preventing sexual abuse, since early parental intervention seems to do the most good. Toward the end of the chapter, however, I also will discuss both how to tell if your child has been abused and what you as a parent can do about it.

How to Talk with Your Child About Preventing Sexual Abuse

1. Talk About Sex Comfortably.

Talks about sex can begin very early in your child's life; even a toddler can be told the names of body parts. Certainly two-year-olds begin to understand the physical differences between girls and boys. If your child hasn't asked any questions about sex by about age five or six, however, it's time for you to bring it up. Start out with the most basic of explanations—the differences between boys and girls and how it takes both a man and a woman (or a mommy and a daddy) to make a baby—and take cues from your child as to when he's ready for more. (See the Readings for Parents section at the end of this chapter for some good, basic books on discussing the facts of life with your child.)

No matter when you begin educating your youngster about sex, however, strive to adopt a relaxed attitude. Using the words "penis" or "vagina" as comfortably as you would the word "shoulder" and answering your child's questions simply and honestly no matter how direct they are lets your child know that you are willing and able to talk about sexual matters. It also tells her that she need never be ashamed or embarrassed to come to you with her sexual questions—or problems—no matter what they may be.

Although some experts disagree, I also think it's okay to use family names for body parts. I don't see the necessity for it, but I don't think it can do any harm, as long as at some point you also tell your youngster the real names for his sexual organs. What *is* important, at least in terms of preventing sexual abuse, is giving your child the vocabulary he might need to tell you if and how someone is sexually mistreating him.

2. Take the Initiative.

Most kids will raise their sexual questions a lot sooner than parents feel "ready" to answer them. But few children, particularly those under the age of seven or eight, will ask about how they can prevent sexual abuse. Since the average age of child victims is somewhere between six and nine, it is important for parents to initiate discussion at a very early age. You can use an appropriate moment—a TV commercial or program involving sexual abuse, for instance—to raise the issue, or, as I will explain in a moment, discuss it in the context of your child's privacy and safety. The point is to go on the offensive in teaching your children about sexual abuse; if you don't, it may be too late to protect them.

3. Include Prevention Messages in Talks About Privacy.

Talking to your child about privacy issues offers an ideal framework in which to discuss sexual abuse prevention. Even a child as young as four can begin learning that when the door to the bathroom, bedroom, den, or home office is shut, it means that the person inside wants to be alone and that you should knock to get his or her permission before entering. Simply explain, "When a door is closed, it usually means that the person inside wants some privacy—that he doesn't want to be disturbed. So you have to ask the person if you can come in. That's why when you close your door, I always knock before I come in, because I respect your privacy."

In this context, a child can better understand that certain parts of the body—the penis, vagina, buttocks, and breasts—are private, too. When you're helping your four- or five-year-old with her bath, you can say, "You know, your vagina and your buttocks are private parts. That's why when you go swimming at the lake, you wear a bathing suit. The suit covers your private parts so that nobody else can see them. They are yours and they are private."

Parents also need to demonstrate to children that there are boundaries and limits to acceptable public behavior. Of course, one of the best ways to demonstrate suitable boundaries is to set a good example. While parents should feel free to show their affection for each other by holding hands or exchanging a few brief hugs and kisses in front of the children, they should not engage in sexually explicit behavior within the child's view. Such behavior can confuse and frighten youngsters and shows a lack of respect for the boundaries between what is personal and private behavior and what is not.

4. Talk About General Safety.

Prevention tactics also can be worked into a conversation about general safety. Suppose, for instance, you are taking your five-year-old to the mall. You can say, "Now remember, there are lots of strangers at the mall, and I want you to hold on to my hand so you won't get lost among them. Do you know what a stranger is?"

Most four- to six-year-olds will answer that "a stranger is a bad guy" to which you can respond by saying, "No, a stranger doesn't have to be a bad guy. A stranger is just someone you don't know. You should not talk to a stranger unless Mommy or Daddy is right there with you."

Here's another example. Suppose you're going to drop your nine-year-old off for a first visit at a new friend's house. Beforehand you could say, "I'm going to drop you off at Janie's house after school today, and I'll pick you up at five o'clock. Here's the telephone number where I'll be. Call me if for any reason you want me to pick you up earlier. If anybody else offers to drive you home, just say no, thank you, that Mommy's coming to pick you up. If you're not sure what to do, call me. Okay?"

Angela Marshall is a prevention specialist at the League Against Child Abuse in Ohio. She recommends reinforcing these safety lessons by role-playing with your child. For instance, while sharing an after-school snack with your eight-year-old, you might say, "Let's use our imaginations. Suppose you were at a friend's house after school and her big brother asked you to come into his room and take your

skirt off. What would you do?" Then listen to your child's
explanation. If it is fine, say, "That's great! You know exactly how to handle things. I'm very proud of you." But if
she doesn't seem to know what to do, you could say, "If
that were to happen, you need to try and get away. Just tell
him in a big, loud, important voice, 'No, I don't want to do
that! We don't do that in our family. I'm leaving!' and get
away from him. Then come home as soon as you can and
tell me about it."

5. Don't Overemphasize Strangers.

While it is certainly important to explain what a stranger
is and to emphasize that your children should never accept
gifts or candy or get into a car with someone they don't
know, don't limit discussions to warnings about outsiders.
Most child sexual abusers are people the child knows well,
such as family members, family friends, neighbors, baby-
sitters, and child-care workers. It may be difficult to do, but
you need to explain to your child that *nobody*, not even
someone she knows very well, not even a relative or a
parent she loves, has a right to touch her where she
shouldn't be touched.

You can say something like "Sometimes, even people
you know, like an uncle or aunt or baby-sitter—maybe even
some daddies and mommies—have a problem and want to
touch your private parts. Or they may ask you to touch their
private parts. But even if you know the person very well,
you don't *ever* have to let anyone touch you that way, or let
anyone make you touch them. Now, if you have a rash or
sore on your private parts, sometimes Mommy or Daddy or
the doctor has to touch you there to put medication or
powder on you, and that's okay. But otherwise, nobody

needs to touch you in those private places and you can always say no."

6. Give Your Child Permission to Say No.

If your child is at least two years old, teaching him to say no may seem a little superfluous, since most kids are willing and able to say no frequently and without any coaxing from parents. That kind of naysaying is normal, a part of the developmental process in which youngsters are learning that they are individuals, separate from Mom and Dad.

But the way in which you respond to those "no's" is what's most important, because it can help give your child a sense of empowerment and self-esteem. Remember, the children most at risk for sexual abuse are those who do not have a strong sense of their own power and worth. They have been taught not to speak out if something bothers them and to try to please others, despite the cost to themselves. Abusers are much less likely to try to manipulate a psychologically strong child with a solid sense of self-esteem than they are a vulnerable, needy youngster who will comply readily with their wishes.

Here's a simple example of how you can give your child permission to say no. Suppose it's lunchtime and you ask your youngster, "Would you like tuna fish for lunch? It has lots of protein that's good for your body," but your child says, "No. I hate tuna fish." Well, don't fight him. Instead, you can say, "Okay, you don't want tuna fish. Then the choices are peanut butter and jelly or grilled cheese. Take your pick."

Allowing your child to say no—while still maintaining your parental role—tells your youngster that he is a real, solid, important little person whose feelings have validity and power. Offering your child a reason why he needs to do something you ask of him, and giving him the opportunity to think for himself, rather than demanding unquestioning obedience, lets your child know that adult authority can be questioned.

7. Define Touch Along a Safety Continuum.

Abuse-prevention specialists have found that one of the best ways you can help young kids protect themselves against sexual abuse is to explain the difference between various kinds of touching. Find a relaxed, comfortable moment when you can sit and talk with your child, even if she is only four (or younger), and say something like "You know, there are all kinds of touches in this world. Some make you feel good, some make you feel bad, and some can make you feel confused." Then, ask your child if she can think of examples of each. Usually, kids answer "hugs" and "kisses" for good touches, and "punches" or "hitting" for bad touches, and "beard rubs" and "cheek pinching" for confusing touches that don't exactly hurt but don't feel good, either.

Then, either in this conversation or one that takes place a day or two later, you need to explain that everybody, even children, can decide if they want to be touched in any way. Stress that children can say no to *anybody* who touches them in a confusing or bad way—that is, in a way that makes them feel confused, scared, unsafe, or just uncomfortable. Finally, you can sum up by saying, "No one has the right to touch you if you don't want them to. So if someone tries, just say no."

8. Never Force Children to Express Physical Affection.

Teaching children the difference between various kinds of touches and encouraging them to refuse to be touched in ways that make them feel hurt or uneasy won't work in a vacuum. You've got to demonstrate that when they say no, you, an adult, will respect their wishes. And that can be done simply by not pressuring your child to express physical affection. When Aunt Annie comes for a visit, don't push your youngster to give her a welcoming kiss unless he wants to. If your child doesn't want Uncle Dave to tickle her or toss her in the air, let her know it's okay to refuse. Respecting your child's right to govern his or her own body teaches them a critical lesson in self-protection.

9. Explain the Difference Between Good and Bad Secrets.

Because most abusers are highly manipulative, and frequently tell their victim that "what we are doing is a special secret, just between you and me," some child-rearing experts believe that you should teach your children *never* to keep any secrets from you. But I feel that such advice goes a bit too far, because some confidences—like Daddy's surprise birthday party—are not only harmless, but fun to keep. So instead of making secrets completely verboten, try helping your child discriminate between good and bad ones. Just say something like "Do you know what a good secret is? It's something that is fun to keep, like the time it was Daddy's birthday and we kept his surprise party a secret for a whole week. But there are lots of bad secrets, too."

If your child is around five, you might continue with: "A bad secret is not telling Mommy about something that hurts you or makes you feel bad, like the time you fell off the swing at Amanda's house and didn't tell Mommy and you got a big headache that night." To a ten-year-old you might explain, "A bad secret is one that makes you sad, uneasy, or frightened, like the time you tried to hide your F in math on your last report card. You should always come and tell Mommy about any bad secrets. Even if someone tells you not to tell, you can still come and tell Mommy. Nothing you tell me could ever make me stop loving you. I love you very, very much and I always will."

10. Identify "Safe" Adults.

Sometimes you may not be around when your child needs help. Or your youngster may not feel comfortable telling you about a particular situation (for instance, that her father molested her). As hard as it may be to accept, it's your job to offer your children other safe adults to whom they can turn for help.

Sally Cooper, the executive director of the National Assault Prevention Center, finds that brainstorming with your child about adults they can talk with in any given situation is extremely helpful. You can say, "Suppose something happened at Bobby's house that you didn't like. Who could you tell?" Then help your child to identify Bobby's mother or another person you know who would listen to your child. Or you can be less specific and say something like "Suppose someone did something that made you feel frightened and confused; who could you tell?" Most kids will automatically say "Mom or Dad," to which you can respond, "Well, that's true. But suppose we weren't around, who else could you tell?" Then help your child construct a mental list of reliable people, from his teacher to the rabbi to Aunt Sue. The objective here is to let your child know that she never has to contend with a difficult situation all by herself.

11. Plan a Series of Talks.

Teaching kids all they need to know to protect themselves from sexual abuse takes many, many little discussions. That's because children "dose themselves"; that is, they take in only as much information as they are ready to absorb at any given time. So be patient and repeat safety rules over and over again until they become second nature to your kids. Only then will your children be sufficiently prepared to protect themselves.

How to Tell If Your Child Has Been Abused

As unnerving as the thought may be, parents need to be vigilant when it comes to sexual abuse. Any one (or a combination) of the following signs may indicate that your child is a victim:

• Pain, redness, itching, bleeding, or bruises in genital or anal areas.

• Spontaneous statements made by your child. I learned of a five-year-old girl who was eating mussels at a restaurant with her mom when she said, "Mommy, these mussels feel like Daddy's pee-pee in my mouth." That was this mom's first indication that her husband was abusing their child.

• Precocious sex play or talk. Children are sexual creatures who, depending on their stage of development, show various levels of interest in sex. Four-year-olds may engage in a game of "show" and display curiosity about different bathroom activities. Five-year-olds (and even younger kids) often become modest about showing their bodies in public, and six- and seven-year-olds frequently engage in investigative sex play such as "doctor." Kids eight to eleven find "dirty" jokes and bathroom humor hilarious, and may giggle and evince curiosity over love scenes on TV or in the movies.

All of these behaviors are perfectly appropriate for normal, healthy children. Victims of abuse, however, may engage in *precocious* sex play; for instance, a four-year-old who, when playing with her dolls, makes them copulate or perform fellatio, or an eight-year-old who asks explicit questions about anal or oral sex, is exhibiting behavior far beyond what is appropriate for that age child. Additionally, kids who are sexually aggressive with other youngsters, or who repeatedly draw sexually graphic pictures, also may be victims of sexual abuse.

• Infantile or regressive behavior. Children who are being sexually abused often become clingy and babyish in their actions, and regress to previously outgrown behaviors, such as bed-wetting or thumb-sucking. They may also withdraw from playing physical games or sports with friends.

• Uncharacteristic fearfulness. A child who suddenly starts crying or acting fearful over the prospect of spending time with a once-adored baby-sitter or relative may be telling you something about what is going on between the youngster and that caretaker.

• Secretiveness or vigilance. If your child begins to evade conversations and questions and/or becomes extremely watchful when in the company of adults, it may indicate that he is being sexually victimized. As Leona Tockey, a trainer for Parents United, a guided self-help group for sexually abused families, explained to me, "Children sense that abuse is a secret, or they have been told by their abuser not to tell. So they tend to become secretive and vigilant around other adults as they work hard to keep their secret."

• Any other sudden changes in mood or actions. Children under stress often will suddenly behave in uncharacteristic ways. A normally cheerful, outgoing child might become sullen and withdrawn; an excellent student may suffer a sudden drop in grades; a well-behaved child could begin fighting or disobeying parents or teachers; or a usually healthy child might complain of stomachaches or headaches.

While the above red flags often signal that a child is being sexually abused, they may also occur in nonabusive situations. So you need to strike a delicate balance: stay open to and alert for any signals of abuse, but try not to jump to any conclusions.

What to Do If You Suspect Your Child Has Been Abused

1. Believe Your Child.

If your child makes a spontaneous comment that suggests she is being abused—"I held Uncle Steve's penis, Mommy"—believe her. Children rarely make up such statements; they need to be taken seriously. What's more, therapist Tockey points out, "One of the most traumatizing things about sexual abuse occurs when the child finally tells the secret and is not believed. This discounts the child's experience and her perception of reality, and that alone can be extremely upsetting."

2. Reassure Your Child.

If your child tells you about some abuse, assure him that he was right to tell you and let him know that he will be safe. You can say, "I know it must have been hard to tell me that, but I am so glad that you did. You are a very smart and brave boy and you were right to tell. Now we can look into the problem and make sure that no one hurts you anymore. I love you very much."

3. Stay Calm.

Any parent who discovers that her child has been sexually abused can be overwhelmed by anger, fear, and disgust. It's perfectly natural to feel this way, but it's also important to stay as calm as possible in front of your child. If your youngster sees you distraught, she may begin to blame herself for making you so upset. So try hard to remain unruffled.

4. Seek Professional Help.

If you suspect your child has been abused, take her to a pediatrician for a medical examination immediately. This may help to confirm your suspicions. You also need to contact a mental health professional who will evaluate your child to determine if she was mentally abused and recommend the best way to minimize any traumatic effects. Ask your pediatrician for the name of a professional who is skilled in this area, or get a referral from your local medical, psychological, or psychiatric society; you can also contact the organizations listed at the end of this chapter. The mental health expert will contact your local child protective services agency to report the abuse, or you can contact the agency yourself and the professionals there will help to direct you to the proper resources.

5. Assure Your Child It Wasn't Her Fault.

A child is *never* at fault when she has been sexually abused. *Never.* Although the abuser might claim that "she wanted it; she enjoyed it" and thus the perpetrator couldn't help himself, don't believe it. Even if a tiny part of you is angry at the child for allowing this to happen, know that your youngster, not the abuser, is the victim here. And convey this certainty to your child. As calmly as possible explain that "what Daddy [in the case of incest] did to you was very bad. He has a problem and we are going to try to get him some help. I'm very sorry this happened to you and I want you to know that you did nothing wrong. You're a wonderful little girl and I love you very much."

Sample Questions and Answers

Q: Why do people try to hurt children?

A: People who try to hurt or molest children have a big problem. They need to get help. But the only way they can get help is if the children tell somebody what is happening. If anyone ever does anything that hurts you or makes you feel uncomfortable, you should tell Mommy or Daddy [or another trustworthy adult] right away.

Q: Is it okay to tell a secret?

A: Yes. When a secret is a bad secret—when it makes you feel hurt or angry or confused or sad—then you should tell someone. It's usually best to tell Mom or Dad, but you can also tell Grandma or Aunt Sally or even your teacher, Mrs. Jackson. You'll never get in trouble for telling a bad secret.

Q: What are my private parts?

A: Well, your private parts are your vagina, breasts [penis, testicles], and buttocks. That's why we cover them up whenever we go out in public; even when we swim, we wear a bathing suit. Sometimes Mommy [or Daddy] has to touch them so she can help you get clean when she helps you take a bath. And sometimes the doctor has to touch them when he examines you, but Mommy will always be in the room when the doctor examines you. Other than that, no one is allowed to touch your private parts if you don't want them to. They are yours and they are private.

Q: You told me never to get into a car with a stranger. But what if you tell someone I don't know to pick me up at school because you or Daddy can't?

A: Mommy and Daddy would never tell someone you don't know to pick you up. So if a stranger tells you that Mommy or Daddy said it was okay, don't believe them. Just run to your teacher or your principal and tell her what happened. Never get into a car with anyone you don't know.

Q: What if I'm wrestling or playing with a friend and by accident his arm brushes up against my private parts or I brush up against his?

A: There may be lots of times when someone accidentally brushes up against your private parts. It's just an accident and that's okay. But if your friend says, "Let's pull down our pants and show each other our parts," then you should say, "No, I don't want to do that. Let's play another game instead."

Helpful Resources

ORGANIZATIONS

Childhelp
Box 630
Hollywood, CA 90028
Childhelp's National Child Abuse Hotline:
(800) 422-4453

Children's Rights of America, Inc.
12551 Indian Rocks Road, suite 9
Largo, FL 34644
(813) 593-0090 (for information)
(800) 874-1111 (to report abuse)

The Clearinghouse on Child Abuse and Neglect
Information
P.O. Box 1182
Washington, DC 20013
(203) 821-2086

National Assault Prevention Center and Child Assault
Prevention Project
P.O. Box 02005
Columbus, OH 43202
(614) 291-2540

National Center for Missing and Exploited Children
2101 Wilson Boulevard, suite 550
Arlington, VA 22201

National Committee for Prevention of Child Abuse
P.O. Box 2866
Chicago, IL 60690
(312) 663-3520

The National Exchange Club Foundation for the
Prevention of Child Abuse
3050 Central Avenue
Toledo, OH 43606
(419) 535-3232

National Organization for Victim Assistance
1757 Park Road, NW
Washington, D.C. 20010-2101
(202) 232-6682

READINGS FOR PARENTS

Adams, Karen, and Jennifer Fay. *No More Secrets*. San Luis
    Obispo, Calif.: Impact Publishers, 1981.
Benedict, Helen. *Safe, Strong and Streetwise*. Boston: Little,
    Brown, 1987.
Calderone, Mary, and J. Ramey. *Talking With Your Child
    About Sex: Questions and Answers for Children from Birth to
    Puberty*. New York: Ballantine, 1982.
"Childhelp Information Guide," 2d ed. Woodland Hills,
    Calif.: Childhelp USA, 1991.

"Common Sense Information for Parents of Young Children," 2d ed. Columbus, Ohio: Action for Children, 1985.

Crewdson, John. *By Silence Betrayed: Sexual Abuse of Children in America.* Boston: Little, Brown, 1988.

Crowley, Patricia. *Not My Child: A Mother Confronts Her Child's Sexual Abuse.* New York: Avon Books, 1990.

Dziech, Billie Wright, and Judge Charles Schudson. *On Trial: America's Courts and Their Treatment of Sexually Abused Children.* Boston: Beacon Press, 1989.

Hagans, Kathryn, and Joyce Case. *When Your Child Has Been Molested: A Parent's Guide to Healing and Recovery.* Lexington, Mass.: Lexington Books, 1988.

Hart-Rossi, Janie. *Protect Your Child from Sexual Abuse: A Parent's Guide.* Seattle: Parenting Press, 1984.

Hillman, Donald, and Janice Solek-Tefft. *Spiders and Flies: Help for Parents and Teachers of Sexually Abused Children.* Lexington, Mass.: Lexington Books, 1988.

Sanford, Linda. *Come Tell Me Right Away.* Fayetteville, N.C.: Ed-U Press, 1982.

———. *The Silent Children.* Garden City, N.Y.: Anchor Press, 1980.

Terr, Lenore. *Too Scared to Cry: Psychic Trauma in Childhood.* New York: Harper & Row, 1990.

Townley, Roderick. *Safe and Sound: A Parent's Guide to Child Protection.* New York: Simon & Schuster, 1985.

Webster, Linda, ed. *Sexual Assault and Child Sexual Abuse: A National Directory of Victim Services and Prevention.* Phoenix: Oryx Press, 1989.

READINGS FOR CHILDREN

Aho, Jennifer Sowle, and John W. Petras. *Learning About Sexual Abuse.* Hillside, N.J.: Enslow Publishers, Inc., 1985. (Ages 10 and up)

Bassett, Kerry. *My Very Own Special Body Book.* Redding, Calif.: Hawthorne Press, 1982. (Ages 5–9)

Freeman, Lory. *It's My Body.* Seattle: Parenting Press, 1982. (Ages 3–6)

Girard, Linda Walvoord. *My Body Is Private.* Niles, Ill.: Albert Whitman & Co., 1984. (Ages 6–10)

Gordon, Sol, and Judith Gordon. *Did the Sun Shine Before You Were Born?* Fayetteville, N.C.: Ed-U Press, 1982. (Up to age 6)

——————. *A Better Safe Than Sorry Book: A Family Guide for Sexual Assault Prevention.* Fayetteville, N.C.: Ed-U Press, 1984. (Ages 6–11)

Johnsen, Karen. *The Trouble with Secrets.* Seattle: Parenting Press, 1986. (Ages 4–10)

Spider-Man & Power Pack Child Sexual Abuse Prevention Comic Books. Chicago: National Committee for the Prevention of Child Abuse, in conjunction with Marvel Comics, 1984. (Ages 8–11)

Sweet, Phyllis. *Something Happened to Me.* Racine, Wis.: Mother Courage Press, 1981. (Ages 4–7)

Wachter, Oralee. *No More Secrets for Me.* Boston: Little, Brown, 1984. (Ages 4–11)

Special thanks to the following experts for their input into this chapter: Cordelia Anderson, director of Illusion Theatre's Prevention Program; Sally Cooper, executive director, the National Assault Prevention Center; Arthur Green, M.D., medical director, The Family Center and Therapeutic Nursery of Presbyterian Hospital, and clinical professor of psychiatry, Columbia University College of Physicians and Surgeons; Hecht Lacky, Ph.D., director of psychological services, Fairfax Hospital; Angela Marshall, prevention specialist, League Against Child Abuse; Diane Schetky, M.D., child and adolescent psychiatrist; Leona Tockey, primary trainer, Parents United.

Chapter 13

"DADDY, AM I GAY?"

Talking with Your Child About
Homosexuality

Instead of bursting though the front door, shouting "I'm home!" and wolfing down a fistful of Oreos, today nine-year-old Brian went immediately to his room after school and quietly shut the door. Something was up, surmised Brian's dad, but the problem didn't surface until dinnertime. "Dad," said Brian, "David and Teddy were fooling around in gym today, and David called Ted gay. Coach Simmons got really mad and told them to cut it out. He said that gay means when men love each other and that Ted wasn't gay. But the thing is," Brian said, his voice quavering, "I *really* like lots of guys—I mean Christopher's a guy and he's my best friend. Does that mean I'm gay?"

The careless, pejorative and, sometimes homophobic way in which many people in our society use the term "gay" leads to a good deal of confusion and concern in parents and kids alike. In the above scenario, young Brian became quite anxious because he felt that he might be homosexual. Brian's dad also felt uncomfortable, not so much because he was worried that his son might be gay—although he did feel a tug of anxiety—but because he felt so awkward and uneasy with the subject. Should he explain homosexuality to his young son? Could talking about it prompt Brian to experiment with homosexual behavior? Should he simply reassure the youngster that he was not gay and dismiss any further discussion?

Most parents feel a little uneasy talking about sexuality with their young children, but when it comes to homosexuality, the going gets even rougher. The reasons for their discomfort vary. Some feel that homosexuality is deviant, immoral behavior and that to discuss it with their kids is to convey the message that they condone it. Others feel unclear about their own feelings toward homosexuality and thus don't know what they would say to their kids should any discussion arise. Still others, like Brian's father, believe that homosexuals are normal, healthy adults whose only difference from heterosexual individuals is their sexual orientation; even so, these parents worry that homosexuality is too complex and confusing a subject for young children to understand.

No matter where you fit in, one thing is certain: Homosexuality is an issue with which contemporary parents need to deal. The media's references to and depiction of gay lifestyles and issues have brought the terms "homosexual" and "gay" into young children's awareness. Since youngsters are already hearing about homosexuality, it's best that you, the parents, be the ones to explain it. That way you can put homosexuality into the context with which you feel most comfortable.

Another reason parents need to discuss homosexuality with their kids is that many children now have relatives or family friends who are openly lesbian or gay. To insure that these youngsters can accept homosexuals in their lives and feel at ease with them, they need to understand, at a level appropriate to their cognitive and emotional development, what homosexuality means.

But perhaps the most important and sensitive reason parents need to talk about homosexuality is this: Since it is difficult to ascertain whether your child will be homosexual until adolescence, when his/her sexual orientation usually becomes clear, it is essential for the development of your child's self-esteem that you let him/her know that it is okay to discuss all aspects of sexuality in your home. As child and adolescent psychiatrist Dennis Anderson explained to me, "Kids hear about homosexuals in almost exclusively pejorative ways. Imagine what it's like for an adolescent who, throughout his childhood, has heard that homosexuals are horrible, immoral 'fags'—then one day he has to say to himself, 'Oh my God. That's me!' "

This brings up a host of questions surrounding homosexuality: What determines sexual orientation? Are people born gay? If my son likes to play with dolls, or play with my makeup, will he be gay? If my daughter refuses to wear dresses, will she be a lesbian? Is it my fault if my child becomes gay? To answer these and other such queries, we need to examine the issue of homosexuality in greater detail.

The Issue in Focus

Homosexuals are people who have an emotional and sexual attraction to individuals of the same sex. Homosexual men are often referred to as "gay," but many homosexuals prefer to reserve that term for those who live an openly homosexual life-style rather than to describe a sexual orientation. Homosexual women are often called lesbians after the Greek island of Lesbos, home of Sappho, whose poetry spoke of love between women. Various studies, including those carried out by the Kinsey Institute, reveal that approximately 10 percent of the male U.S. population is homosexual; numbers are not available for female homosexuals, though estimates range from 5 to 10 percent. (NOTE: Kinsey research shows that sexual behavior exists on a continuum, with exclusive heterosexuality at one end, exclusive homosexuality at the other, and many variations in between. The 10 percent figure, however, refers to that percentage of the population that has lived an exclusively homosexual life-style for a number of years.)

What determines homosexuality—or heterosexuality, for that matter? This simple question stirs so much controversy that even the experts can't agree. In fact, when a major association of mental health professionals asked five hundred of its members to pinpoint that stage in an individual's life at which sexual orientation becomes "irreversible," it found no consensus. Many scientists believe that an individual's sexual orientation is determined at birth. That is, that your hormonal and/or chemical makeup determines whether or not you will be homosexual or heterosexual. Some even believe that sexual orientation is inherited, though studies suggesting this concept have not, to my knowledge, been replicated.

Others assert that homosexuality is determined by an individual's environment and, most specifically, by his relationship with his parents. At the risk of oversimplification, the basic thinking is that boys with an overbearing mother and a distant and/or passive father are not permitted to properly resolve their Oedipal conflict. The boy therefore identifies more with his mother than his father and becomes a homosexual. (Opponents of this philosophy, however, point out that while many homosexual men do have domineering mothers and passive fathers, so do many heterosexual men.)

The most recent thinking is that whatever the origins of homosexuality, a child's predisposition toward sexual orientation, either homosexual or heterosexual, seems to appear at a very early age—as young as five or six. And while proponents of this theory may not believe that parents can change their children's sexual orientation, they believe moms and dads can influence how comfortably their kids accept that orientation and integrate it into a healthy and positive life-style once they reach young adulthood.

But here's what I think is most important: Whatever the theories posit, the fact is that many people, some of them friends or members of our families, are homosexual. And as with any group of people, they deserve our understanding and respect.

With this in mind, then, let's erase a few common misconceptions:

• *Myth:* All homosexuals engage in irresponsible sex.

• *Fact:* Because AIDS has hit the homosexual population so hard, the myth of the irresponsible, promiscuous homosexual has found increased popularity. But the fact is that while some homosexuals do engage in irresponsible sex, so do some heterosexuals. Sexual orientation has little to do with a sense of morality or responsibility.

• *Myth:* All gays are deviant or maladjusted.

• *Fact:* This myth was fueled by early studies that showed homosexual men to be psychologically and psychosocially maladjusted. A closer look at the research, however, shows that the studies' subjects were homosexuals who were in prison or under treatment for psychiatric problems; thus, any conclusions regarding homosexuals' psychological health are spurious, to say the least.

More recent research reveals that homosexual populations contain no more and no fewer deviant or poorly adjusted individuals than heterosexual ones. Further, in 1973 the well-respected American Psychiatric Association deleted homosexuality from its official listing of mental disorders. Two years later, the American Psychological Association asked its membership also to help "remove the stigma of mental illness" from homosexuality.

• *Myth:* Young boys can be "recruited" or "seduced" into homosexuality by homosexual adults.

• *Fact:* Research by the Kinsey Institute and others has offered no evidence whatsoever that boys can be "turned into" homosexuals via sexual encounters, or that homosexuality is in any way "contagious." Nor does evidence exist to support the belief that homosexual adult males are any more attracted to or interested in seducing young boys than heterosexuals are young girls. Actually, the overwhelming amount of child molestation occurs between adult males and young females.

• *Myth:* People choose to become homosexuals and can choose to "undo" their homosexuality.

• *Fact:* Current opinion suggests that an individual's sexual orientation is not a matter of choice: persons do not *choose* to be homosexuals and cannot "refuse" to accept their orientation. Homosexuals can, however, choose not to engage in sexual activity with members of their own sex. Thousands of admittedly homosexual men do marry women; some even live exclusively heterosexual lives, at least for some time. But research indicates that most attempts to deny one's sexual orientation completely, both publicly and privately, not only don't work but fail to lead to long-term happiness and fulfillment.

• *Myth:* You can tell if someone is homosexual without knowing who their sexual partners are.

• *Fact:* When Bell and Weinberg of the Kinsey Institute for Sex Research interviewed approximately fifteen hundred homosexual men, they found that most homosexuals "are indistinguishable from the heterosexual majority with respect to most of the nonsexual aspects of their lives. . . ." (For more information on this study, see the Readings for Parents section at the end of this chapter.)

Often parents, and especially fathers whose sons seem to prefer such "sissy" behavior (at least, in their fathers' eyes) as playing with dolls, drawing, or helping out in the kitchen to participating in sports or any other rough-and-tumble play, worry that their child is going to become a homosexual. So they try to turn their sons into "men" by insisting that they get involved in more aggressive activities while denigrating the more "gentle" pastimes the child genuinely favors.

Not only are such parental efforts futile—you can't force a child to like activities he simply does not like, and even if you could, it would not change his eventual sexual orientation—but they can have harmful consequences for your youngster's emotional health. At the very least, denying your child's individuality as expressed by his activity preferences can alienate your youngster from you. Even if he goes along with your wishes and starts participating in the kinds of activities you approve of, he won't like them and his resentment toward you will grow.

Even more disturbing is the possibility that your child, knowing that you don't approve of who he is, will develop self-hatred. After all, if his own parent doesn't like him, why should he like himself? During adolescence, the time when a youngster may identify himself as homosexual, he might even feel enough self-loathing brought on by your disapproval and societal homophobia to take his own life. According to a paper presented to the National Institute of Mental Health and reported on by the Sexual Minority Youth Assistance League, lesbian and gay youth are two to three times more likely to attempt suicide than their heterosexual counterparts.

If your child withdraws from rough-and-tumble play to such an extent that he gets teased by his peers, you may want to intervene; we'll explore how to do this later. But for now, suffice it to say that parents who try to force their sons to "be a man" may be doing much more harm than they ever realized.

How to Talk with Your Child About Homosexuality

1. Get Yourself Comfortable with the Topic.

Homosexuality is one of those topics that makes many an adult squirm. So before you broach the subject with your youngster, try to become comfortable with the issue yourself. Peruse a few of the books I recommend at the end of this chapter—particularly the ones on sexuality in general—so that you're at ease with your own feelings. Remember, if you are homophobic, or so uneasy with the entire issue of homosexuality that you simply can't discuss it, your youngster may pick up on that and keep his questions—and concerns—to himself.

2. Bring It Out in the Open.

Talking about homosexuality will not increase your child's chances of becoming gay. But refusing to discuss it conveys the message that homosexuality and, in its broader context, sexuality are taboo, and *that* can inhibit your child's sexual feelings and healthy sexual development.

One way to avoid unhappy consequences is to talk with your child about friends or family members who are homosexuals (provided, of course, that those individuals have made their sexual identities public). I don't mean you need to sit around and gossip about them. But if your child asks why Uncle Al lives with a man, explain it to her. You can simply say, "Uncle Al is gay—that means he loves another man much the same way that Mommy and Daddy love each other." You don't have to go into any more detail than that unless your child asks—but that's highly unlikely in kids under the age of ten or eleven.

It's only when you refuse to acknowledge Uncle Al and his homosexuality or to answer questions your child may have about homosexuality that you can hurt her. And keep this in mind: If your youngster is already feeling some anxiety about his sexual identity, he'll get even more anxious if you make the subject taboo.

3. Be a Sleuth.

When young children, under the age of about nine or ten, start asking very graphic questions about homosexual behavior, investigate why. It would be an extremely precocious five-year-old who wanted to know the explicit details of anal or oral sex. As awful as it is to consider, such questions may be a tip-off that your child is being sexually molested or is observing these sexual acts. Another possibility, particularly for a child of ten or eleven, is that he is part of a group who are masturbating or fellating each other, and that may be upsetting him. It's important, therefore, to do a little sleuthing and find out why your child is asking this particular question. Don't panic, though—his queries may stem from something he saw on TV or in the movies. But if it becomes clear that there is more to his question than it first appeared, you will need to be prepared to take some remedial action.

4. Offer Age-appropriate Detail.

Always try to fit any answers to your child's questions to the youngster's ability to understand. While you don't have to worry that what you say to a child may scar her for life—kids have a protective tendency to tune out what gets to be too much for them—you don't want to overwhelm a youngster with information that she cannot cognitively or emotionally integrate and that might confuse the issue.

Most four- to seven-year-olds, for instance, will be satisfied with explanations of homosexuality that center on the idea of two men or women being together and loving each other. Even at that tender age kids can understand what it means for two people to care for each other. Children in the eight-to-eleven age range may push for more detail, like one ten-year-old who asked, "But how do gay people have sex?" In that case, you can say something like "There are lots of ways people can show affection for each other, like touching or hugging or kissing. And that's what gay people do to show that they care about each other." I would *not* go into greater detail *unless your child asks a specific question and you feel he is emotionally ready to handle it.* Too much graphic detail can confuse a young child and/or make him anxious enough to inhibit his own natural sexual development.

5. Discourage Name Calling and Negative Stereotyping.

Through contact with parents, teachers, family, friends, and the media, kids pick up on our society's homophobia at a very early age. They learn that any gender atypicality is bad, and that the young boy who doesn't know how to throw a ball well is a "sissy" and, later on, a "fag." I've heard children as young as six and seven call each other "faggot" and "queer," even though they haven't the slightest idea what those words mean other than being put-downs. When we don't try to stop such name calling, we give it approval through our silence. As children grow up and learn that those words refer to homosexuals, they may continue to use them because they've also learned, both directly and indirectly, that it's okay to put homosexuals down.

But this doesn't have to happen. One simple approach is to let your child know that words like "queer" and "faggot" are mean names that can hurt people's feelings. If you have an older child who uses the words in context—suppose, for instance, you have neighbors who are gay—be direct. If your youngster says, "You know those two fags who live next door?" you can say, "It's not nice to use the word fag. It's a mean word that can be hurtful. The people next door are homosexuals." Then you can allow the conversation to proceed. Letting your child know that name calling and jokes that denigrate homosexuals are not tolerated in your home goes a long way toward teaching him that homosexuals are people, too, and worthy of respect. It almost goes without saying that you need to set an example by refraining from name calling and joke telling yourself. It's simply a matter of refusing to perpetuate negative stereotypes.

6. Talk About Diversity.

Answers to your kids' questions about homosexuality are most effective when they include a discussion of our world's diversity. You can explain, for instance, that "our world is like a beautiful rainbow—it has people of many different colors, religions, and beliefs. It also has people who love others in various ways. Mostly, men fall in love with women and women fall in love with men—that's what happened with Mommy and Daddy. But there are some men who fall in love with men and women who fall in love with women. These people are homosexuals and they are also part of the big rainbow that makes up our world."

7. Don't Jump to Conclusions.

Lots of young boys and girls enjoy "gender-atypical" behavior. Some young boys may prefer playing with dolls to Little League; some young girls prefer climbing trees to playing with Barbie. Yet these behaviors don't necessarily indicate that your child is heading toward homosexuality.

Dr. Gary Remafedi has spent years studying adolescent homosexuality at the University of Minnesota. Although his work shows that adolescent and adult homosexuals do recall not being interested in stereotypical male or female behaviors during childhood, it reveals that many heterosexuals recall similar impatience with such roles. Thus, Dr. Remafedi concludes, "Being somewhat different as a child is a poor predictor of what that child's sex orientation will be."

Another reason parents shouldn't jump to conclusions: Overly quick assessments may blur your objectivity and make you unable to understand what *is* behind your child's behavior. Here's what I mean.

Dr. Myron Belfer, a child psychiatrist at Harvard Medical School, told me of a mother and father who were very worried about their five-year-old son's preoccupation with dolls. But what Dr. Belfer discovered was that the youngster had a baby sister who was playing with dolls and getting lots of attention for it. So the little boy just followed suit. And although it's hard to tell at such a young age, he feels this youngster will be fine in his long-term sexual development.

Also keep in mind that lots of young children experiment with homosexual behaviors. It's not unusual for little boys to play games occasionally that involve touching each other's penises, or for preteen girls to "practice kissing" on each other. As long as you feel confident that such behavior is not coercive (which might be a signal of sexual abuse by another child), persistent, or pervasive, don't worry about it; it's really quite normal. Rather than punishing your child and making a big deal out of it, you can stop the behavior by saying something like "Okay, it's time to come downstairs now. Which game do you want to play?" You may also take your child's actions as your cue to talk with him, at a later time, about sex and sexuality and to offer some guidelines as to acceptable public behavior.

If you notice that your child is engaging in activities atypical for his/her sex—a young girl who loves to rough-house or a young boy who'd rather help Mom bake cookies than play soccer with the boys—don't draw attention to it. Fussing about such behavior can make your child feel self-conscious, incompetent, and humiliated and, in the long run, damage self-esteem. Instead, accept your child's preferences and skills. Who knows? Maybe your cookie-baking son will become a wonderful chef some day.

8. Help Your Child Negotiate in the Real World.

If your child is suffering because of his preferred behaviors—that is, if he's being picked on by his peers and being called a "sissy" at school—you may need to help him negotiate ways to get along better with his same-sex friends. I find the technique recommended by Dr. William Womak, a child psychiatrist who headed up the task force on gay and lesbian issues for the American Academy of Child and Adolescent Psychiatry, particularly effective. He suggests you tell your child something like "You know, I noticed that your friends are teasing you and that bothers you. I don't blame you; it would bother me, too. But you know what? I think there are some things we could do to help you make friends. You can bake cookies whenever you want to at home, but maybe when you're with your friends you could try to do some of the things that they like to do. In fact, why don't you and I go outside and toss a ball around? I can give you some pointers on how to do that pretty well."

Preschoolers having this trouble, however, may be too young to learn such negotiation skills. In that case, it's important to find a more appropriate peer group, one in which the children's activity preferences and behavioral styles are similar to your child's. That way, your son or daughter won't feel like an "outcast" and can begin to achieve a sense of competence, belonging, and a healthy sense of self-esteem.

9. Expect More Teasing with Boys.

In our society, girls who love to roughhouse are called "tomboys," but the word is usually said with affection and, in a certain sense, pride. After all, studies show that girls who are competitive and aggressive (stereotypically male traits) are often more successful in their adult, and particularly professional, lives than their more passive, submissive counterparts. However, little boys who shun typical "boy" activities in favor of "girl" games, or who behave in an effeminate manner, are labeled with the pejorative "sissy" and are the subject of much hurtful teasing. Parents need to be alert to this gender discrimination and to be prepared to handle any problems, particularly with their sons, as they arise.

10. Keep an Open Mind.

All parents have a set of beliefs and attitudes about what is correct moral behavior, and they work hard at passing those beliefs on to their children. And I am aware that some parents may believe that homosexuality is immoral. But I ask you here to try and keep an open mind. Read some of the books I recommend at the end of the chapter; hopefully they will give you more insight into homosexuality and help you to view it not as aberrant and immoral social behavior but as a certain kind of sexual orientation.

Letting your child know that you are an open-minded, tolerant adult helps her learn that all human beings, whatever their sexual orientation, are valuable and encourages her to perpetuate your values and become a tolerant adult. Also, if your child is already feeling "different" (and if he becomes aware of his or her homosexual orientation during adolescence or even later), your open-minded attitude lets him know that however his life unfolds, you will always love and accept him.

Sample Questions and Answers

Q: What does "gay" mean?
A: Being gay means that two men love each other or

two women love each other, the way that mommies and daddies love each other.

Q: How come Aunt Sally lives with Jane?

A: Aunt Sally is a homosexual; when two people of the same sex—two men or two women—love each other, they are homosexuals. Aunt Sally loves Jane and that's why she lives with her.

Q: I think about Miss Jones, my teacher, a lot and I like being around her a lot. But I'm a girl; does that mean I'm a lesbian?

A: No. Lots of girls have crushes on female teachers; it's perfectly normal. And Miss Jones is such a nice person. Being a lesbian is much more complex than just liking someone a lot. It has to do with your feelings and thoughts, your emotions and actions. Most people don't know whether they're homosexual until they're much older than you, at least till they're in their teens. So I don't think you have to worry about it for now. All you have to know now is that you're a terrific kid and that I'll always love you very much.

Q: How do I know if I'm a homosexual?

A: It's hard to know now. As you get older, you may have feelings that are hard to explain or that seem different from those of your friends. If you do have these feelings at some point, come and talk with me about them and we can see if they are like the feelings that homosexual people have. When you get to be a teenager, if you are really having homosexual feelings, it will become clearer to you. But right now, you really don't need to be concerned. And remember that no matter what feelings you have now or when you get older, I'll always love you very, very much.

Q: Are gay people bad?

A: There are good gay people and bad gay people just as there are good straight people and bad straight people. But there are lots more nice gay people in the world than bad ones. Some gay people are doctors and teachers and football players and bus drivers and actors.

Q: How come Johnny has two daddies?

A: There are all kinds of families in this world. Our family has a mommy and a daddy, you, and your sister. Some kids have just one mommy and no daddy, or a daddy and no mommy. And some kids, like Johnny, even have two daddies. His two daddies love each other very much and they love Johnny. And that's what makes them a happy family.

Helpful Resources

ORGANIZATIONS

Federation of Parents and Friends of Lesbians and Gays
P.O. Box 27605
Washington, DC 20038

Hetrick-Martin Institute
Clinical Program
401 West Street
New York, NY 10014
(212) 633-8920 (counseling and referrals only)

Lambda Legal Defense and Education Fund, Inc.
666 Broadway, 12th floor
New York, NY 10012
(212) 995-8585

National Gay and Lesbian Task Force Policy Institute
1734 Fourteenth Street, NW
Washington, DC 20005

Sexual Minority Youth Assistance League (SMYAL)
1621 Connecticut Ave., NW, 5th floor
Washington, DC 20009
(202) 483-9587

READINGS FOR PARENTS

Bell, Alan P., and Martin S. Weinberg. *Homosexualities: A Study of Diversity Among Men and Women.* New York: Simon & Schuster, 1978.

Bjorklund, David, and Barbara Bjorklund. "Straight or Gay." *Parents Magazine,* October 1988, 93–98.

Blumenfeld, Warren J., and Diane Raymond. *Looking At Gay and Lesbian Life.* Boston: Beacon Press, 1989.

Bozett, Frederick W., ed. *Gay and Lesbian Parents.* New York: Praeger Publishers, 1987.

Calderone, Mary, M.D., and Eric Johnson. *The Family Book About Sexuality.* New York: Harper & Row, 1981.

Carrera, Michael. *Sex: The Facts, the Acts and Your Feelings.* New York: Crown Publishers, 1981.

D'Emilio, John, and Estelle B. Friedman. *Intimate Matters—A History of Sexuality in America.* New York: Harper & Row, 1988.

Kleinberg, Seymour. *Alienated Affections.* New York: St. Martin's, 1988.

Whitney, Catherine. *Uncommon Lives: Gay Men & Straight Women.* New York: New American Library, 1990.

READINGS FOR CHILDREN

Jennes, Aylette. *Families: A Celebration of Diversity, Commitment, and Love.* Boston: Houghton Mifflin, 1990. (Ages 10 and up)

Johnson, Phyllis Hacken. *The Boy Toy.* Durham, N.C.: Carolina Wren Press, 1988. (Ages 4–6)

Newman, Leslea. *Heather Has Two Mommies.* Boston: Alyson Publications, 1989. (Ages 3–8)

Simon, Norma. *All Kinds of Families.* Niles, Ill.: Albert Whitman, 1976. (Ages 4–8)

Wilhoite, Michael. *Daddy's Roommate.* Boston: Alyson Publications, 1990. (Ages 2–6)

Special thanks to the following experts for their input into this chapter: Dennis Anderson, M.D., assistant professor of psychiatry, Albert Einstein College of Medicine; Myron Belfer, M.D., professor of psychiatry, Harvard Medical School; Susan Bradley, M.D., consulting psychiatrist, The Child and Adolescent Gender Identity Clinic, Clark Institute of Psychiatry, Toronto; Jacqueline Etemad, M.D., associate clinical professor of psychiatry, University of

California at San Francisco; Harold Kooden, Ph.D., co-chair, Citywide Committee on Lesbian and Gay Issues in Mental Health of the NYC Federation for Mental Health; Gary Remafedi, M.D., medical coordinator of the Adolescent Health Program, University of Minnesota; Wayne Steinman, co-chair of Center Kids, the family project of the Lesbian and Gay Community Services Center of New York; Marilyn Volker, Ed.D., sexologist and adjunct professor of sexuality, University of Miami; William Womack, M.D., associate professor, Division of Child Psychiatry, the University of Washington School of Medicine.

Chapter Fourteen

"WHY CAN'T WE SWIM AT THE BEACH ANYMORE?"

Talking with Your Child About the Environment

Ten-year-old Kevin didn't get to go to camp this year. "Too many expenses," his mother had explained, "what with the new roof on the house, Barbara's braces, and Daddy's being out of work this winter." But his mom had assured him that the whole family would go on a special camping trip to the youngster's favorite beach; they'd taken the same trip two years ago and Kevin had loved it, even though he'd been too young to do much more than wade. Now, though, Kevin knew how to swim and couldn't wait to hit the surf. For two whole months he thought of nothing else. Finally, summer arrived; the family loaded up the van and headed out. But when they reached the campgrounds, the manager informed them that the health department had shut down the beach. Apparently, raw sewage and medical waste had washed ashore. "I don't understand," said Kevin, crestfallen. "Why can't we swim at the beach anymore?"

When I was a little girl back in the fifties, the environment wasn't an "issue." We went to the beach on summer weekends and never gave its clear blue water and sparkling white sand a second thought. We drank tap water and breathed the air without concern; when our drafty houses turned chilly, we just turned up the thermostat full blast. Gas was less than twenty-five cents a gallon and the family car guzzled it down.

But as the children in young Kevin's generation are learning, things have changed. Today's children and adults are realizing that the earth is neither evergreen nor impervious to our demands. The reality is clear: our environment is a fragile one, and unless we begin to change our attitudes and behaviors, the world our kids will inherit may well be ugly, unclean, and unfit.

For many youngsters, such a possibility causes great concern. As Professor Milton Schwebel, who has spent years exploring children's reactions to the nuclear age, said to me, "In a sense, now that the cold war seems to be over, environmental concerns are displacing the fear of nuclear war as the thing kids believe most threatens their future." I agree. When a twelve-year-old announces that "my future—our future—is plop," and another youngster predicts that "my generation will be the last because we've ruined the world," you begin to understand just how distressed many children feel.

To be fair, not all kids have such a doomsday attitude. But most do get upset when their beaches are closed or when a favorite tree-filled stretch of land is sacrificed for another office complex. They watch TV, see the effects of a disaster like the Exxon Valdez horror, and become disturbed by the images of oil-soaked seals and birds.

Well, you say, so do we. But the difference between children's upset and our own is that kids haven't yet developed a sense of their own ability to effect change. As Charles Roth, who has worked on environmental curriculum development and assessment for children, explains, "Kids hear about a world that's falling apart. They hear about the hole in the ozone layer, about the rainforest, but they don't understand what they can do to correct things. So understandably they feel a sense of hopelessness."

Many parents, trying to shield their children from all this distressing news, choose not to discuss the environment with their kids. They believe that young children should be more concerned with what kind of bike to get than with the effects of acid rain. But other adults, and I am one of them, believe that talking to kids about the environment, and helping them learn what they can do to make things better, is empowering. Furthermore, says child psychiatrist David Fassler, "Kids like the fact that when it comes to the environment, their parents didn't do everything right and don't have all the answers. They know that adults may have caused the problems, but kids can be part of the solution."

Young children look to their parents when upsetting questions and concerns about anything, including the environment, arise. And that means that you, as parents, need to understand the issues at hand. To get you started, here's a brief look at some of the most important environmental problems of the day.

The Issue in Focus

So many environmental difficulties plague our contemporary world that it is impossible to enumerate, much less explain, all of them in a single chapter. But we can begin to explore the issues that, according to my talks with child-care experts, parents, and kids themselves, seem to be most distressing to our children.

Endangered Species.*

Most children love animals, so it isn't surprising that when wildlife is threatened, kids take note. But the facts are harsh indeed: as man encroaches upon and destroys such wildlife habitats as the rainforest, grasslands, and coral reefs, animals lose their homelands. Too, poaching, hunting and environmental pollutants are killing off whole species of wildlife; some may well become extinct within our lifetimes. A few troubling examples:

—Only two hundred years ago, some ten million elephants lived in Africa. Today, so many have been exterminated that they may be extinct by the year 2000;

—Ninety-five percent of the world's rhinoceroses have been destroyed in the last fifteen years, mostly to obtain

---

*Data on endangered species has been gleaned from information provided by Greenpeace USA, The Humane Society of the U.S., Animal Welfare Institute, World Wildlife Fund, Africa Wildlife Foundation, and the Center for Marine Conservation.

their horns, which are thought to have powerful medicinal and aphrodisiac properties;

—The destruction of bamboo, the food source of the Chinese giant panda, is endangering the fate of this spectacular creature.

These facts depict not only a heartbreaking scenario— imagine how you'd feel if your grandchildren's only chance to see an elephant was in a picture book or movie—but a practical dilemma as well. Extinction of the species can upset the balance of nature and disturb the food chain. Pests multiply, crops are damaged, disease spreads, and, finally, people can die.

Air and Water Pollution.*

Automobile emissions, smoke and chemicals from industry and consumer products are making the air less and less healthful. Our oceans, lakes, rivers, and streams are being polluted by sewage, toxic chemicals, oil, and garbage. Illegal dumping is rampant; for example, more than twenty thousand tons of sewage, detergents, and chemicals are poured into Lake Erie each day. Some pollutants, as well as radioactive materials, have seeped into groundwater (which provides water we will eventually drink) and contaminated it. In some parts of our country, the drinking water contains high levels of benzene, solvents, chloroform, nitrates, and other substances.

---

*Information on air and water pollution is from Concerned Educators Allied for a Safe Environment.

The Destruction of the Rainforest.*

Although tropical rainforests account for only 7 percent of the earth's land surface, they shelter 50 percent of the entire world's species of plant and animal life. But the rainforest is being destroyed so fast—an area as big as West Virginia is wiped out by mankind every year—that at that rate, by the year 2032 all the rainforests will be gone. And the plants and animals will go with them.

The Greenhouse Effect.†

In 1896, a Swedish chemist coined the term "greenhouse effect" to refer to the action of carbon dioxide and other gases in the atmosphere. These gases, emitted by the burning of fossil fuels, act like the glass in a greenhouse, which permits the sun's rays to pass through while trapping some of the heat. The result is a warming of the world's climate and a change in global climatic conditions. The potential effect? One possibility is that as the world heats up, ice will melt and expand the waters in the oceans. Then, experts say, a rise in the sea level of merely one meter could cause 200 million people worldwide to be left homeless because of coastal flooding. Another potential problem is the upsetting of global agriculture. That is, places where food is now being raised will no longer be able to support farming (thanks to the changed temperature), which could bring about a major shift in food production.

*Rainforest data are from the Environmental Defense Fund.
†Information on the greenhouse effect, the ozone layer, and acid rain comes from the World Wildlife Fund's *Atlas of the Environment* (Prentice Hall, 1990).

The Hole in the Ozone Layer.

A layer of ozone in the stratosphere forms a protective screen that filters out the sun's damaging ultraviolet rays. But our extensive use of substances called chlorofluorocarbons (CFCs), found in such everyday items as aerosol sprays, has begun to damage this protective shield. As recently as 1982, scientists discovered a "hole" as wide as the U.S. in the ozone layer that seems to open up periodically over Antarctica. This "hole" could have a potentially devastating effect because, simply put, without a sufficient ozone layer, we have no protection from the sun's ultraviolet radiation—radiation that could destroy terrestrial life.

Acid Rain.

Burning such fossil fuels as oil and coal to produce electricity and heat our homes emits sulfur and nitrogen oxides into the air. When these chemicals combine with water vapor, sunlight, and oxygen, they create a "soup" of sulfuric and nitric acids known as acid rain. Acid rain so increases the acidity of freshwater lakes and streams that it can make them uninhabitable for fish and other aquatic life. But it also hurts man-made structures; experts report, for example, that over the last twenty-five years, acid rain has caused more damage to the great monuments in Athens, Greece, than those structures have suffered in the previous 2,400 years combined.

Waste and Trash.*

It wasn't too long ago that the infamous "garbage barge" floated in and around New York's waterways trying to find a place to dump its unwelcome cargo. That fiasco served as a vivid illustration of an important environmental plight: we are running out of space to dispose of waste.

We can see the results of our "use it once and throw it away" mentality nationwide. Over three thousand dumps have been shut down since 1985. Medical waste, dumped illegally, is washing up on our shores and forcing numerous beaches to close.

Where is all this garbage coming from? Each year, we Americans toss out 18 billion disposable diapers, 220 million tires, and "enough aluminum to rebuild the entire commercial airline fleet every three months," reports Diane MacEachern in *Save Our Planet*. Further, we use 2.5 million plastic bottles every hour, and could build a twelve-foot-high wall running from Los Angeles to New York City with the office and writing paper we throw away each year (and just think of all the trees destroyed to make that amount of paper!).

Fortunately, effectively managed recycling programs can do a great deal to ease our waste problems, as can safe incineration. In fact, each of these environmental predicaments has a solution *if* we are willing to pay attention, devote resources (which means time *and* money), and work actively to reverse the process of global destruction.

Children have the greatest stake in seeing that we all begin to adopt an environmentally sound way of life; after

---

*Unless otherwise noted, data on solid waste comes from information provided by the Environmental Defense Fund.

all, the planet is theirs to inherit. No wonder they have concerns; no wonder they raise questions. Now, let's learn how we can answer them.

How to Talk with Your Child About the Environment

1. Stay Informed.

As the environment becomes an increasingly cogent issue, children will have more and more questions. So you won't find yourself stumped by their queries—by such sticklers as "Why do we recycle?" or, as a young friend of mine asked recently, "Will the acid in rain burn my skin?"— you need to stay informed about the environmental issues of the day. The Issue in Focus section will get you started, but for a more in-depth education, check out the list of books at the end of this chapter or spend some time in the library or bookstore. These days, there are a plethora of books and magazines available on every environmental concern.

2. Correct Misinformation.

The terminology of the environment can be a little confusing, especially to young children. Some kids, for instance, typically mix up "rainforest" and "acid rain." Others absorb odd bits and pieces of information and can't put them in perspective; for instance, they may hear that the earth is heating up and worry we may all become incinerated in a matter of weeks.

When questions or discussions arise, try to ascertain

just how much your child understands and correct any misconceptions. If, for instance, on a warm, sticky day your child suddenly announces, "See, the world is getting hotter," you might respond with "What does that mean to you?" to try and see just how much your child understands. If necessary, you can explain that "yes, the earth is getting warmer, but slowly, and by very small amounts. Today just happens to be a very warm day, but that's not because the earth is getting warmer. It's just today's weather. It will take many, many years before you notice any real change in the earth's temperature."

3. Admit the Problems Honestly.

Sugarcoating our world's environmental predicaments does your child an injustice. First of all, it's dishonest. And when your child discovers that you distorted the facts, as he will when he gets older and learns the truth, it may damage the foundation of trust you are working so hard to establish.

Second, whitewashing today's environmental issues is not fair. The attitude expressed in such parental comments as "Oh, don't worry about recycling our cans and newspapers. All this talk about the trash problem is exaggerated" not only shows a lack of sensitivity to the earth's problems, but gives your children a false sense of security as to their planet's future. If your kids grow up believing that nothing's wrong, then you deny them the opportunity to make things better. A better tack would be to offer enough simple, objective facts to help them become informed individuals who have the information and motivation they need to alleviate the difficulties at hand.

4. Offer a Sense of Hope.

When children reach an age or cognitive level at which they can begin to understand the seriousness of the earth's environmental dilemmas, they sometimes react with a sense of hopelessness. But it's not necessary to adopt such a doomsday attitude, and as a parent, you shouldn't encourage it.

Try to counter such a gloomy outlook by offering words of hope. You can say something like "I know that you're worried about the future of the earth. But throughout history, people have faced difficult problems and found ways to solve them. There are lots of people working very hard to fix these problems, and everybody, including you and I, can do his part to make things better."

5. Offer Age-appropriate Explanations.

Throughout this book, I've stressed the importance of talking to your children in a manner appropriate to their age and developmental level. This same advice holds true when discussing the environment. The five- or six-year-old who asks, "What's recycling?" can be answered with a simple "It's when we return cans and bottles and newspapers so that they can be made into other things instead of just making more garbage." A nine- or ten-year-old can understand a more sophisticated response like "Recycling is using the same materials over and over again to make other things. Aluminum cans can be recycled to make other products; newspapers can be recycled and made into magazines. When you recycle newspapers, you save trees because you don't need to cut down more trees to make the paper for the magazines."

6. Foster an Appreciation of the Natural World.

Here's a familiar scenario: Dad is watching the football game on TV when his eight-year-old son pops in and says, "Dad, come look at the sky. There are a million colors in it!" Dad, annoyed at the interruption, replies, "Can't you see I'm watching the game? Go tell your mother." The message conveyed: Nature isn't important; nature isn't worth caring for.

Young children, even those as young as three and four, have an innate curiosity and sense of wonder about the natural world around them. Nurture it. Take the time to watch a sunset. Go camping with your kids. Take them for walks in a nearby park and watch the birds and insects; get to know the various plants and flowers. Allowing your child's natural appreciation to flourish is a simple, fun, and important way to help your child become an environmentally conscious—and conscientious—adult.

7. Encourage Your Child to Problem-solve.

Learning to problem-solve is an important basic skill for any young child, and environmental issues offer an excellent opportunity to practice. Here's what I mean. Suppose your eight-year-old is watching a TV show that mentions the importance of conserving energy. After the program, you might try make a game of the subject by saying to your child, "Let's have some fun. Let's think of all the ways we can save energy. I can think of one way—we can turn off the lights when we're not in the room. How many ways can you think of?"

You'll find that children are extremely inventive in finding creative solutions. Here were a few suggestions from some youngsters I know: from Jeanie, age ten: "riding a bicycle to school instead of taking the bus"; from Ramon, age six: "using a spoon to help Mommy stir brownies, not the electric mixer"; and from Sam, age eight: "only taking a bath once a week to cut down on the electricity that heats the water." (Okay, so Sam may have had an ulterior motive!)

8. Explain that Actions Have Consequences.

It's important to teach your children that whatever they do affects someone or something else. For instance, you can explain that when they don't return a library book on time, they prevent someone else from reading that book. When they forget to feed the cat, the cat goes hungry. When we ride in cars, we use up fuel. Explaining that people's actions have consequences, that what *they* do *counts,* goes a long way toward helping your children begin to understand that their own actions can either help or hurt the environment.

9. Take Advantage of "Teachable Moments."

Talking to your kids about the environment, or about any other important issue for that matter, is least effective when done in an arbitrary and artificial way—a lecture, for instance. Instead, you need to be sensitive to opportunities that arise spontaneously, to "teachable moments" that can lead to worthwhile discussions. Suppose, for instance, you're driving your kids to school when your daughter says, "Mom, look at all the smoke coming out of that big smokestack. It's making the air turn black!" You can respond with "Well, that plant is burning fuel to make electricity. And we like electricity to give us light, to watch TV, to use the computer. But maybe if everyone cut down on the electricity they used, there wouldn't have to be so much smoke. What do you think?"

10. Demonstrate Your Beliefs.

When you carpool, recycle, or make a family rule to limit the amount of time spent in the shower—and then explain why—you let your child know by your actions as well as your words that you care about the environment. You also convey the message that every person can make a difference, a lesson that even young children can learn, as long as you make it age appropriate. For instance, kids love to crush cans. Making your six-year-old the "official can crusher" for your household shows him that he, too, can help the world around him.

Getting personally involved in the environment—and encouraging your kids to follow your lead—whether by using both sides of the paper when drawing, collecting newspapers for the neighborhood recycling program, or writing a letter to your congressman urging him to support a local bird sanctuary, can empower your children and help them generate positive feelings of self-worth.

11. Expect to Be Challenged.

As your kids learn more about what they can do to save the planet, they may well become relentless environmental watchdogs. The eight-year-old daughter of a friend of mine became such a rabid recycler that whenever anyone in the family would drink a can of soda, she would sit right next to him and, as soon as he was finished, snatch the can away and put it in the recycling container. A nine-year-old insisted on talking to the manager whenever he and his mom went to the drug store because "that store has too many nonbiodegradable containers on the shelves." One exasperated parent complained to me that his ten-year-old son "keeps showing me statistics about how many trees are being cut down every time I try to read a newspaper. It's driving me crazy!"

Well, all I can say is be patient. When and if it goes too far, you can (and probably should) explain that sometimes, environmental concerns need to be balanced by other considerations—and then explain what those are. You might say, "I know you're upset about my driving the car to work everyday because the car fumes pollute the air. But it's the only way I can get to the plant; and I need to work and earn money to help support the family. I do carpool with Uncle Joe to cut down on the problem." And again, remember: Learning that they can take action to help the environment makes your kids feel more confident and secure about themselves and their future. And that's worth a little inconvenience, don't you think?

Sample Questions and Answers

Q: Can we go outside when it rains or will the acid rain burn our skin?

A: It's true that the rain is changing, but it takes a very, very long time before the rain may become really dangerous to us. You can still go outside in the rain and be safe.

Q: Will there be enough food to eat when we grow up?

A: Yes, because people are working hard to learn how to grow plenty of food. They're trying to make sure that there's enough for everyone to eat.

Q: Why did grown-ups let the air get so dirty?

A: For years, people did not realize that things like car exhausts and smoke from coal and oil would hurt the air.

But now that we understand that, lots of people are working hard to figure out ways to keep the air clean.

Q: When oil spills into the ocean, do all the fish die? Can the water ever get clean again?

A: Sometimes, when a great deal of oil spills into the ocean, some of the fish and birds and plants that live in the ocean do die. But scientists are working on ways to clean up the water. It's a hard problem but people are trying very hard to solve it.

Helpful Resources

ORGANIZATIONS

Acid Rain Foundation
1410 Varsity Drive
Raleigh, NC 27606
(919) 828-9443

Animal Welfare Institute
P.O. Box 3650
Washington, DC 20007
(202) 337-2333

Center for Clean Air Policy
444 North Capital Street, suite 526
Washington, DC 20001
(202) 624-7709

Center for Marine Conservation
1725 DeSales Street, NW
Washington, DC 20036
(202) 429-5609

Concerned Educators Allied for a Safe Environment
(CEASE)
17 Gerry Street
Cambridge, MA 02138
617-864-0999

Environmental Action Foundation
1525 New Hampshire Avenue, NW
Washington, DC 20036
(202) 745-4870

Environmental Defense Fund
257 Park Avenue South
New York, NY 10010

Fish & Wildlife Service
Publications Unit
Dept. of the Interior
Washington, DC 20240
(703) 358-1711

Global ReLeaf Program
American Forestry Association
P.O. Box 2000
Washington, DC 20013

Keep America Beautiful
9 West Broad Street
Stamford, CT 06902
(203) 323-8987

National Parks & Conservation Association
1015 31st Street, NW
Washington, DC 20007
(202) 944-8530

National Recycling Coalition
1101 30th Street, NW, suite 305
Washington, DC 20007

National Wildlife Federation
1400 16th Street, NW
Washington, DC 20036
(202) 797-6800

Rainforest Alliance
270 Lafayette Street, suite 512
New York, NY 10012
(212) 941-1900

Sierra Club
730 Polk Street
San Francisco, CA 94109

Treepeople
12601 Mulholland Drive
Beverly Hills, CA 90210
(818) 753-4600

The Wilderness Society
900 17th Street, NW
Washington, DC 20006
(202) 833-2300

World Watch Institute
1776 Massachusetts Avenue, NW
Washington, DC 20036
(202) 452-1999

World Wildlife Fund
1250 24th Street, NW
Washington, DC 20037
(202) 293-4800

READINGS FOR PARENTS

Blumberg, Louis, and Robert Gottlieb. *War on Waste: Can America Win Its Battle with Garbage?* Washington, D.C.: Island Press, 1989.

Caplan, Ruth, et al. *Our Earth, Ourselves.* New York: Bantam, 1990.

Carson, Rachel. *Silent Spring.* Twenty-fifth anniversary ed. Boston: Houghton Mifflin, 1987.

Cornell, Joseph. *Sharing Nature with Children.* Nevada City, Calif.: Ananda Publications, 1979.

The Earthworks Group. *50 Simple Things You Can Do to Save the Earth*. Berkeley, Calif.: Earthworks Press, 1989.

The Global Tomorrow Coalition. *The Global Ecology Handbook: What You Can Do About the Environmental Crisis*. Boston: Beacon Press, 1990.

Lean, Geoffrey, Don Hinrichsen, and Adam Markham. *World Wildlife Fund's Atlas of the Environment*. Englewood Cliffs, N.J.: Prentice Hall, 1990.

MacEachern, Diane. *Save Our Planet*. New York: Dell Publishing, 1990.

Naar, John. *Design for a Livable Planet*. New York: Harper & Row, 1990.

Newkirk, Ingrid. *Save the Animals! 101 Easy Thing You Can Do*. New York: Warner Books, 1990.

Nilsson, Greta. *The Endangered Species Handbook*. Washington, D.C.: Animal Welfare Institute, 1990.

Roan, Sharon L. *Ozone Crisis*. New York: John Wiley & Sons, 1989.

Schneider, Stephen H. *Global Warming*. New York: Random House, 1989.

Sisson, Edith. *Nature with Children of All Ages*. Englewood Cliffs, N.J.: Prentice-Hall, 1982.

Timberlake, L. Thomas. *When the Bough Breaks: Our Children, Our Environment*. London: Earthscan, 1990.

Viner, Michael, with Pat Hilton. *365 Ways for You and Your Children to Save the Earth One Day at a Time*. New York: Warner Books, 1991.

Weiner, Jonathan. *The Next Hundred Years: Shaping the Fate of Our Living Earth*. New York: Bantam, 1990.

READINGS FOR CHILDREN

Bellamy, David. *How Green Are You?* New York: Clarkson
N. Potter, 1991. (Ages 5–9)

Bowden, Marcia. *Nature for the Very Young.* New York: John
Wiley & Sons, 1989. (Ages 4–8)

Caduto, Michael J., and Joseph Bruchac. *Keepers of the Earth.*
Golden, Colo.: Fulcrum, Inc., 1989. (Ages 5–12)

The Earthworks Group. *50 Simple Things Kids Can Do to Save
the Earth.* Kansas City, Mo.: Andrews & McMeel, 1990.
(Ages 7 and up)

Elkington, John, Julia Hailes, Douglas Hill, and Joel Ma-
kower. *Going Green: A Kid's Handbook to Saving the Planet.*
New York: Viking, 1990. (Ages 11–14)

Goodman, Billy. *A Kid's Guide to How to Save the Planet.* New
York: Avon Books, 1990. (Ages 8–14)

Hadingham, Evan, and Janet Hadingham. *Garbage! Where It
Comes From, Where It Goes.* New York: Simon &
Schuster, 1990. (Ages 9–12)

Harrar, George, and Linda Harrar. *Signs of the Apes, Songs of
the Whales: Adventures in Human-Animal Communication.*
New York: Simon & Schuster, 1986. (Ages 9–12)

Heilman, Joan Rattner. *Tons of Trash.* New York: Avon,
1992. (Ages 7–12)

Koral, April. *Our Global Greenhouse.* New York: Franklin
Watts, 1989. (Ages 10–14)

Lewis, Barbara. *The Kids' Guide to Social Action.* Minneapolis:
Free Spirit Publishing, 1991. (Ages 10–14)

McQueen, Kelly, and David Fassler. *Let's Talk Trash: The
Kids' Book About Recycling.* Burlington, Vt.: Waterfront
Books, 1991. (Ages 4–7)

Michel, Francois, and Larvor Yves. *The Restless Earth*. New York: Viking, 1990. (Ages 8–12)

National Wildlife Federation. *Endangered Animals* (Ranger Rick Books). Washington, D.C.: National Wildlife Foundation, 1989. (Ages 6–12)

O'Brien, Michael. *I Helped Save the Earth: 55 Ways Kids Can Make a World of Difference*. New York: Berkley Books, 1991. (Ages 8–11)

Ruis, Maria, and J. M. Parramon. *Air*. Woodbury, N.Y.: Barron's Educational Series, 1985. (Ages 3–5)

Schwartz, Linda. *Earth Book for Kids: Activities to Help Heal the Environment*. Santa Barbara, Calif.: The Learning Works, 1990. (Ages 9–12)

—————. *My Earth Book: Puzzles, Projects, Facts & Fun*. Santa Barbara, Calif.: The Learning Works, 1991. (Ages 6–9)

Seuss, Dr. *The Lorax*. New York: Random House, 1971. (Ages 7–9)

Snow, Theodore P. *Global Change*. Chicago: Children's Press, 1990. (Ages 7–9)

Stille, Darlene R. *Air Pollution*. Chicago: Children's Press, 1990. (Ages 7–9)

—————. *The Greenhouse Effect*. Chicago: Children's Press, 1990. (Ages 7–9)

—————. *Water Pollution*. Chicago: Children's Press, 1990. (Ages 7–9)

Vendrell, Carme Sole, and J. M. Parramon. *Water*. Woodbury, N.Y.: Barron's Educational Series, 1985. (Ages 3–5)

—————. *Earth*. Woodbury, N.Y.: Barron's Educational Series, 1985. (Ages 3–5)

————

Special thanks to the following experts for their input into this chapter: Anne M. Blackburn, educator; David Fassler, M.D., clinical director, Otter Creek Associates; Jackie Kaufman, editor and publisher, *P-3* magazine; Joseph Kiefer, executive director, Food Works; Charles Roth, senior research development associate, Education Development Center; Milton Schwebel, Ph.D., professor emeritus, Rutgers University, and senior research scholar, Center for Psychological Studies in the Nuclear Age; Alan Stern, D.P.H., environmental toxicologist; Harriett Stubbs, Ph.D., executive director, Acid Rain Foundation; Christopher Taranta, teacher, The Philadelphia School; Nancy Wolf, executive director, Environmental Action Coalition.

AFTERWORD

AIDS, homelessness, war, divorce, drugs. Without question, the topics I've addressed in the preceding chapters are among the most sensitive and difficult for you to talk about with your children. And I hope that the advice I've offered here will help you discuss them with your child clearly and sensitively. But keep in mind that these guidelines will also help you communicate about less profound topics, the ones that pop up in everyday life.

Speaking with your children about any subject—how your son feels about turning five, for example, or why your daughter wants to quit Brownies—isn't always easy. Finding out what's *really* on your child's mind takes a great deal of time, patience, caring, and sensitivity. It also requires some basic parent-child communication skills—the very skills that I've presented throughout this book.

So let me make one final point: Don't save whatever tips you may have picked up here for those special discussions of delicate issues. Instead, put them to work whenever you can—tonight at the dinner table, or tomorrow when you drive your child to school. Remember: Talking with your child isn't just about providing information. It's about creating a foundation of love and trust that will last a lifetime.

ABOUT THE AUTHOR

Lynne S. Dumas, a former teacher in both private and public schools, has worked with children of all ages. Now a journalist and social researcher, she has written for many national parenting magazines, including *Working Mother, Woman's Day Magazine's* "Your Child's Health," and *Woman's Day Magazine's* "Mother and Child." Ms. Dumas, co-author of *Congratulations! You've Been Fired,* lives with her husband, Dominick Scotto, in New York City.